The Ultimate Guide to
DOG BREEDS

The Ultimate Guide to
DOG BREEDS

Derek Hall

CHARTWELL
BOOKS, INC.

Published in 2002 by
Chartwell Books, Inc.
A division of Book Sales, Inc.
Raritan Center
114 Northfield Avenue
Edison. NJ 08837 USA

ISBN 0-7858-1460-4

Printed in China by Sino Publishing House Limited

All photographs are supplied by kind permission of the
RSPCA Photo Library, with the exception of those on
the following pages which are courtesy of Cogis:
168, 189, 200, 378 Guazargues/Cogis: 48, 62, 63, 70
right, 176, 184, 192 left, 232, 233, 379 Français/Cogis:
82, 83 both, 86, 87, 92, 182, 197 left, 199, 201
Hermeline/Cogis: 133 left, 137 bottom right, 193 right,
360 Lanceau/Cogis: 70 left, 230, 231 Labat/Cogis

CONTENTS

RIGHT

Dogs make wonderful pets for people of all ages, not least the elderly. They offer protection, encourage activity by asking to be taken for walks, and even help people cope with their disabilities.

Mankind's relationship with the dog can be traced back for thousands of years. Indeed, the dog is probably our oldest non-human companion. Excavations of Middle Eastern fossils, believed to be at least 12,000 years old, reveal a touching reminder of the bond between humans and dogs, for on this site was found the skeleton of a dog, lying next to the remains of its master.

Interestingly, for an animal that has been so important to us for so very long, there is uncertainty as to the exact way in which domestication of the dog occurred. We cannot even be absolutely sure of the evolutionary route by which the dog itself came about – although most experts are in agreement that the wolf is the most probable ancestor. Later, we shall look in more detail at the most likely theories of dog evolution. We shall also explore some of the ways in which the dog may have begun to befriend humans.

DOGS OF MANY KINDS

Despite the huge variations in size and appearance, all breeds of domestic dog belong to a single species, *Canis familiaris*. No other species of animal in the world exists in so many different forms, and this is because the majority of breeds have come about as the result of man's almost ceaseless attempts to create the perfect dog for every task and every fancy. The smallest dog breed in the world today is the Chihuahua. It measures no more than 9in (23cm) in height and weighs a maximum of 6lb (less than 3kg). At the other end of the scale is the Irish Wolfhound. This gentle giant towers above the Chihuahua and can reach 32in (81cm) or more at the shoulder. Standing on its back legs it is taller than an average-sized person.

Between these two extremes is found a bewildering array of diverse breeds. Some are built for speed or endurance, and others are designed to guard people and property – just as they have done for centuries. Some are prized for their herding abilities, and others for their skill in detecting or retrieving game for the hunter. Despite all of these admirable working qualities, many dogs are owned simply because they fulfil another important role for man – they have adapted perfectly to become a good and faithful friend. In this, the dog excels

The Labrador is one of the first choices when it comes to training dogs for the blind. It is noted for its equable temperament and faithful attention to duty.

RIGHT

The Bernese Mountain Dog is a working dog, used for herding and pulling farm carts in its native Switzerland. It is an old breed, probably descended from the time of the Romans.

OPPOSITE

Bringing a dog to a peak of fitness, and grooming it to perfection for showing and competition, adds another exciting dimension to the lives of both a dog and its owner.

like no other animal. Intelligent, affectionate, playful, resourceful and loyal, many a dog would give its own life in defence of its owner. And for most owners, no expense or effort is too great to ensure the health, safety and comfort of their pets.

Today, there are about 400 different breeds of dog in the world. It is impossible to be exact about this figure, because new ones still emerge from time to time. Some dog breeds are common and familiar to many people, wherever they live. For example, many of us could probably recognize well-known breeds such as German Shepherd Dogs (otherwise known as Alsatians), Dachshunds (the familiar 'sausage dog') or Greyhounds. However, few people outside their native countries would be able to name with certainty dogs such as the Norwegian Buhund or the Neapolitan Mastiff – although many of these breeds are now becoming established in countries far beyond their original homeland as breeders seek to encourage wider ownership of more unusual breeds.

A breed is described as a purebred dog of predictable size and shape. What this means in reality is that if two dogs of the same breed are mated, the offspring will look exactly like their parents. The offspring will have inherited the genes that determine certain physical

10

characteristics. They will also have inherited the parents' natural instincts. Therefore, for example, an Afghan Hound will have a natural tendency to hunt by sight, because the genes that determine this behaviour were passed on to it by its parents.

Sometimes changes do manifest themselves during the reproductive process. Some of these may be subtle, such as a slight variation in coat pattern or a change in colouring. Other changes, or mutations, can be more profound; a wire-coated dog may appear in a litter of normally smooth-coated dogs, for example. Because characteristics are usually passed from one generation to the next, breeders have long sought ways of improving the line by selecting the very best examples from which to breed. So, for example, the strongest, fastest hounds will be mated together to maintain the qualities of the breed in the next generation.

Many of today's breeds have come about by crossing different types of dogs in the hope that the offspring will reflect the best or most desired characteristics of each of the parents. Thus, for example, the Bracco Italiano came about as the result of crossing gundogs with hounds to produce a breed with the best features of both types – in this instance, a pointing dog with extra stamina.

DOG SHOWS

For centuries, humans have come together to compare and buy and sell their dogs. In time, this activity led to the formation of the dog show – an activity that really took off during the latter part of the 19th century. Now, dogs were judged against recognizable criteria, or standards, with the winners being the dogs that most closely conformed to the accepted standard in each breed category. Enthusiasts formed clubs dedicated to the promotion and excellence of particular breeds. In 1873 the Kennel Club was formed in Great Britain, and in 1884 the American Kennel Club was created, followed by the Canadian Kennel Club in 1888. Pedigree breeds could be registered with these clubs, and stud records were kept which documented the lineage of breeds.

Not all shows are designed simply to cater for breed excellence, however. There are shows that judge working skills, obedience and agility, for example. Many shows are far more informal than, say, an international championship event such as Crufts. There are even shows dedicated to cross-breeds (mongrels) and some in which any type of dog is welcome to enter, the winner simply being the best example chosen from all the entrants. Anyone with an interest in showing their dog

11

BELOW
Children love dogs and dogs love children. However, children must be taught from an early age to respect all animals and treat them with kindness and sensitivity.

would be well advised to visit as many shows as possible, so that an understanding can be gained of what the judges look for and to seek advice from the various breeders and other experts on hand.

DOGS AND HUMANS

Throughout recorded history, mankind's enduring association with the dog has been well documented in many ways – in sculpture, in art, on film and in literature. Art from the Babylonian Empire over 5,000 years ago clearly depicts huge, mastiff-type dogs. There can be little doubt that these animals were valued comrades in battle and probably performed guard duties as well.

Fleet-footed sighthounds like the Greyhound and the Pharaoh Hound feature as drawings on the walls of Egyptian tombs dating back to 4000BC, indicating clearly not only the presence of such breeds at that time, but also their significance in the lives of the people in these ancient empires. Indeed, so important was the dog considered during this period that it was worshipped in the form of the god Anubis, which is represented as a dog-headed human.

In the Middle Ages, dogs were frequently depicted in scenes, and the Bayeux Tapestry clearly shows Bloodhound-type dogs riding into battle with the Norman army. Later, in the 18th and 19th centuries, for example, it often seems that scarcely a painting was commissioned without a dog appearing in it somewhere – sitting diligently at its owner's feet, lying resplendent by the fire, or joining the hunters with their guns. Van Eyck, Gainsborough, Hogarth and Landseer were among the many famous artists whose work has helped to immortalize dogs in art.

More recently, dogs have featured in literature. No one who has ever read Dodie Smith's book *A Hundred and One Dalmatians*, or watched the film, will ever forget these endearing dogs and their antics as they try to escape from being made into an overcoat by the

their side when dealing with a rowdy gathering than any other sort of deterrent. Rounding up a flock of hillside sheep without a dog such as a Collie would be an almost impossible task. Many blind people would face an isolated and lonely future without the intelligent seeing eyes of a kindly Labrador to help them. The list is endless.

Today, interest in dogs and all things canine is as great as it has ever been. As we find ourselves increasingly under pressure at work or because of the tensions in the world, so the simpler things in life – like a relaxing country

LEFT and BELOW
Dogs are rewarding creatures; they inspire love and return it with interest. In fact, 'loyal' and 'faithful' are the adjectives most often used to describe the dog's sterling qualities.

villainous Cruella De Vil. Then there is Buck, the half St Bernard and half shepherd dog that is the hero of Jack London's bittersweet epic tale *Call of the Wild.*

Although many dogs make delightful pets, the huge range of breeds seen today has not come about because humans wanted a bigger choice of house companions! It is because most breeds of dog were designed to perform a particular duty – the fact that many of

these breeds also have a friendly nature and adapt well to living in our houses as pets is something of a bonus. Although the need for dogs to carry out certain types of work has diminished, in other working situations they are as valued and important as ever they were.

No one has yet discovered a better all-round detector of drugs or explosives than the canine nose. The police forces of the world would probably rather have a well-trained German Shepherd Dog by

13

ramble with a dog – take on a greater significance. Dogs fulfil a need in a way that no other animal can; we need them and we feel gratified that they seem to need us, too. For people living alone, a dog is a perfect companion, and for a growing family a dog is the instant playmate that expects to join in every bit of fun.

A well trained and happy dog makes a loving friend; it is always willing to participate in whatever you want to do, it won't criticize, it won't sulk for too long if it can't get its own way, it guards the house and alerts you to visitors, it gets you out and about, and each has its own unique character that can amuse for hours. The therapeutic value of dogs is well known, too, and their usefulness in reducing stress and encouraging calmness in people around them cannot be overemphasized. However, for this happy coexistence to occur, it takes effort on both parts and a degree of dedication and a lot of common sense and patience from you. Choosing the right sort of dog at the outset is one of the most important aspects of ownership, and this is examined in more detail later on in this book .

Inevitably, a huge industry has grown up to cater for our love of dogs. Unfortunately, this has not always worked to the advantage of dogs or their owners.

Unscrupulous breeders have sometimes offered poor-quality animals, particularly if the breed is popular and in demand. This practice reduces the quality of the breed overall – especially if such animals are then bred on – and may even result in dogs with behavioural problems. Happily, it should be possible to avoid difficulties like this by buying a pedigree dog only from a reputable breeder. On the positive side, there has never been more choice of potential canine pets or working companions available to the would-be buyer. Once purchased, every aspect of a dog's nutrition, entertainment and general

well-being can easily be provided for – there are even companies specializing in offering holiday accommodation designed to give a welcome to our dogs, too!

The descriptions found later in this book cover over 170 of the most popular breeds from all over the world. They will hopefully provide an insight into the varied world of dogs, helping you to choose the right animal for your situation.

DOG EVOLUTION AND THE DOG FAMILY

The dog is a carnivorous, or meat-eating, mammal belonging to the family *Canidae*. The ancestor of all the world's

meat-eating mammals (including the dog) is thought to be a small, primitive carnivore called *Miacis,* that appeared about 40 million years ago in what is now North America. About 30 million years ago, *Miacis* gave rise to a creature called *Cynodictis* which, about 10 million years ago, gave rise to *Cynodesmus* and *Tomoritus* – possibly the direct ancestors of the dog family. The development of the canid, or doglike group of carnivores, continued throughout the Pliocene and Pleistocene periods and in due course culminated in the appearance of the members of the present-day dog family. By now, dog species had spread to all parts of the world – except for the southernmost

The modern dog retains many of the traits of its wild ancestors. When running free with other dogs, it quickly becomes aware of its position in the pack, displaying many of the characteristics of wolves in the wild and submitting to a similar 'pecking' order.

RIGHT

The Dingo is a feral or semi-domesticated dog with a sandy-coloured coat. It is a native of Australia and is believed to have been introduced by early aboriginal immigrants to the country. This example was photographed on the Nullarbor Plain of South-Western Australia.

the *Canidae* is the ancestor of the domestic dog, but which of them is it? The fox certainly resembles many of the modern dog breeds in general appearance, but it is not a pack animal and other factors – such as differences in chromosome numbers making the offspring resulting from dog/fox matings infertile – would tend to eliminate the fox from the list of possible ancestors. Hyenas can also be discounted as potential ancestors, despite their superficially similar resemblance to dogs, since the evolutionary line that gave rise to them is different from the one that produced the dogs. Jackals and coyotes are very similar to domestic dogs, and

RIGHT

The African wild dog is one of 37 species of the family Canidae *which also includes wolves, foxes, hyenas and jackals, among others.*

regions such as Australasia and Antarctica from which they were isolated because of the vast oceans that separated the land masses at that time.

Today, the *Canidae*, or dog family, is represented by 37 different species. Included among them are the foxes (of which there are about 20 species), the grey wolf and the red wolf, the jackals, the raccoon dog and the African wild dog. (Dingoes, thought for so long to be naturally occurring wild dogs are, in fact, feral animals – in other words, domestic dogs that have gone back to living in the wild.)

Somewhere among the members of

crosses between dogs and these wild animals are fertile. However, there are sufficient internal differences between them to suggest that, although they are close relatives, they are not the same species.

This leaves us with the wolf. Although there is still no undeniable scientific or archaeological proof about the direct ancestor of the domestic dog, the evidence that exists is strong enough for most scientists to believe that the dog lying by your fireside is in many ways no more than a highly evolved wolf. Let's look at some of this evidence. First, anatomical features of dogs and wolves, such as the teeth, show almost no differences. Second, like coyotes and jackals, wolves and dogs can mate to produce fertile offspring. There are variations in the periods during which wolves and dogs come on heat, but these may have been caused by man's selective breeding of dogs. Perhaps more subjective evidence comes from our own eyes. We only need to look at a wolf and then to compare it with a breed of dog such as the Alaskan Malamute to see the almost uncanny resemblance between the two.

Other important similarities exist in the way in which both wolves and dogs behave. Each is a social pack animal, and even thousands of years of domestication have not eradicated this behaviour from the domestic dog. As we shall see later, it

demonstrates this aspect of its nature in almost everything it does.

Even if we accept that the dog arose from its wolf ancestor, there is still some conjecture about the precise way in which this occurred. Is the dog simply a modified wolf that has come about through the production of countless generations of domesticated animals? If so, then not only have we seen domestication occur, but also huge changes in the nature of the animal itself – far more than could be accounted for by natural evolutionary processes over this timescale. Thus, for example, we have seen the appearance of massive breeds like the Wolfhound and tiny breeds such as the Chihuahua. We have also seen the results of man altering the breeding cycle itself, so that the domestic dog now comes to maturity at six months or so, whereas the wolf is not ready to mate until at least two years of age.

Another theory suggests that there was a wolf-dog mutant that gave rise directly to the domestic dog. It has even been proposed that the Asiatic wolf is the animal in question, and that it was first domesticated by prehistoric northern Asian tribes.

DOMESTICATION OF THE DOG
Even if all of the foregoing questions still await definitive answers, what is not in doubt is mankind's profound influence on

the dog, who discovered in this animal the blueprint for a creature that could change his life forever. For the first time in our history, here was an animal that could become a friend and ally, rather than just another creature to be hunted or to be feared. Here was an animal that appeared intelligent, expressed emotions and appealed to the human soul. The

The Black-backed Jackal is slender and long-legged, feeds on carrion, game and fruit, and hunts cooperatively. This animal is in Botswana, but other species can be found in southern Asia as well as Africa.

The Golden Retriever has all the right instincts to enable it to search out casualties in difficult situations.

dog became a vital piece of the jigsaw that helped us to understand the natural world. However, while man was changing the dog, the dog was also imperceptibly changing the life of man.

With the help of the dog, humans could travel faster and more efficiently than before. With the help of the dog, humans could protect their livestock and even their own lives from

marauding predators. In time, the dog became an invaluable helper in a multitude of different tasks. There is no doubt that the dog altered both the speed and the direction of human development, and helped set the pattern for a relationship that endures to the present day.

It is quite possible that domestication took place several times and in different locations throughout prehistory. Fossils of domestic dogs dating from between 8,000 and 12,000 years ago have been found in localities as widespread as Iraq, Israel, America, Turkey, Denmark, Switzerland and England, although it is thought that the relationship between man and dog may have begun even earlier than these finds suggest.

In the same way that there are uncertainties about the true ancestor of the dog, there is plenty of conjecture, too, about the way in which domestication actually occurred. Domestication, however it happens, is a slow process. The affectionate, obedient, human-oriented dog did not suddenly appear on the scene. For domestication to be achieved, generations of animals showing the propensity to socialize must be selectively bred. Domestication is also different from tameness. Tameness can

Among the many benefits of the human-dog relationship was that the dog enabled man to travel faster than he would be able to under his own steam. These Huskies seem to positively relish their work as they speed across the ice.

This German Shepherd (Alsatian) will eventually become a police dog, indispensable in many tasks that would be difficult or dangerous for his handler to accomplish unaided. Here he is being trained to deal with a potentially dangerous assailant.

be taught to an individual animal, but this behaviour will not pass to the next generation. A domesticated animal, on the other hand, will produce offspring with the same traits as its parents. Once a domesticated dog puppy reaches a certain age it will not only instinctively show friendliness towards humans, but will actively seek out their company. Contrast this behaviour with that of, say, a naturally born hyena puppy of the same age; it will act aggressively towards humans and will do all it can to avoid contact with them.

The domestication of the dog is clearly more than simply a process whereby the animal and man became tolerant, even friendly, towards each other. As we saw earlier, man recognized in the dog an adaptable and versatile creature that was not only capable of becoming sociable but which exhibited a variety of useful traits. These include the natural ability to hunt, to guard, to haul loads and to retrieve. By carefully selecting animals with desired traits and breeding for these qualities, man was able to produce dogs which excelled at certain tasks. One could say that this was the beginning of the categorization of dogs into groups according to human needs.

But what is it about the nature of the dog that made it a suitable subject for domestication in the first place? To begin with, the dog was the right size to become a companion of man. Big enough to be a useful pack, guard and hunting animal, it was nevertheless not too big for it to live inside caves and other homes with humans. The dog is also a strong, agile and alert animal with a powerful range of senses. It is able to breed fairly soon after it reaches adulthood and produces a litter containing a useful number of offspring. Moreover, the dog is an intelligent creature, with a willingness to do man's bidding. This meant that not only could the task of training be achieved much more rapidly, but that the animal could to some degree bring this intelligence to the task in hand.

In all of this, we must remember that the relationship between man and dog is unlike the relationship between man and any other animal. We see in the dog a willingness to please and a desire to socialize with us. It is clear that the dog finds reward in the process of living with man and accepts without question its place as part of the human 'pack'. In return, it receives food, protection, shelter and stimulation. The dog clearly also receives, and enjoys, the attention and love that is bestowed upon it by its human owner.

THE ORIGINS OF DOMESTICATION

Let us now look at the possible ways in which the domestication process occurred. Several theories exist that try to explain this. One of the most popular and easy to imagine scenarios would be the one in which the dog began to scavenge around the edges of camps used by early man. Scraps of food discarded by the humans, such as bones, would have been taken and eaten by the dogs. This 'clearing up' process would have been beneficial for the humans, too, for it helped to remove items that may have attracted rats and other unwanted food raiders. The dogs may have hung around close to the camp, and their barks would have proved useful in raising the alarm when any other animal or human intruder came close.

Over time, some of these dogs may have become less timid and may even have begun to recognize humans as food providers; this would have been a powerful factor helping to promote the domestication process. The dogs may even have accompanied man on his hunting expeditions, again hoping for a chance to feed off any leftovers. It is even possible that some form of cooperation took place during the actual hunt.

Perhaps around this stage, humans began to recognize individual dogs that showed more friendliness or more ability to be effective in the hunt or act as guard dogs. These dogs might be encouraged by being rewarded with extra food, reinforcing the bonding process.

Alternatively, it could be that wolves or wild dogs were chased from their kills by stick-wielding or stone-throwing humans. Having taken from the carcase all they required, the humans then left the remains to be picked over by the animals they had chased away. In time, generations of these animals may have come somehow to regard humans as a part of the hunting process.

It has also been suggested that the association started with dogs being companions for humans. Orphan wolf cubs could have been raised by children as pets, for example – although the reasons why this would have taken place are somewhat hard to imagine, since the

Feral dogs photographed in Goa, India. These are usually animals which have escaped from a domesticated situation to fend for themselves, where they soon revert to the wild state. This can also occur in cats.

easily from pasture to pasture and possibly guarded from marauders. With so many qualities, it is little wonder that ancient civilizations, even prior to the Ancient Egyptians, revered the dog and raised it to the level of a deity.

WHAT IS A DOG?

We have already seen that the dog is a member of the family of mammals called *Canidae*. The *Canidae* are placed in a yet larger group of mammals – the *Carnivora* or carnivores. Carnivores are meat-eating animals that catch their food by hunting, and then despatch and eat their prey using powerful teeth and jaws. Other well known carnivores include bears (which are closely related to dogs), cats, pandas, raccoons and seals. All of the physical features of a typical carnivore are present in a domestic dog, although some have been selectively modified by man in certain breeds.

wolf was probably an animal to fear and would have been regarded as a competitor for food.

Whatever the actual process, the mutual bond between man and dog was slowly forged. Over time, dogs showing different traits came to be regarded as useful for different tasks. Thus a swift, quiet dog might be chosen for accompanying humans hunting a timid prey such as a deer. Hunting wild boar

and other strong or dangerous game would require the services of powerful dogs which could bring the prey down. Dogs whose alert senses caused them to bark at the approach of intruders, and which may also have been of impressive size and naturally protective, would be prized as guard dogs. The herding instincts shown by certain breeds would have been valued and developed so that livestock could be moved about more

THE SKELETON, TISSUES AND ORGANS

Most dog skeletons are remarkably similar in general appearance, although skull shape and limb length varies according to breed. The skeleton consists of two parts. The skull and the bones that form the spinal column and ribs make up what is known as the axial skeleton. The ribcage is usually deep in dogs, and it encloses the heart and the lungs. The leg bones and their associated bones, the shoulder blades and the pelvis, are called the appendicular skeleton. Typically, the legs of a canine are long and strong, allowing for effortless strides over great distances. If you examine the back leg of a dog you will see that the leg juts outwards about three-quarters of the way down. This part is called the hock, and it is actually the dog's heel, for dogs walk on their toes, which makes them very nimble and agile.

The skull is attached to the neck by the atlas and axis bones, and these bones permit great mobility. The nasal region of the skull may be very short in breeds such as the Pug, Bulldog and Pekingese – a condition that can lead to respiratory problems. At the other extreme, dogs like the Rough Collie and the Saluki have extremely long skulls. The skull houses the brain, eyes and the organs associated with the sense of smell. The jaws are armed with powerful, deep-rooted teeth. At the front of the jaws are the incisors. In the wild, these are used to cut skin and nibble at flesh and other soft body parts. To the side of the incisors are the sharp, dagger-like canine teeth. These are used to grip the prey tightly during the hunt and are the main weapons that a dog uses when fighting. Along each side of the jaw, the premolars and molars are used to slice up the food prior to swallowing. They are shaped in such a way that the food is sheared by them as the dog chews, rather like a pair of scissors cuts material. This action can be seen quite clearly when a dog gnaws meat off a bone, for example.

The dog has powerful muscles controlling its limbs and strong heart muscles to pump the blood around the body. The muscles are richly supplied with blood vessels and nerves. The locomotor muscles provide the means for moving the limbs, and these muscles are attached firmly to the bones. Muscles always act in pairs or groups; during movement, some of the muscles contract to pull the bone in one direction, and then an opposing set of muscles contracts to pull the bone back in the opposite direction.

The paired lungs provide the oxygen necessary for life. Air is drawn into the lungs, and the oxygen then diffuses through the walls of the lungs and into the bloodstream. The lungs also provide

LEFT
The owner of this German Shepherd periodically examines his dog's teeth and will refer any problems that are detected to a vet. As a carnivore, a dog's teeth are one of his most important pieces of natural equipment, especially vital to a dog in his wild state, when his powerful jaws with their pointed incisors and dagger-like canines would have been used to tear a prey to pieces.

a means of expelling waste gases such as nitrogen and carbon dioxide from the body when the dog breathes out. The nostrils that draw air into the body also take air over the sensitive cells of the nasal cavity so that the dog can register smells. Panting is also associated with the respiratory system, and is a mechanism by which the dog can lose excess heat from the body.

The dog's digestive system, like many other parts of its body, is a fairly robust affair. It is often a source of amazement to us that a dog can eat so fast when food is offered and can sample or closely examine so many dubious-looking items on its travels without showing any ill-effects. Food taken into the mouth is roughly chewed by the teeth and then passes down the oesophagus to the stomach. In the stomach, the food is broken down by a mixture of strong acids, enzymes and muscular action before it goes into the small intestine. Here, nutrients are extracted and passed into the bloodstream. Next, the remains pass into the large intestine where water is extracted. The waste that is left is passed to the rectum and leaves the anus as faeces.

Various organs are associated with the digestion of food, the largest of which is the liver. The liver also has many other functions, one of which is to produce bile. As well as being voided as faeces, other waste matter is removed by the kidneys, which act as a filtering mechanism to produce liquid urine.

The main external parts of the male dog's sex organs consist of a penis, and the two testes which lie in the scrotal sac between the thighs. Most of the seminal fluid which is ejaculated through the penis during mating is produced by the prostate gland within the abdomen. The sex organs of the female dog are largely internal. Only the slit-like vulva is visible externally. The other reproductive organs, the vagina, cervix and uterus are all located in the abdomen. Each of the two horns of the uterus lead to a fallopian tube and an ovary. The ovaries produce eggs which, when fertilized by the male sperm, develop into embryos.

A few bitches come into season or heat once a year, but most do so twice-yearly. Puberty is reached between 6 and 14 months of age, depending on the breed as well as on external factors such as food availability. A season lasts approximately 21 days, and a bitch signals her readiness to mate by standing with her tail pulled over to one side.

OPPOSITE
The owner of a team of Huskies likes to involve his child in the task of caring for his animals. This could be the start of a lifelong love affair.

BELOW
Four dogs interacting socially and learning all about each other, which is usually achieved by giving one another a good sniff.

During mating, the male dog mounts the female from the rear, inserts his penis into her vagina and ejaculates his sperm. Following successful mating, the bitch gives birth to puppies about 63 days later.

Apart from general body shape, one of the major features that helps to distinguish many dog breeds from one another is their fur. Like all mammals, some of the cells in the skin of a dog produce hairs that cover the body. The hair grows longer in some parts of the body than in others, and it also differs greatly in overall length, colour and texture depending on the breed. The main function of fur is to keep the body warm, but in many wild carnivores it also has an important role in helping to camouflage the animal in its habitat.

Man has selectively bred dogs in order to produce many different coat patterns and types, although many breeds still display the type of coat that evolved to best suit their natural surroundings. Thus, for example, Spitz-type breeds such as the Samoyed have a thick, stand-off coat that helps to keep them warm in Arctic conditions. Some northern breeds also have fur between their toes to help keep them warm and to obtain a better grip in the snow. On the other hand, the rough, short fur of a typical terrier is a much more suitable

body covering for a dog that was intended to spend much of its time beneath the ground.

THE SENSES

As in many other animals, the brain of a dog is the command centre for its whole body. The brain controls and coordinates all of the body's functions, and to do this it receives a constant influx of information from the sense organs. Dogs are intelligent, social creatures with well developed brains, capable of a wide range of different activities and with the ability to quickly learn new patterns of behaviour.

Among all the dog's senses, it is the sense of smell that seems to us to be the most acute and remarkable. At its most extreme, a dog's ability to detect scent is 100 million times better than a human's! This remarkable feature enables the dog in the wild not only to track prey successfully, but also to read the scent messages left by others of the same species informing the recipient about territorial boundaries, the readiness to mate, and so on. Clearly, the sense of smell was an important factor in the natural selection of the dog, for an animal with a well-developed ability to detect prey or its enemies would stand a better chance of survival.

The sense of smell is well developed

in most dogs, but in some breeds this ability has been blended with other attributes to produce, for example, superb hunters such as the Foxhound, the Basset, the Otterhound and the Pointer. In order to maximize any scent it receives, a dog has a long nasal passage and special scroll-shaped bones in the nasal cavity called turbinates. These help to increase the surface area of scent-detecting cells. It is likely, therefore, that dogs with foreshortened nasal regions, such as Boxers, have inferior scenting abilities than dogs with longer muzzles. When a scent is passed to the cells responsible for detection, the message travels to the brain as an electrical impulse along the olfactory nerve. At the part of the brain called the rhinencephalon, the message is received and processed. In the roof of the mouth dogs have another structure, Jacobson's organ, which is also used to detect scent particles.

In humans, vision is usually our primary sense. In other words, we use sight to tell us about our surroundings before we use any of our other senses. The role that vision plays in the life of the dog varies from breed to breed, but it is unlikely that this sense is ever as crucial or even as finely developed as ours.

In a dog's eyes, as in our own, the

positioned in the skull varies from breed to breed and has a profound effect on the way a dog sees. Sighthounds such as the Saluki have narrow skulls with forward-facing eyes set close together and almost no stop. These features combine to give the Saluki, and others like it, excellent overlapping binocular vision – a vital aid when judging distance and focusing on the prey prior to going in for the kill. Many of the sighthounds, or gazehounds as they are also known, have a reputation for aloofness, but it may be partly because they are more concerned with scanning the distant horizon for some imaginary prey than concentrating on matters closer to hand!

By comparison, many of the sheepdog and retriever breeds have eyes positioned more laterally. In the case of sheepdogs, this would be an advantage when trying to keep an eye on wandering sheep or watching for predators that might attack the flock; for a gundog such as a Golden Retriever, wide-placed eyes help it to see falling prey more easily and thus make retrieval a quicker and easier task.

Interestingly, all puppies are born blind. Not only do their eyes remain tightly shut until they are ten or more days old, but the visual cortex in the brain is so poorly developed at birth that they would be unable to discern

LEFT

The Borzoi is another example of a sighthound, or gazehound which, having a narrow skull and closely-set eyes, has excellent binocular vision, helping it to judge distance and pinpoint its prey before going in for the kill. Their habit of scanning the distant horizon gives then a reputation for aloofness which is not entirely justified.

light-sensitive cells on the retina at the back of the eye are of two types – rods and cones. Rods are concerned with night vision, and a dog has many more of these rods than cones. This explains why the dog can see so well at night. The cones are responsible for high-intensity daylight vision, in which colour is important. The fact that a dog has far fewer cones than a human helps to explain why scientists have concluded that a dog has almost no capacity to see in colour.

For a dog's vision to work most

effectively, there needs to be movement. You may have noticed that a dog appears to lose sight of someone standing still at some distance from it. However, once the person moves, it seems that the dog can again detect their presence. The importance of being able to detect movement obviously has its roots in the natural behaviour of the wild carnivore. Similarly, a stationary prey has a much better chance of avoiding detection than one that is moving in the dog's line of vision.

The manner in which the eyes are

When compared with the sighthounds, the Golden Retriever's eyes are placed more laterally, enabling it to spot falling prey more easily and making retrieval a simpler task.

anything from the light entering their eyes even if they were open. In these early stages of their lives they rely on other sensations, such as warmth and smell, to help them find their way about in the nest. It usually takes about six weeks before a puppy can see properly.

Good hearing is another of the features that we associate with dogs, and this sense is certainly well developed in canines. Again, hearing is a sense that dogs use to help them find their prey and avoid their enemies. Dogs hear sounds in the low frequency range, but they are also able to detect sounds of much higher frequencies than humans can. The ability to hear high-pitched sounds may be associated with prey detection, and it explains why dogs react to special high-pitched dog whistles that appear silent to us. Just as a dog can distinguish between different smells, it also has a remarkable ability to discriminate between different sounds that would appear almost the same to us. Thus a dog can tell the difference between the footsteps of its owner approaching the house and that of a stranger doing the same thing. One set of footsteps elicits signs of happy expectation and the other provokes a fit of aggressive barking.

So do dogs understand what we say to them? Clever though dogs undoubtedly are, it is unlikely that they have the capacity to actually understand our language. However, they are experts at both picking up the visual clues we adopt when we speak and also at associating the tones we use when we say different things. For instance, if we ask a dog if it wants to go for a walk, we probably use a light, questioning tone. We may even make specific hand or body gestures as we speak. On the other hand, if the dog is being scolded, we would probably use a lower, sharper tone of voice. We might also use dismissive arm movements, banishing the dog from the scene of its 'crime'. The dog, a quick learner, soon comes to link your actions and voice with either a pleasant or an unpleasant moment in its life and reacts accordingly, giving us the impression that it understands what we are saying. The ability of a dog to discriminate sounds can go much further than this, of course, and many dogs are taught to respond appropriately to a variety of different commands, such as SIT, COME, LIE DOWN, and so on.

Dogs have other senses, too. Like other mammals, they have receptors and nerve endings in their skin that can detect changes in temperature and can help them feel pressure or pain, for example.

DOG BEHAVIOUR

One of the great delights of dog ownership is to be had by watching your pet as it goes about its everyday life. Dogs are highly social pack animals by nature. They inherited, and still retain, many of the behavioural traits associated with their wolf ancestors, and these are clearly seen in the domestic dog today. A dog will display these characteristics whether it is interacting with another of its kind, amusing itself by following a trail when out on a country walk, or in its behaviour towards its owner.

This last point is a particularly important one to remember when training a dog. For the dog considers its owner as part of its pack, and in order for it to obey commands correctly and to avoid it trying to become the dominant

This Border Collie is obeying the command to LIE DOWN or lie low. In the working Collie, this is an important part of the herding instinct, when it will assume a low profile to avoid alarming the sheep in its charge.

RIGHT

*Dogs love repetitive
games which are also
important for exercise,
reinforcing natural
behaviour and visual
coordination. This
Border Collie is waiting
for his owner to throw a
stick for him so that he
can retrieve it.*

member of the pack, the dog must first
come to regard its owner as pack leader.
As soon as a puppy is introduced into a
household, it starts to look for clues
about where it stands in the pack
hierarchy. During the time a puppy
matures, it must learn that it ranks at the
bottom of the pack, below all the
humans in the family. This is important
for everyone's future harmony, including
the dog's, for if the dog considers itself to
be in charge it can become wilful and
even aggressive as it tries to assume
command. Therefore a young puppy
must learn, for example, that it cannot
do just as it pleases and that it must wait
until everyone else has eaten before it
gets its own food. Show the puppy, on
the other hand, that you can do whatever
you want to do, such as grooming it or
sitting in its bed, and that the time for
feeding is when you choose and not
when the animal demands it.

During the time that the puppy is
maturing, it is important to reinforce the
fact that you, and not it, are 'top dog'.
Make sure that the dog ultimately obeys
all your commands, even if it takes time
for it to respond correctly. If you tell it to
sit, keep gently pushing the hindquarters
while repeating the command until it
complies. A rewarding word and
perhaps a titbit will help to reinforce
good behaviour. Tug-of-war and rough

and tumble games with your dog are fine, but it is important that the games usually end with you as winner. Remember, throughout your relationship with your dog, that firmness and kindness work better than anything else where training is concerned.

There are two types of behaviour that a dog will exhibit. The first form is instinctive behaviour. This includes not only life-sustaining activities like feeding, but also the sorts of things that make a dog a dog – mutual sniffing of rear ends when two individuals meet, marking territory, a tendency to want to protect owner and property from intruders, the desire to sit next to you on the sofa given the chance, and so on. Although an individual dog can be trained to modify or suppress some of these behavioural traits, they are deeply rooted in the canine psyche from birth.

The second type of behaviour is learned. Some behaviour is learned by all wild animals as they react with their environment, but a pet dog, subjected to so much stimulation and conditioning, will quickly acquire forms of behaviour designed to make its life easier – even if some of these are cunningly disguised as a desire to please others! For example, a dog is not born with the tendency to carry a newspaper to its master, but as soon as a dog has learned that bringing a

newspaper results in praise, perhaps even a titbit, this piece of behaviour may become a regular part of its repertoire.

Although there are many kinds of animals that socialize with others of their own species, the dog is one of only a small number of animals that also socialize with different species, and it is perfectly happy to consider humans as one of these other creatures. In fact, the dog's whole ancestry is built around close cooperation as a means of ensuring

survival – hunting together to help bring down large prey and warning each other of dangers to the pack as a whole, for example. The dog expects to be part of the group, which is why it is always ready to dash outside with the children or join in their games, and why some dogs left behind when you go out shopping become so miserable and even destructive. In its own mind, the dog is unable to understand why it cannot go where the rest of the pack is going.

It is fun teaching a puppy new skills, even if they are not particularly useful, like shaking paws! It does demonstrate, however, that the dog is one of the few animals which will happily socialize with us, its survival depending on its being a member of the family or human 'pack'.

RIGHT

In order to facilitate its own survival, the dog will happily adjust itself to the lifestyle of its owner, even to the point of tolerating the family cat!

BELOW

This dog is gazing intently at his owners, willing them to part with food. However, he must be taught to mind his manners and refrain from making a nuisance of himself at mealtimes.

It would require a whole book to deal adequately with the complexities of dog behaviour, but here we only have space to mention the subject briefly. Listed below are some of the more common aspects of dog behaviour that are easy to observe.

PACK INSTINCT

The dog, as we have frequently said, is a pack animal. Cooperative behaviour helps the wolf to capture large prey, and dogs retain this characteristic. This is one of the reasons why dogs make good companions; they fit into our lifestyles and happily go along with whatever we want to do, because they

realize that this helps their survival. The members of a wolf pack do not take kindly to wolves from other packs invading their territory, and neither do domestic dogs appreciate intruders – hence the frenzied barking and other signs of aggressive behaviour whenever a stranger approaches your home. Your dog is simply defending its pack and its territory.

The look of intense devotion on the face of a dog as it looks up at its master in the expectation of attention or food is another example of pack behaviour – this is precisely the way a puppy looks up at its mother.

COMMUNICATION AND BODY LANGUAGE

Communication is everything to a dog. Dogs tell each other about their mood, their willingness to mate or to play and their ownership of territory. They also show each other who is boss. Dogs use a variety of different methods to convey all of these, and many other, important pieces of canine information – not just to other dogs, but also to their owners.

Scent is one of the most powerful mechanisms of communication in dogs. Male dogs mark their territory by urinating, and may also 'wipe' soil or grass with the scent glands in their paws. A male dog will usually cock its leg and urinate on a part of an object some distance off the ground; this is intentionally designed to leave the scent at nose height for the benefit of other dogs investigating it. Dogs also urinate at intervals to provide them with an odour trail to remind them how to get home again. Droppings may be impregnated with an odour from the anal glands. The urine from a bitch on heat can tell other dogs in the area when she is ready to mate. Dogs, of course, read the scent from other animals, too, and use this when tracking.

The mutual sniffing inspection that takes place when two dogs first meet – usually at each other's front end first and then at the rear – is another example of scent being used to convey information.

Your dog also uses its tail as a signalling flag. A furiously wagging tail is an indication of pleasure or excitement, although a tail held stiffly with just the tip wagging is more likely to be an aggressive posture and is often adopted when confronting an unknown dog. The tail can also be used to signal other moods; tucked firmly between the legs it indicates submission.

The dog also employs a whole range of other body language. As part of the submission posture described above, a

dog will attempt to make itself look smaller by flattening its ears, dropping its head and shoulders and crouching. In extreme cases, to really make the point, it will roll over, raise a hind leg and present its vulnerable belly. This posture is often adopted by your pet when it wants to show you that you are the leader of the pack – this action normally elicits a pleasant tummy rub from its owner at the same time!

By contrast, a dog wanting to exert dominance will do all it can to make itself appear bigger. Ears, tail and hackles (the hairs running down the centre of the neck and back) are raised, the neck is arched and the animal may even snarl. The dominant animal may try to reinforce its position by towering over the other dog or placing a paw firmly on its back.

PLAY AND ATTENTION

Play is an important part of a dog's life, especially when it is growing. Many animals use play as a way of learning how to survive. Puppies play-fight with each other, and with their human family, as a means of improving their skills at defending territory and settling

Dogs are social animals and after the first sniffing ritual is over like to play. One of them will usually assume the dominant role, and it is usually immediately apparent which one it is. By the look of its tail, the larger dog seems to be adopting the aggressive posture assumed when confronting another dog it does not know.

RIGHT

A dog is very clever at getting what he wants, whether it be supper or a walk, when he will make his wishes known to us in no uncertain terms. Then, the only course of action is to don boots and overcoats and put on his leash.

OPPOSITE

Even in later life, many dogs still retain the urge to play, and remain fond of having their bellies tickled, playing tug of war or jumping into water to retrieve sticks. It is important to play with your dog in order to stimulate him and prevent boredom.

disputes. Toys often represent prey, and a puppy hones its hunting skills by dashing after balls and other toys, and then by preventing them from being taken by running away with them. As they grow, most dogs seem to retain their playful instincts, and will often play just for the fun of it. Playing with your dog helps to keep it stimulated and thus prevents boredom. During play, or in an attempt to get its owner or another dog to play, the play stance is often adopted. This involves the dog crouching down with its front legs bent but with its hind legs held straight.

This attention-seeking behaviour is one of many strategies a dog will use when it wants something. The fixed stare accompanied by the furiously wagging tail can tell us in no uncertain terms that supper or a walk are overdue; a sharp, impatient bark reminds us that the dog has been outside for long enough and would now like to come in; a head pressed heavily on the knee or leg at mealtimes is a begging gesture (and not to be encouraged!); a paw pulling or patting at our arm is also a way of attracting our attention; a toy dropped ostentatiously at our feet is another invitation for a game. Obviously, you cannot always resist these pleas for attention, and so you comply. Do we train dogs or is it the other way round?

OTHER NATURAL INSTINCTS

We share our homes with our dogs and we treat them as members of the family. In some ways we even regard them as 'honorary humans'. However, despite domestication, a dog is still a dog, and given a chance most dogs will soon show plenty of examples of basic canine behaviour. Breeds with strong hunting instincts, such as hounds, will dash off on the scent of possible prey – often oblivious to the 'return' commands of their owners. This instinct to hunt is so strong in Greyhounds that they are often muzzled when out walking in case they spot the local cat!

Digging is a form of behaviour shown by many breeds, especially terriers. This is often related to finding prey that has gone to earth. Some dogs dig to hide bones from rivals, or to dig them up again. Digging can also be an effective way for a dog to escape the confines of the garden if it has the urge to wander.

We have already seen how the strong guarding instincts of some breeds are put to use, and a dog that may appear a submissive animal towards its family can become an aggressive and highly protective creature when confronted by a real or supposed threat from a stranger.

The desire to mate can make dogs completely focused and uninhibited, too. When a nearby bitch is on heat, male dogs (who are always ready sexually) can undergo a complete character change, much to the exasperation of their owners.

CHOOSING A DOG

Choosing to own a dog is a decision that should not be taken lightly. It is an unfortunate fact that many people choose dogs entirely unsuited to their

RIGHT

Although dogs are adaptable creatures, it is most unkind to get a dog, then leave it alone all day when you go to work. They are sensitive creatures and need to fully interact with human beings to develop their potential. In other words, they like to be with you most of the time, so don't get a dog if you can't give it all the attention it needs.

own particular lifestyles or personalities. A large, boisterous breed can be a disaster in a small urban flat, for instance. Although dogs are infinitely adaptable creatures, one kept in an unsuitable environment may not show its true character and may make life miserable for you. There are also many people who should not own a dog at all. It is unkind to keep a dog simply as a burglar deterrent because you are out all day or just because you like the look of a particular breed and regard it as some kind of status symbol. A dog is an intelligent, sensitive creature that needs to be properly understood, given the chance to express itself naturally, and become an integrated part of your life.

There are, in fact, several factors that need to be considered almost simultaneously when choosing a dog, but you need to start somewhere! Some of what follows can apply to both cross-breeds and pedigree dogs, but some is more relevant to pedigrees because it is easier to predict the behaviour and characteristics of known breeds. Breed behaviour is possibly the most important factor to consider when choosing a dog. The breed sections which follow in this book are a useful way of gauging the appearance and general temperament of specific varieties, as well as indicating the size of the dog (the height is measured at

the withers). Some potential owners have no special breed in mind when deciding to own a dog, and the breed sections of this book may help them decide on a type they would like to consider.

Unless you own and work a dog such as a sheepdog, the chances are that your purpose in getting a dog is because of the companionship that it provides. The size of the dog is an important initial consideration, but some big dogs seem bigger than others! A Deerhound is a big, tall dog but it can take up a remarkably small amount of space when lying down, and it can also move about the house with quietness and ease. Some large dogs, however, can seem like walking disaster areas in homes and are prone to knocking things off tables whenever they pass. A St Bernard will make even a moderate-sized house feel small when it sprawls across the floor asleep. Interestingly, among the top most popular dog breeds in Britain and America are Golden Retrievers, Labrador Retrievers, Rottweilers and German Shepherd Dogs – none of them exactly small dogs!

Similarly, some big dogs have relatively modest appetites, whereas a few have enormous ones. The cost of feeding a dog is a significant factor when choosing – even some medium-sized

LEFT
The owner of this Spaniel is aware that a dog craves constant companionship and should not be left at home to fend for himself. Consequently, he has decided to take his dog to work with him; indeed, the dog seems quite happy to be a driver's mate!

Be aware, when choosing a dog, that large breeds can present problems of their own in terms of the space they occupy and the amount they eat. Nevertheless, the German Shepherd is one of the most popular dogs around, even though it is not exactly small.

breeds can consume 330lb (150kg) of meat a year, before you add the cost of mixer and other food items.

While on the subject of cost, remember that there will also be vet bills to meet for regular vaccinations and other forms of treatment, equipment such as collar, leash, name tag, grooming tools, food and water bowls, treats, toys, bed, and possibly travelling cages and car harnesses. Unless your pet is going with you, there may also be boarding kennel costs to meet when you go on holiday. It may be worth considering one of the many pet insurance schemes available, since the cost of an unexpected vet bill can be considerable.

Your lifestyle is another important factor. All dogs require some form of regular exercise, but some demand more than others. How much time, and motivation, have you got for giving your dog the exercise it needs? Some toy breeds may be content with a ramble around the garden or a walk to the nearby shops, but many dogs – such as hounds and gundogs – will expect (and require) plenty of vigorous exercise, perhaps a couple of times a day. This will prevent boredom and keep them fit and healthy. Some breeds, such as Border Collies, need lots of interest and stimulation to keep them out of trouble. Provided they get sufficient exercise, most dogs will then be quite happy to fit into your routine and will look forward to their home comforts.

Do you choose a dog (male) or a bitch (female)? There is something to be said for either sex, and ultimately the choice is purely personal. Dogs of a particular breed can be a little more aggressive and dominant than bitches. They are usually more outgoing and tend to be bigger. Sometimes harder to train, dogs are also more inclined to get wanderlust – especially when a local bitch is in season. Bitches, unless they are neutered, come into season twice yearly and may attract the unwanted attention of all the neighbourhood canine suitors. Bitches tend to be quieter, less aggressive or territorial and are less likely to wander off. Many people say that bitches make more affectionate pets, but perhaps they are biased!

Pedigree dogs are usually classified according to the tasks they perform – although many of these breeds today perform a role no more arduous than that of being the family pet, even if originally they were bred for hunting, guarding or other duties. In this book, we adopt the system of grouping dogs into six categories based on their original uses. These are: hounds, gundogs, terriers, utility dogs, working dogs and toy dogs.

When it comes to temperament, some breeds are definitely a better choices than others, especially where young children are concerned. Many small or toy breeds are not very tolerant of children, who may not realize how much care needs to be taken when handling a small dog, or may make a lot of noise which frightens it. Terriers, on the other hand, are usually pretty good at standing up to a bit of rough and tumble, and seem to enjoy the busy, lively environment that exists when children are around.

Exercise requirements notwithstanding, many of the hound group make good choices as pets on the whole. A few of the breeds in this group, such as Borzois and Afghan Hounds, will not suit everyone perhaps, and of course the giants of the group such as Wolfhounds tend to need plenty of space. Some large breeds also have much shorter lives than medium-sized or smaller breeds.

Many of the best-known pet dogs come from the gundog group. On the whole, they are easy to train and naturally willing to please, and most fit into home life with ease and enjoyment. Among the ranks of this group we find such perennial favourites as the various setters, retrievers and spaniels. More recently, breeds such as the Italian Spinone have been gaining new fans, too.

If dogs in the utility group have a common link, it is to have been used as guards. This characteristic is very apparent in some breeds, especially those that were originally bred for fighting. Although today this more pugilistic side of their behaviour has been bred out, the dogs in this group are very protective, although they can still make charming pets.

Dogs in the working dog group were usually bred for a variety of different tasks – either to herd flocks of domestic animals or to perform duties ranging from guarding to sled pulling. Among the dogs in this group are some of the most popular pets, such as the German Shepherd and the Corgi, but there are also plenty of other, less well known breeds that have yet to prove their long-term popularity as pets.

Generally, you can obtain dogs in one of several ways. First, if you are not concerned about getting a recognized breed, you can tour your local pet rescue centres. Here you will normally find a heart-rending selection of dogs – mostly cross-breeds (mongrels) – all looking at you with imploring eyes. Many of these dogs are already fully grown, so at least you may not have to worry about how big the dog will become.

However, this fact reveals one of the problems associated with 'rescue' dogs.

OPPOSITE
This striking animal with its dramatic markings should not be regarded as a mere fashion accessory. Dalmations are gentle but fun-loving, and are excellent with children. However, the breed has a tendency towards skin troubles and deafness.

The dog may have been mistreated or badly socialized, and many of its bad habits may not reveal themselves immediately and may subsequently be hard to break. You may need to prepare yourself and your home for a few shocks during the so-called settling-in period! A dog with an unfortunate past may be nervous and insecure, at least to begin with, and this may manifest itself in behaviour such as bouts of howling or furniture chewing whenever it is left alone. Under no circumstances should you ever strike a dog if it behaves in this way. This will only make it more difficult for the dog to bond with you (a vital element for successful dog ownership) and it may even cause the dog to attack you in defence.

There are some dogs that will, sadly, never be the confident and friendly animals they may have been in different circumstances. The other drawback with a rescue dog is that it may already be several years old, which means that your time together is going to be reduced from the start. Occasionally, a dog will be offered for homing simply because its owner has died, but most dogs for homing have either been abandoned or are placed with the centre by owners who were not prepared to put in the effort required to turn a puppy into a well-adjusted adult dog.

Nevertheless, choosing and giving a second chance to a rescue dog can be a rewarding experience for both of you. With kindness and patience – and you may need to show even more patience than with a puppy – even the bad habits of an older dog can often be eradicated. Cross-bred dogs are invariably entertaining and intelligent animals, and their mixed parentage often expresses itself in a wide variety of different behaviour. Cross-breeds also enjoy what is known as hybrid vigour; they are less prone to the specific ailments that often affect pedigree dogs, and they generally seem to have robust constitutions.

When you see a dog that appeals to you at a rescue centre, you will probably be given the opportunity to walk it on a leash within the grounds of the centre. Be prepared for your arm to be stretched! Dogs kept in rescue centres, however well looked after, simply cannot get the exercise and attention that you would give your own pet, and so the dog may be highly excited and desperate to stretch its legs. Don't let this exuberance put you off; most dogs will calm down once they have adjusted to normal life again. Use this 'getting to know each other' period to see if you like the way the dog moves, if it shows any interest in you or

your family, and so on. It won't be a full test of its character, but it may give you an idea as to whether or not you might be compatible.

Before you can take a dog from a rescue centre, you may be required to fill in various forms, and some centres even insist on checking your home to make sure it is suitable for a dog. There will normally be a charge for obtaining a dog in this way. These are all good measures, designed to prevent dogs being homed with unsuitable owners. Most rescue centres neuter dogs before releasing them, and a vet will have examined the dog and inoculated it against canine diseases before it is even presented for homing.

Although most of the dogs available from rescue centres are cross-breeds, the occasional pedigree also turns up. Some centres operate a register, whereby potential owners can go on a waiting list of people hoping to obtain an unwanted pedigree dog of a particular breed.

You can also obtain dogs from local pet stores and from advertisements in magazines, local papers and so on – especially if you are looking for a particular breed. Although many of the dogs offered for sale in this way are perfectly good and healthy animals, some are not, and therefore it is wise to

The Jack Russell Terrier, although not universally recognized as an official breed, is small but brave, and is an excellent watchdog.

do some research before making a purchase which may involve some considerable cost. Organizations such as breed clubs can provide lists of breeders in your area, and you can check to see if the advertisers are among those recommended by the club. In any event, if you looking to obtain an expensive pedigree dog, it is advisable to discuss your requirements with several breeders first if possible.

Try to have a list of questions written down before you call, so that you get the information you require. The kind of things you might ask could include information concerning the breed's temperament: the cost of keeping the dog; how much exercise it requires; whether or not it is good with children; whether the parents have been shown and won any certificates; whether the puppy can be returned if it has defects; and when the next litter of available puppies is due. The answers to some of these questions may help you to decide not only if this is the right breeder for you but also if it is a breed that will suit you. Let the breeder know if you are looking for a dog to breed from, or to show, or simply as a pet.

Having decided on a breeder, you should arrange to visit the litter and the bitch – perhaps more than once if possible. Always ask to see the mother; her temperament may provide clues about her offspring. Check to see that the animals are not showing signs of anxiety or any other dubious traits. They should all look healthy and confident. Notice how the puppies react to you and their surroundings. Finally, you will need to make your choice. You will probably know instinctively which one is right for you!

Puppies do not normally leave the litter until they are about eight or nine

weeks old. During the time it is in the litter, the puppy will have learned basic pack behaviour and communication. A puppy that has remained in the litter for more than 12 weeks may have begun to develop some poor socialization habits. When you take your puppy, the breeder should provide you with full information about its vaccination programme, its diet, its worming treatments and any other details that may help the puppy settle down quickly in its new home. Ask about exercise routines, the best way to begin house-training, and advice on any other matters on which you are unsure. Most breeders are very knowledgeable and are willing to provide as much help as they can.

Whatever dog you finally choose, remember that it is going to be around for many years and will become an important part of your life. Treat a dog with kindness and understanding, and it will repay you a hundred times over.

WHAT TO LOOK FOR IN A HEALTHY PUPPY

Nose Should be cold and wet when awake, with no discharge, or sneezing.

Mouth Breath should be pleasant-smelling, the teeth straight and white, and the gums pink.

Coat Should be clean and shiny, with no bald itchy patches. Check for evidence of fleas.

Body Should be symmetrical and well grown. Body movements should be agile and supple.

Ears Should be clean and pink inside, free of discharge or redness and with no unpleasant odour.

Eyes Should be clear and bright, and the under-lids should be a healthy pink. There should be no redness or watering.

Anus Should be free from swelling or irritation as well as clean and dry.

Skin Should be clean and free from dandruff, blemishes and sore patches.

Limbs There should be no evidence of lameness. The puppy should be able to stand squarely and should be active and fluid in all his movements.

HOUNDS

BELOW
*One of the oldest of all
British breeds, the
impressive-looking
Deerhound was
developed in the Scottish
Highlands, having
perhaps been brought to
the country by
Phoenician traders.
(Page 66.)*

The common feature of all the dogs in this group is that they pursue game. If necessary, they then prevent the quarry from escaping, and may bark to pinpoint its location for the hunter before he arrives to despatch it. Being able to corner the quarry in this way was a particularly important requisite before the advent of efficient guns.

Most of the dogs in this group are hounds that hunt by sniffing the ground to pick up and then follow a scent, calling and barking all the while. Dogs of this type include Foxhounds, Beagles and Bassets. The sport of hunting game on horseback – using a pack of hounds to track down the quarry – was a popular pastime in medieval France. There, kings and rich noblemen hunted in the extensive broadleaved forests for foxes, wild boar and deer. Later, following the Norman Conquest, this pursuit was introduced to England.

Keeping packs of hounds became a highly developed activity. Dogs were carefully bred to ensure continuity of the best strains for working over the terrain and to pursue a particular quarry. Furthermore, specific colours and type were selected in order to produce a uniform appearance throughout the pack. Large hounds with great strength and stamina were used to accompany hunters on horseback, chiefly in pursuit of foxes, deer and wild boar. In due course, smaller mutations and basset-type hounds were developed; these were used by hunters following on foot to capture smaller game such as badgers, rabbits and hares. The dogs would usually be sent underground to flush the animal out of its lair. For such work, dogs with specific features would be obtained through selective breeding. These features included shorter legs to enable them to tunnel underground and powerful jaws for dealing with the quarry.

The ancestor of the pack hound is the Chien de Saint Hubert. For many centuries it was bred in a monastery in the Ardennes region of Belgium, and until the 1780s the monks there were required to give six hounds each year to the king. Although purebred specimens of the breed ceased to be found any longer in Belgium or France, in England it continued to flourish in the form of the Bloodhound. This breed was believed to have been brought to England by William the Conqueror. Despite popular belief, the name "bloodhound' does not indicate that the hound can follow a blood trail – although its powers of scent detection are phenomenal – but refers to the fact that the breed has pure blood.

Some hounds hunt primarily by sight. Among the best-known of the sighthounds is the Greyhound. Sighthounds rely on their eyes, rather than their noses, to detect prey before giving chase. Then, the dogs use their enormous speed and power to overtake and despatch the quarry. In some Middle Eastern countries hunters on horseback take with them their sighthounds, which are released once a quarry is sighted. Other typical sighthounds include Salukis, Whippets and Afghan Hounds – all characterized by their long-legged, supple and slender bodies capable of carrying the dog at speed.

In Russia, during the time of the tzars, noblemen and royalty would keep packs of fast-running hounds that were capable of bringing down wolves. Usually the wolves were pursued first by

Greyhounds and other lightly built hounds, before they were overcome by a second wave of stronger hounds such as Borzois.

There are some hounds that encompass both the virtues of the scenthounds and the sighthounds. They include the Pharaoh Hound and the Ibizan Hound, characterized by their sleek appearance and large, erect ears. Some of these breeds are of very ancient origin; similar-looking animals adorn artefacts found buried in the tombs of the Egyptian pharaohs thousands of years ago, proving that dogs such as these were prized by the rulers of these early civilizations.

Another group of hounds, the spitz dogs, are multipurpose hounds. The group includes breeds such as the Elkhound and the Finnish Spitz. Typically, these dogs are large and stocky, with erect ears and bushy, curled tails. Their thick coats help them to keep warm in very cold weather. These large, tough dogs were bred to give chase to game such as wolves, elks and bears in frozen, wooded terrain and then to hold the game at bay, signalling their whereabouts with loud and distinctive calls. Today they are more commonly used for hunting gamebirds.

In addition to their skills as hunters and trackers, many hounds make

excellent guard dogs, too. Apart from a few breeds – such as Foxhounds, which are better suited to life as part of a hunting pack – members of the hound group are also friendly, gregarious, affectionate and loyal companions. However, many can get so absorbed by the work in hand that they tend to be a little deaf to the 'return' commands of their owners!

Powerful and agile, the Rhodesian Ridgeback is a loyal and protective dog towards its family. However, it may not be the ideal choice for people unused to dogs. (Page 94.)

The elegant Afghan requires a good deal of exercise and has a natural tendency to chase small animals. However, they are very attached to their owners and make excellent pets, though regular grooming is important.

AFGHAN HOUND

Origins As its name suggests, this sighthound originates from the mountains and plains of Afghanistan. One of the most glamorous breeds of dogs, with a regal air about it, the Afghan is in fact a powerful hunter. In its native country it is also prized as a watchdog and herding dog. The first Afghans arrived in Britain in the early 1900s, and the breed achieved great acclaim at the 1907 Crystal Palace show. Afghans were imported into America in 1926.

Appearance Large and dignified, but with the impression of power and speed. The head is held proudly. The skull should be long but not too narrow. The nose should be black, although liver is permissible in dogs with lighter-coloured coats. Dark eyes are preferred, but golden-coloured eyes are also found. The almond-shaped eyes slant upward slightly at the outer corners. The ears should be carried close to the head and are covered with long, silky fur. The well muscled, moderate-length body with deep chest is offset by long, strongly boned legs and a long tail with a ring at the tip.

Coat Long and fine, except on the foreface, and with a silky 'topknot'.

Both fore and hind feet should be covered with long fur. All colours are acceptable.

Size *Height:* dog 27–29in (68.5–74cm); bitch 25–27in (63.5–68.5cm). *Weight:* dog 60lb (27kg); bitch 50lb (23kg).

Characteristics and Temperament
Intelligent and with a distinct oriental expression, these dogs appear reserved and aloof. However, they are quite capable of playing the fool if the mood takes them. Afghans are also affectionate toward their owners, although they are one of the more demanding breeds to keep. The high-stepping gait and long, flowing coat are characteristics of this breed. Afghans enjoy plenty of exercise – with a natural tendency to chase small animals – and need regular grooming.

The American Foxhound is a good-natured dog, but does have a wilful side to its nature which requires careful training.

AMERICAN FOXHOUND

Origins The American Foxhound is the result of crossings between a pack of hounds brought from Britain to Maryland in America in 1650 and dogs imported later from countries such as England, France and Ireland. Over time, the distinctive American Foxhound of today was developed. The sport of foxhunting in America differs greatly from foxhunting elsewhere, and this breed reflects those differences. American Foxhounds are used in field trials and for racing, as well as for foxhunting with a gun.

Appearance The skull is fairly long and domed, and the muzzle is longish with a moderate stop. The large eyes must be brown and should have a gentle expression. The moderately low-set ears should be long and pendulous, and with fine texture. The deep-chested body with well sprung ribs is narrower than in the English Foxhound. The long, strongly boned legs terminate in short feet. The tail is long, held high, and has a slight brush.

Coat Medium length, close and hard to the touch. All colours are acceptable.

Size *Height:* dog 22–25in (56–63.5cm); bitch 21–24in (53–61cm). *Weight:* 65–75lb (30–34kg).

Characteristics and Temperament These are friendly and non-aggressive dogs, but sometimes with a rather determined and ill-disciplined nature. Their natural stamina and endurance stand them in good stead as hunters.

BASENJI

Origins The Basenji has its origins in what is now called the Democratic Republic of Congo, although dogs similar in appearance to this breed are found throughout central Africa and were even depicted as palace dogs at the time of the pharaohs. In its native country, the Basenji is still used as a guard dog, companion and hunter. It is adept at catching rats and other vermin. The first two examples were brought to Britain in 1895, but it was not until 1937 that imports bred successfully in Britain. The breed was imported to America in 1941. Today, the Basenji has a small but enthusiastic fan club.

Appearance A fine-boned and lightly built animal, the Basenji always looks poised, aristocratic and alert. The well chiselled, wrinkled head narrows towards the point of the nose. The nose should be black. The dark, almond-shaped eyes have a fixed, somewhat inscrutable expression. The ears are small, pointed and pricked. The neck is well arched, long and strong. The body is short and deep, with a level back. The tail curls tightly over the back and lies to one side of the thigh in a single or a double curl.

Coat Short, smooth and fine. Colours range from black-and-white, red-and-white, black, tan-and-white, or black. There should be white present on the feet, chest and tail tip. White legs, blaze and collar are optional.

Size *Height:* dog 17in (43cm); bitch 16in (41cm). *Weight:* dog 24lb (11g); bitch 21lb (9.5kg).

Characteristics and Temperament

Renowned for its cleanliness and lack of odour, the Basenji is an ideal pet. Intelligent and curious, this dog can become very bonded to its family. Basenjis do not bark, but instead make an unusual yodelling sound when they want to express themselves. The wrinkled brow gives the dog a somewhat quizzical expression. Basenjis love to chew, even when past puppy stage, so it is a wise precaution to give them plenty of toys to destroy instead.

The Basenji has been known to wash itself like a cat, so fastidious is it about its appearance.

The Basset Fauve de Bretagne is becoming very popular as a house pet because it isn't too big and has a kindly, playful nature.

BASSET FAUVE DE BRETAGNE

Origins This little dog comes originally from Brittany, France. It is likely that the breed was created by crossing the Griffon Fauve de Bretagne with Brittany Bassets – both hunting breeds of dog. The Basset Fauve de Bretagne is a relatively recent introduction into Britain.

Appearance A neat, nimble animal with a moderately broad and long skull. The fairly long muzzle ends in a slight stop. The nose should be black or at least dark. The dark eyes should bear a lively expression. The ears are thin and pendulous. The body should be broad, with a fairly deep chest and a level back. The short, muscular legs can be straight or slightly crooked and end in short, strong feet. The tail is long.

Coat Harsh and dense, but not long or woolly. Colours are golden-wheaten, red-wheaten, or fawn. A white spot on the chest is allowed.

Size *Height:* 12.5–15in (32–38cm).
Weight: 35–40lb (16–18kg).

Characteristics and Temperament
Lively, friendly and not too big for even
a small home, this dog is gaining
popularity as a house pet. Tough and
always ready for exercise or play, the
breed is easy to groom and feed.

The Basset Hound may look mournful but it is an accommodating animal, as happy ambling through fields and sniffing out prey as it is idling away hours by the fireside.

BASSET HOUND

Origins The ancestor of the Basset Hound was believed to have been bred by French monks in the Middle Ages for hunting. A close relative of the French Bassets, the breed was nevertheless developed separately in Britain by crossings with Bloodhounds. The breed was introduced to shows in Britain in 1875. Lighter types of Basset are used as pack dogs in hunting hares, but the heavier ones are bred just for the show ring and as pets.

Appearance A heavily-built, slow-moving and sometimes ponderous dog with a somewhat comical, worried expression. The long, broad head is heavily domed and bears long, pendulous ears. There is loose skin around the head and muzzle. The nose should be black, although it can be brown or liver in lighter-coloured dogs. The eyes are brown or hazel; the red coloration of the lower lids should be visible. The low-slung body is long and with a broad, deep chest and arched loins. Short, heavy legs end in massive feet. When moving, the long and tapering tail is held well up and slightly curving.

Coat Short and smooth, without being too fine. Usually black, white and tan; any recognized hound colour is acceptable.

Size *Height:* 13–15in (33–38cm). *Weight:* 70lb (32kg).

Characteristics and Temperament This is a dog that loves to paddle through wet fields sniffing for prey – being tenacious and full of endurance – but is equally at home idling its time away by the fireside with its family. The Basset Hound's deep-chested bark may suggest an unfriendly nature, but this is a false impression, for this amiable dog is good-natured and placid. On the move, the Basset usually proceeds at a steady, lumbering pace, although it can break into a run if needed.

BEAGLE

Origins The smallest of the pack hounds, the Beagle is an English breed used for hunting hares with followers on foot. The breed has been in existence since at least the reign of Henry VIII of England. The Beagle is deservedly popular in many countries including America, Britain and France.

Appearance A bustling, active and enthusiastic dog of compact build. The head is medium-broad with a slightly domed skull. The nose should preferably be black. The ears hang down to the cheeks and are thin, fairly long and rounded. The eyes are brown or hazel with a friendly expression. The medium-length neck is carried on a short, deep-chested body. The strongly boned, muscular legs end in round feet. The tail is moderately long and carried high.

Coat Dense, short and waterproof. Any recognized hound colour is acceptable except liver.

Size *Height:* 13–16in (33–41cm). *Weight:* 20lb (9kg).

Characteristics and Temperament Ever ready for action, the Beagle is equally happy hunting in a pack or simply being the pampered family pet. Bold, lively and affectionate, this dog is also blessed with stamina and intelligence. The short coat is quick to wash and dry, after even the muddiest of romps. Once free of the leash, a Beagle may take off after a scent trail, seemingly deaf to its owner's calls.

The Beagle's smooth shorthaired coat is easy to maintain and needs little grooming to keep it looking smart.

In films and stories, the Bloodhound is always depicted as a kind of sleuth or detective, which is due to its supposed ability to follow a blood trail. However, the word actually refers to its aristocratic bloodline.

BLOODHOUND

Origins The origins of the Bloodhound can be traced back to Belgium, where legend has it that the breed was used for hunting in the Ardennes region as long ago as the 7th century. The Bloodhound was introduced to England by William the Conqueror in 1066. The name 'bloodhound' has been incorrectly attributed to the dog's legendary ability to follow a blood trail. In fact, the name is used to mean 'bloodstock' – and is a reference to aristocratic breeding.

Appearance A huge hound with great presence. The long, narrow head has characteristic hanging folds of pendulous skin, giving a somewhat lugubrious expression to the face. Eyes are brown or hazel. The long ears fall in graceful folds and feel soft to the touch. A long, throaty neck is carried on a short, deep-chested body. Long, muscular legs contribute to the dog's imposing size. The long, thick tail is carried high on the move.

Coat Smooth, short and waterproof. Colours are black-and tan; liver (red)-and-tan; and solid red. Small areas of white are allowed on the tail tip, chest and feet.

Size *Height:* dog 26in (66cm); bitch 24in (61cm). *Weight:* dog 110lb (50kg); bitch 100lb (45kg).

In films and stories, the Bloodhound is always depicted as a kind of sleuth or detective, which is due to its supposed ability to follow a blood trail. However, the word actually refers to its aristocratic bloodline.

BLOODHOUND

Origins The origins of the Bloodhound can be traced back to Belgium, where legend has it that the breed was used for hunting in the Ardennes region as long ago as the 7th century. The Bloodhound was introduced to England by William the Conqueror in 1066. The name 'bloodhound' has been incorrectly attributed to the dog's legendary ability to follow a blood trail. In fact, the name is used to mean 'bloodstock' – and is a reference to aristocratic breeding.

Appearance A huge hound with great presence. The long, narrow head has characteristic hanging folds of pendulous skin, giving a somewhat lugubrious expression to the face. Eyes are brown or hazel. The long ears fall in graceful folds and feel soft to the touch. A long, throaty neck is carried on a short, deep-chested body. Long, muscular legs contribute to the dog's imposing size. The long, thick tail is carried high on the move.

Coat Smooth, short and waterproof. Colours are black-and tan; liver (red)-and-tan; and solid red. Small areas of white are allowed on the tail tip, chest and feet.

Size *Height:* dog 26in (66cm); bitch 24in (61cm). *Weight:* dog 110lb (50kg); bitch 100lb (45kg).

FINAL

The Borzoi, though the personification of elegance, is not the ideal pet for everyone. It is quiet and reserved, with a distrust of strangers and children.

BORZOI

Origins An ancient Russian breed, packs of Borzoi were once kept by almost all Russian noblemen. The largest Borzoi were used, in pairs, for bringing down wolves – as their original name 'Russian Wolfhound' suggests. The first Borzoi seen in England were presented to Queen Alexandra by the Russian tsar.

Appearance A graceful, aristocratic dog whose body suggests great power and speed. The long, lean head has a slightly domed skull. The jaws are long and powerful, and the nose is large and black. Eyes are dark, with an intelligent expression. The ears are small and pointed. The neck is slightly arched and muscular. A Borzoi's body should be comparatively short and rising to an arch at the loins, and with a deep chest. The long, narrow legs are strong and muscular. The long tail is well feathered.

Coat Silky, flat, curly or wavy; much longer on the body and with feathering on legs, chest, hindquarters and tail. Any colour is acceptable.

Size *Height:* dog 29in (74cm); bitch 27in (68.5cm). *Weight:* dog 75–105lb (34–48kg); bitch 60–90lb (27–41kg).

Characteristics and Temperament
Rather aloof and self-possessed, this is not by any means a typical pet dog. Some examples may be rather temperamental, and ownership should be considered carefully. The Borzoi expresses its affection for its owners but is distrustful of strangers. For such a large animal, the Borzoi does not have a huge appetite, however.

The Coonhound is a large, robust dog with Bloodhound ancestry, the most important development being its black-and-tan coat.

COONHOUND

Origins In the 17th century, British colonists imported Bloodhounds into the state of Virginia in America to be used as guards for the settlements. During the second half of the 18th century, with the aid of progeny from these early Bloodhounds, dogs were bred with the intention of hunting opossums and raccoons – especially at night. These dogs were given the name of Coonhounds. Of the various Coonhounds that have been developed, the most important one is the black-and-tan variety.

Appearance A large, powerful and alert dog with obvious Bloodhound ancestry. The head has a long, moderately-broad skull and a long, broad muzzle. The eyes are dark brown or hazel. The ears are long, pendulous and folded. The fairly long neck is carried on a medium-length body with a deep chest. Long, well boned legs terminate in short, powerful feet. The tail is long and held up when on the move.

Coat Short and dense. Colour is very black with rich tan markings.

Size *Height:* dog 25in (63.5cm); bitch 24in (61cm). *Weight:* dog 90lb (41kg); bitch 80lb (36kg).

Characteristics and Temperament Keen and ready for action, this is a dog bred to withstand the cold of winter as well as the heat of summer. Coonhounds are friendly by nature but can be aggressive when required.

DACHSHUND

Origins The word Dachshund means 'badger dog' and describes the purpose for which these tough little dogs were originally bred in their native Germany. Their short legs and powerful jaws are ideal adaptations for entering setts and taking on their quarry underground. In fact, only the larger varieties were used for hunting badgers; the smaller ones hunted stoats and weasels. Not only did Dachshunds vary in size, however. A range of coat types was also developed, and each coat type is available in each size. Today, Dachshunds are popular show dogs as well as working dogs.

Appearance A long and low dog with a muscular body. The long, lean head has a narrow skull and a long, fine muzzle. The eyes are medium-sized, almond-shaped and coloured dark reddish brown to brown-black. The ears are broad and well rounded and hang flat. The neck is rather long and muscular. A long body with a deep chest and level back must be held sufficiently clear of the ground to allow free movement. Legs are short and strong. The tail is long.

Coat *Smoothhaired:* Short, glossy and dense. *Longhaired:* Soft and straight or slightly waved; abundant feathering on underside and behind legs. *Wirehaired:* Whole body, except for the chin, ears, jaws and eyebrows should be covered with short, straight, harsh hair. All colours are permissible.

Size *Weight:* large varieties 26lb (12kg); small varieties 10lb (4.5kg).

Characteristics and Temperament Intelligent and lively, Dachshunds need firm training to prevent disobedience. Despite their small size, they make admirable watchdogs and are fearless in the protection of their family and friends, to whom they are very loyal. The Dachschund will normally eat whatever is placed before it – or whatever it may secure by its own means – so its diet should be controlled.

Because they are so near to the ground, care should be taken not to step upon the little Dachshund. They are also prone to weight gain, so diet must be carefully monitored.

The Deerhound resembles a large, hairy Greyhound. It is a noble breed with ancient origins which continues to be admired and respected to this day.

DEERHOUND

Origins One of the oldest of all British breeds, the impressive-looking Deerhound was developed in the Scottish Highlands, having perhaps been brought originally to the country by Phoenician traders. Formally used to bring deer to bay, the ending of the clan system in Scotland following the Battle of Culloden in 1746 also meant the virtual demise of this noble breed. However, a few enthusiasts ensured the survival of the breed, which still commands admiration and respect wherever it is seen.

Appearance The overall impression is of a larger, bigger-boned, rough-coated Greyhound. The head is long with a broad skull, pointed muzzle and no stop. The nose should be black. The dark eyes appear gentle at rest but keen when aroused. The ears are small and folded back at rest. A long, muscular neck is carried on a long body with well arched loins and a deep chest. The legs are long and strongly boned. The tail is long and tapering and almost reaches the ground.

Coat Shaggy and thick; hard or crisp to the touch. The preferred colour is dark blue-grey, but it also appears in darker or lighter greys, brindles and yellows, sandy-red or red-fawn.

Size *Height:* dog 30in (76cm); bitch 28in (71cm). *Weight:* dog 100lb (45kg); bitch 80lb (36kg).

Characteristics and Temperament
Speed, power and endurance are all suggested by the breed's build, but this is allied to a calmness and dignity. The Deerhound is a gentle and friendly animal, ready to play and eager to please – and remarkably easy about the house, considering its large size.

The Elkhound is a friendly, confident dog, with a dense waterproof coat that insulates it from both heat and cold. It is hardy, has a very good appetite, and suffers few genetic disorders.

ELKHOUND

Origins An ancient Norwegian dog of the spitz type, which was used for hunting game, particularly elk. The Elkhound was developed for working in intensely cold conditions and over rough terrain, and it is no surprise that this dog is therefore strong and hardy.

Appearance The head has a broad skull with a long, broad muzzle. There is a marked stop. The slightly oval eyes should have a fearless, yet friendly, expression. The ears are erect and pricked. The powerful neck holds the head high. The short body has a deep chest with well sprung ribs. Moderately long, strongly boned legs terminate in

comparatively small, oval feet. The tail is held curled tightly over the back.

Coat Coarse, straight, waterproof outercoat with a dense, soft, woolly undercoat. Colour can be various shades of grey with black tips to the outercoat; lighter on the chest, stomach, legs and underside of the tail.

Size *Height:* dog 20.5in (52cm); bitch 19.5in (49.5cm). *Weight:* dog 50lb (23kg); bitch 43lb (20kg).

Characteristics and Temperament
Hardy, bold and intelligent, the Elkhound is also friendly and independent with no signs of nervousness. This breed has a loud and distinctive bark. A fairly hearty appetite is a feature of Elkhounds.

The foxy Finnish Spitz is lively and intelligent and makes a good pet, despite the fact that it was once used to track bear and elk in remote woodlands.

FINNISH SPITZ

Origins The national dog of Finland, with a breed standard going back to at least 1812, the Finnish Spitz is one of several spitz breeds. Originally the dog was bred to track game such as bear and elk in Finnish woodlands and then to keep it at bay and mark its position with a piercing bark. Nowadays it is mainly used to track birds such as black grouse. The breed was introduced to Britain in 1927. Puppies tend to resemble fox cubs.

Appearance The head is fox-like, with a gradually tapering muzzle. The medium-large eyes should be dark and with a lively expression. The nose should be completely black. The pricked ears are small and sharply pointed. A muscular, medium-length neck is carried on the deep, almost square, body. The strong legs should terminate in round feet. The bushy tail is held curled, typically spitz-like, over the back.

Coat This is fairly long, with a short, dense undercoat which is shorter on the head and legs. Colour is a reddish-brown or red-gold on the back while other parts have lighter shades.

Size *Height:* dog 17–20in (43–51cm); bitch 15.5–18in (39.5–46cm). *Weight:* dog 31–36lb (14–16kg); bitch 23–29lb (10–13kg).

Characteristics and Temperament Eager, courageous and intelligent, the Finnish Spitz is also lively and friendly. A good family pet but one that likes plenty of exercise. It is a rather vocal dog with an undemanding appetite.

FOXHOUND

Origins The Foxhound is a handsome dog whose purpose is exclusively to hunt – usually as part of a pack. As a result, this breed is seldom seen in the show ring and is not generally regarded as a potential household pet. Intense selection and careful breeding, free from the influences of fashion, have kept the Foxhound at the peak of perfection.

Appearance A well balanced dog with a rather broad, medium-length skull and a fairly long muzzle. The medium-sized hazel or brown eyes should have a keen expression. The broad, moderately-long ears hang down flat. The neck is long and lean, and the body short and deep-chested. Long, well boned legs terminate in round feet. The tail is long and held high.

Coat Short, dense and waterproof. Any recognized hound colour is permissible, such as combinations of black, tan and white.

Size *Height:* 23–25in (58.5–63.5cm). *Weight:* 67lb (30kg).

Characteristics and Temperament The Foxhound is a dog with plenty of endurance and stamina, and with a natural hunting ability. The breed is also friendly and non-aggressive, although somewhat determined and ill-disciplined. With training, this breed can be kept as a house dog, but it needs considerable exercise and feeding.

Foxhounds were bred specifically for hunting and are not usually regarded as household pets. However, with correct training, this is not impossible, but they do require a good deal of exercise as they are accustomed to running with the hunt all day long.

This is a strong and active dog, once used for hare coursing in its native Vendée, where it was bred for stamina and the ability to keep going all day.

GRAND BASSET GRIFFON VENDÉEN

Origins The origins of this breed can be traced back to the Vendée region of southwest France, where it was used for coursing hares and rabbits. The Grand Basset Griffon Vendéen was first introduced to Britain in 1990.

Appearance A well balanced hound, it has a long skull, which is not too broad, with a long, square muzzle and slight stop. The nose should be large and black. The eyes should be large and dark, with an intelligent, friendly expression. The ears are long, thin and pendulous. A long body is carried on large, strong legs. The tail is fairly long and held proudly.

Coat Rough and long, and of a flat nature with a thick undercoat. The colour can be white with any combination of lemon, orange, tricolour or grizzled markings.

Size *Height:* 15.5–17in (39–43cm). *Weight:* 40–44lb (18–20kg).

Characteristics and Temperament A strong and active dog possessing all the stamina necessary for a day's hunting. This is also an undemanding and outgoing breed, which enjoys the company of its owner. Regular grooming will keep the coat in good condition.

GRAND BLEU DE GASCOIGNE

Origins A descendant of the Grands Chiens Courants, it is said that King Henry IV of France owned a pack of these dogs. The Grand Bleu de Gascoigne is a hunter, like all hounds. Originally they hunted wolves, but today they hunt hares. The breed has only fairly recently been introduced as a show dog.

Appearance An aristocratic-looking dog with distinctive blue-tinged coloration. It has a large, long skull and muzzle. The dark, chestnut-coloured eyes have a sad, gentle, but trusting expression. The ears are thin, long and pendulous. The neck is characteristically throaty. The long, deep-chested body is carried on long, strongly boned legs. The tail is long and rather thick.

Coat Smooth and weather-resistant. Colour is white with speckles of black and larger black patches. Black patches encircle the eyes and ears, and there is often a small black patch on the skull. There are tan markings above the eyes, on the cheeks, lips, inside the ears, on the legs and under the tail.

Size *Height:* dog 25–27.5in (63.5–70cm); bitch 23.5–25.5in (60–65cm). *Weight:* 70.5–77lb (32–35kg).

Characteristics and Temperament A dog with a powerful voice but a gentle disposition. The breed is sometimes described as lacking in energy. Although not suitable for all owners, this breed is nevertheless affectionate and friendly.

A pack of Grand Bleu de Gascoigne was said to have been owned by Henry IV of France, when they were used to hunt wolves. Today they have less exciting lives and have recently been introduced to the show ring.

Greyhounds have a natural inclination to chase small animals, which makes them ideal for following a mechanical prey around a track. Unfortunately, their racing days are usually short-lived, but Greyhounds can make excellent pets.

GREYHOUND

Origins Many experts believe that the Greyhound has its origins in the Middle East. Drawings of dogs resembling Greyhounds have been found on the walls of Ancient Egyptian tombs dating back to 4000BC. The first of the so-called sighthounds, or gazehounds, the breed was eventually developed to today's standard in Britain. The racing Greyhound is slightly smaller than the show dog. Racing Greyhounds have been measured at speeds of over 45mph (72kph), making them one of the fastest of all animals.

Appearance A strongly-built, muscular and symmetrical animal. The head is long with a broad skull and a long, strong muzzle. The dark eyes bear an intelligent expression. The ears are small and rose-shaped. The neck is long and muscular. A deep and capacious chest allows for plenty of heart room. The back is long with powerful muscles, and there are slightly arched loins. Long, strongly boned legs terminate in long feet. The tail is long.

Coat The fine coat lies close to the body. Colours may be black, white, red, fawn, brindle or fallow, or any combination of these colours with white.

Size *Height:* dog 28–30in (71–76cm); bitch 27–28in (68.5–71cm). *Weight:* dog 65–70lb (29–32kg); bitch 60–65lb (27–29kg).

Characteristics and Temperament Greyhounds possess remarkable endurance and stamina, and, of course, a turn of speed second to none in the canine world. This is facilitated by the animal's long-reaching movement over the ground. Greyhounds are quiet, calm and affectionate dogs – although with a natural desire to chase other, smaller animals. Nevertheless, they make good companions and pets.

The Hamiltonstovare is an adaptable dog and will tolerate town life. However, with its Foxhound ancestry, it is most at home in the countryside.

HAMILTONSTOVARE

Origins One of the most popular breeds in its native Sweden, the Hamiltonstovare was created by Count Hamilton – the founder of the Swedish Kennel Club – in the 1800s. Also known as the Swedish Foxhound, the breed is used for hunting, but singly rather than as part of a pack.

Appearance The breed's Foxhound ancestry is clearly visible in this handsome and well proportioned dog. The head is longish and rectangular, with a moderately-broad skull. The nose should always be black. The dark brown eyes should convey a calm expression. The soft ears are approximately half the muzzle length. The long, powerful neck merges into the shoulders. The back is straight and powerful and the chest is deep. The strong legs should appear parallel when viewed from front and back. The long tail is held straight or slightly curving up.

Coat The outercoat is waterproof and lies close to the body, the undercoat is short and soft. The back is black, shading to brown on head and legs. There is white on the muzzle, neck, chest, lower legs and tail tip.

Size *Height:* dog 22.5in (57cm); bitch 21in (53cm). *Weight:* 51–59.5lb (23–27kg).

Characteristics and Temperament An active dog which expects to work and exercise, this even-tempered hound also makes an undemanding companion. Happiest out in the countryside chasing a trail, the Hamiltonstovare will also adapt well to town life when the need arises.

This is one of the most ancient of breeds, depicted in artefacts from thousands of years ago. It is still going strong, as intelligent and non-aggressive as ever.

IBIZAN HOUND

Origins In the tomb of the pharaoh Hemako was found a carved dish bearing an image of an Ibizan Hound. The dish was made in the 1st Dynasty, between 3100 and 2700BC, thus indicating that the history of this breed can be traced back at least to the time of the Ancient Egyptians. The tombs of other Ancient Egyptians also bear witness to this. The breed takes its name from the Balearic island of Ibiza, and was probably taken there by Phoenician traders. It has been known on the island, and on nearby Formentera, for 5,000 years at least. The Ibizan Hound is used for hunting hares, partridge and other game, singly or as part of a pack.

Appearance A finely-built dog with upright ears. The head has a long, narrow skull and muzzle. The nose is flesh-coloured. Eyes are amber-coloured and fairly small. The ears are large and

Size *Height:* 22–29in (56–74cm). *Weight:* dog 49lb (22kg); bitch 42lb (19kg).

Characteristics and Temperament A renowned jumper, this breed needs plenty of room to exercise. Sometimes aloof with strangers, the Ibizan Hound is nevertheless devoted to its owner. It is also intelligent, cheerful and non-aggressive.

pricked. A long, lean neck is carried on a body with a long, flat ribcage and arched loins. The legs are long and strong and terminate in hare feet. The tail is long and thin.

Coat The coat may be smooth or rough but always dense and hard; it is longer under the tail. The colour can be white, 'lion' colour; or any combination of these colours.

The Irish Wolfhound is an ancient breed, known since Roman times for its huge size and dignified appearance. But it is a gentle giant, even-tempered and good with children.

IRISH WOLFHOUND

Origins Perhaps no other dog evokes such looks of admiration as the Irish Wolfhound. This magnificent breed was known to the Ancient Romans, and it was held in great esteem from the 12th to the 16th century in Ireland. There it was used to hunt wolf, bear, stag and elk. When the last wolf was wiped out in Ireland, the Irish Wolfhound almost became extinct as well. In the mid 19th century, however, the breed was revived using the few remaining specimens. Now a healthy and enthusiastic following exists for these animals – the tallest of any breed of dog.

Appearance Of commanding size and appearance, coupled with muscular strength. The head is long, and the skull not too broad. The muzzle is long and moderately pointed. The nose is black.

The eyes are dark. The small rose ears have a fine, velvety texture. The neck is long and muscular. A long body with a very deep chest and arched loins is carried on long, well boned legs. The tail is long and slightly curved.

Coat Rough, hard and shaggy; long and wiry over the eyes and under the jaw. Colours are black, grey, red, brindle, fawn, wheaten, steel-grey or pure white.

Size *Height:* dog 31in (79cm); bitch 28in (71cm). *Weight:* dog 120lb (54kg); bitch 90lb (41kg).

Characteristics and Temperament The breed's comparative rarity and huge size, together with its air of dignity, set it apart from others. Despite being such a large dog, the breed is renowned for its calmness and friendly nature. It is also tolerant with children and obedient. As befits such a massive creature, food portions need to be considerable.

The Lundehund is unusual in that it has six toes on each foot, a selective adaptation to help it, in a previous incarnation, to climb rocks.

NORWEGIAN LUNDEHUND

Origins This smallish dog originates from islands off the coast of Norway. It is a recent introduction into Britain and is fairly rare outside its native country. In its native land it has been used to search for puffins and their eggs along the coast – hence the word *Lund*, meaning puffin in Norwegian. The dog is unusual in that it has six toes on each foot – a selective adaptation to help it climb rocks.

Appearance A spitz-type dog of fairly light build. The wedge-shaped head has a fairly broad skull and a medium-length muzzle. The eyes are brown. The mobile ears are pricked and of medium size. The strong neck is carried on a rectangular body with a strong, straight back. The legs are strong and carry double dew claws. The tail is sometimes carried curled up.

Coat A dense, rough outercoat and a softer undercoat. Colours are shades of black, red-brown or grey, with white.

Size *Height:* dog 14–15in (35.5–38cm); bitch 12.5–14in (32–35.5cm). *Weight:* dog 15.5lb (7kg); bitch 13lb (6kg).

Characteristics and Temperament A good-natured, lively dog. Alert and intelligent.

The affable Otterhound isn't the most elegant of creatures, but it has great stamina and its engaging personality makes it a rewarding pet.

OTTERHOUND

Origins With an ancestry that includes French blood mixed with various strains of English hounds, the Otterhound is a long-established breed. A pack of Otterhounds was known to have been kept by the English King John in 1212. When in 1977 the hunting of otters was banned in England and Wales, the breed declined. A campaign to have the breed recognized in Britain for showing purposes helped to restore its fortunes.

Appearance A large, rugged-looking dog, the head is heavy with a medium-broad skull and a deep muzzle. The whole head is covered with rough fur. The eyes are brown and should help to convey an amiable expression. The ears are long and pendulous. A long and powerful neck is carried on a strong, deep-chested body. Moderately long legs terminate in large, round feet which are webbed. The tail is thick at the base and tapers to a point.

Coat A dense, harsh and waterproof double coat. The fur on the head and lower legs is softer. A slight oily texture may be apparent in the coat. All recognized hound colours are permitted.

Size *Height:* dog 27in (68.5cm); bitch 24in (61cm). *Weight:* dog 75–115lb (34–52kg); bitch 65–100lb (29–45kg).

Characteristics and Temperament The Otterhound was developed to spend much time hunting in the water, but the breed can also travel long distances across rough country without tiring. A loud, baying bark and a keen nose for a scent are other features of this dog. The breed is also good-natured, intelligent and friendly. Not the most stylish-looking dog by any means, the Otterhound makes up for this by its engaging character.

This is a country dog at heart and likes nothing better than to sniff around, searching out a trail. An amiable little dog, it would make an ideal pet for a country-dweller.

PETIT BASSET GRIFFON VENDÉEN

Origins A breed that originates from France. The word 'basset' indicates a dog that is low to the ground, and this breed is used by sportsmen for trailing and beating game from cover. Introduced into Britain in 1969, this is still a comparatively rare dog.

Appearance A compact, short-legged hound. The head, carried on a long, strong neck, has a medium-length skull. The nose is black. The large, dark eyes should convey an intelligent and friendly expression. The supple ears end in an oval shape and are covered with long, fine hair. The medium-length body has a deep chest and is carried on thick, well boned legs. The tail is of medium length and carried proudly.

Coat Rough and long with a thick undercoat. Colour is white with any combination of orange, lemon, tricolour or grizzle.

Size *Height:* dog 13–15in (33–38cm); bitch 14in (35.5cm). *Weight:* dog 42lb (19kg); bitch 39.5lb (18kg).

Characteristics and Temperament Like most hounds, this dog is at its most content out in the countryside following trails. The dog's expression exemplifies its character – extrovert, happy and alert.

The Pharoah Hound has a noble bearing and is an excellent hunter that once tracked its prey by scent as well as sound. Originating in warmer climes, and having a short coat, it needs added protection in cold weather.

PHARAOH HOUND

Origins The paintings on pottery and other artefacts found in the tombs of the Ancient Egyptians clearly depict dogs almost identical to the Pharaoh Hound known today. It is thought that the breed then came to Malta from Africa with Phoenician traders. It was from this island that the breed was introduced elsewhere, and it arrived in Britain, for example, in the 1970s.

Appearance A graceful-looking dog with a noble bearing about it. The head has a long skull and a long muzzle with a slight stop. The small, amber-coloured eyes are oval and have an intelligent expression. The ears are pricked. A long, lean and strong neck is carried on a long body with a deep chest. The legs are also long and well boned. The long tail is held high and curved on the move.

Coat Fine or slightly harsh; short and glossy. The colour is basically rich tan but with a white tail tip, white mark on the chest and white toes. A slim white blaze on the centre of the face is also acceptable.

Size *Height:* dog 22–25in (56–63.5cm); bitch 21–24in (53–61cm). *Weight:* dog 44–45lb (20kg).

Characteristics and Temperament An alert hunter that tracks its prey by both scent and sight, this is a true working hound. However, the Pharaoh Hound is also friendly and affectionate, and willing to play. The short coat means the dog should not be exposed to very cold conditions without protection.

The Rhodesian Ridgeback is a large, muscular dog which requires proper training. It is loyal and protective, but is not the first choice for the inexperienced handler.

RHODESIAN RIDGEBACK

Origins The Rhodesian Ridgeback was developed by crossing dogs brought to Southern Africa by European farmers with native hunting dogs. This produced a large breed of dog that was ideal for hunting game and also for guarding. The original native dogs had a ridge on their back, and this feature is a characteristic of the Rhodesian Ridgeback. The dog was introduced to Rhodesia (now Zimbabwe) in the 1870s and was bred there in large numbers – and hence given the name of that country.

Appearance The head has a broad skull with a long, deep muzzle. The nose is black or brown. The eyes are round and bright and should tone with the coat colour. The medium-sized ears are pendulous. The muscular body is fairly long and supports a long, strong neck. The legs are strong and muscular. The tail is carried with a slight upward curve but never curled.

Coat Short and dense, with a glossy, sleek appearance; the ridge of hair on the back should be clearly defined, tapering and symmetrical. Colour is light wheaten to red wheaten, with only small amounts of white on the chest and toes.

Size *Height:* dog 25–27in (63.5–68.5cm); bitch 24–26in (61–66cm). *Weight:* dog 80lb (36kg); bitch 70lb (32kg).

Characteristics and Temperament Powerful and agile, the Rhodesian Ridgeback is a loyal and protective dog towards its family. It is not necessarily an ideal choice for the inexperienced dog owner, however.

SALUKI

Origins One of the oldest of the North African breeds of dog, the Saluki is depicted on the carvings of tombs in Sumeria and Egypt dating from 7000BC. A breed much prized by Arabs, the dog has a keen hunting instinct and is renowned for the speed with which it moves over the variable Middle Eastern terrain. Despite its ancient lineage, the Saluki was not seen in Europe until the 1840s. Its name may come from either the former Arabian city of Saluk or from Seleukia in ancient Syria.

Appearance The overall impression is of grace and speed. The long, narrow head tapers towards the nose. The nose is black or liver. The muzzle is long and strong. The large eyes are dark to light brown in colour, with an intelligent, interested expression. The long, mobile ears are covered with long, silky fur. The body, like the neck, is long. The chest is deep with slightly arched ribs. Long, powerful legs and feet and a long, well feathered tail complement the other features.

Coat Soft and silky, longer on the ears, with feathering on legs, back of thighs and tail. Colours are white, cream, fawn, red, grizzle, silver grizzle, tricolour (black, white and tan), black-and-tan and permutations of these colours.

Size *Height:* dog 23–28in (58.5–71cm); bitch proportionately smaller. *Weight:* 50–66lb (23–30kg).

Characteristics and Temperament A speedy and active hunter, with a far-seeing gaze. The breed is dignified and gentle, but can become bored and destructive if left alone. Although somewhat reserved with strangers, and even highly-strung, the dog is very affectionate towards its owner.

The Saluki is the oldest of the African breeds and has been depicted in ancient artefacts. Loyal to its owners, it is highly-strung and becomes easily bored if left to its own devices.

The Segugio Italiano is an ancient breed that although quiet and affectionate, also has great stamina. It is uncertain with strangers, and needs a firm hand.

SEGUGIO ITALIANO

Origins An ancient breed of hound from the Italian mainland, the dog is descended from Celtic hounds. In its homeland it is used to flush wild boar and hares from cover. The dog is also known as the Italian Hound.

Appearance A medium-sized hound of light build with a squarish outline. The head is fine, long and with a narrow skull and muzzle. The nose is black. The breed has large, dark, oval eyes. The fine, triangular ears can reach to the tip of the nose. A long, lean neck is carried on a moderately long body with a deep chest. The legs are long and strong. The tail is thin and tapering and is carried curved upward when on the move.

Coat The short coat can be either smooth or harsh, and both types are close-lying. Colours are black-and-tan or any tone from deep-red to wheaten. White marks on the head, chest, feet and tail tip are allowed.

Size *Height:* dog 20.5–23in (52–58.5cm); bitch 19–22 (48–56cm). *Weight:* 40–62lb (18–28kg).

Characteristics and Temperament A versatile and active hunter with great stamina. A fairly quiet breed that is both gentle and affectionate, although some individuals have been known to resent the attentions of strangers.

SLOUGHI

Origins This elegant and lean-looking breed has existed in the desert and mountainous regions of North Africa for centuries, where it is employed as a sighthound. It is likely that the dog was a native of the Middle East before being brought to Africa. This is not a common dog on the European scene, nor one that have ever achieved wide popularity.

Appearance The overall impression is of a racy but delicate dog. The head is strong, but not heavy, and the skull is flat and fairly broad. There is a wedge-shaped muzzle. The nose is black or dark brown. The large eyes are set well into their orbits and impart a gentle, if a little sad, expression. The ears are triangular and pendulous. The strong and elegant neck is carried on a deep-chested body with prominent haunches. Legs are long but well muscled. The long tail is never carried higher than back level when on the move.

Coat The coat is smooth and fine. Most usual colours are fawn or sable in all shades; a black mask may be present. Also seen as brindle, white or black with tan points.

Size *Height:* dog 27in (68.5cm); bitch 25.5in (65cm). *Weight:* 27.5–30lb (12.5–13.5kg).

Characteristics and Temperament A calm, clean and graceful-looking dog, much valued as a hunter and a guard. Aloof with strangers but affectionate towards its owner. The standard is for prominent haunches, and this may deter some because of the fine line between this requirement and unattractive thinness.

The Sloughi is an elegant breed from the mountains of North Africa. Slightly wary of strangers, it is always loyal to its owner.

The charming Whippet may appear too slight and delicate to be capable of much, but don't be fooled: it is a highly-valued sporting dog, has a wonderful disposition, and makes an excellent pet.

WHIPPET

Origins Despite appearances, the Whippet is not a small Greyhound. It came about in the 19th century when it was made legal in Britain for working people to hunt small game and vermin. Originally called a 'snap-dog', the term may have been coined either because of the animal's ability to snap up small game such as rabbits, or because of the English word 'snap', meaning food – a reference to the dog's ability to provide food for its owner. The Whippet's speed also made it a popular subject for racing, and races often took place in the alleyways between houses when no other venues were available.

Appearance Muscular and powerful but at the same time graceful and elegant. The head is long and lean with a tapering muzzle. The nose should be black or of a colour toning with the body colour. The oval eyes are bright and lively. The ears are fine and rose-shaped. A long, well muscled neck is supported by a fairly long body with a deep chest and arched loins; the loins should give an impression of power and muscularity. The legs are long and strong. The tail is long and tapering.

Coat The coat is fine, dense and short. Any colour or mixture of colours is allowed.

Size *Height:* dog 18.5–20in (47–51cm); bitch 17–18.5in (43–47cm). *Weight:* 27.5–30lb (12.5–13.5kg).

Characteristics and Temperament A highly adaptable sporting dog that is happy out in the field, at home with the family, or trotting at heel to the shops. A deservedly popular animal, it is both gentle and affectionate. The Whippet is also neat and tidy, easy to care for and has an undemanding appetite.

GUNDOGS

Dogs in this group were all bred to assist in the hunting and retrieving of game. As early as the 6th century BC, there were records of certain types of dog which, instead of pursuing game, sniffed the scent with raised head and then stood completely still. Although originally considered a rather unsatisfactory characteristic in a hunting dog, it was later realized that in fact the behaviour could be very useful in the right circumstances. This was particularly the case when hunters wanted to net partridge or quail, for example. Then, the dogs were trained to crouch, sit or lie down when they had spotted game so that the hunters could draw a net over the birds before they could fly away.

This is the origin of the name 'bird dog', although most gundogs today are employed to help hunt furred quarry as well as feathered. After the invention of the gun, and perhaps in recognition of the wider role the dogs played, the name of bird dog was changed to the more appropriate gundog. A gundog works in several ways. First, it must search around to locate the quarry by scent. Then it indicates the location of the game by standing in full view and pointing – in other words, taking up a static stance in the direction of the game. Next, the gundog must move

forward to put the game up. This means causing the bird or other quarry to move from cover so that the hunter can shoot it. Lastly, the gundog must retrieve the prey without damaging it further.

Among the features exhibited by many gundogs are weatherproof coats that enable them to work in often cold, wet conditions, including freezing water. In order to respond consistently and obediently to commands, gundogs must usually be loyal, willing to please and friendly by nature – features that makes this group the most popular of all in terms of human companions and family pets. The stealthy nature of their work also means that they are less given to vocalization than hounds; again, a considerable attribute in a housedog.

Field trials are held regularly in which the qualities of the various types of gundogs are tested. Certain characteristics necessary for field work, such as speed or stamina, are bred on. Sometimes these same features are considered less important in the show dog – where appearance may be more highly prized – and this explains the divergence that often occurs between the working dog and the show dog of the same breed.

Among the gundogs, different breeds are used for the various tasks in the field. The gundogs that exemplify

pointing behaviour include the various breeds of pointer (such as the Pointer and the English Setter). Dogs such as the Springer Spaniel are prized for their ability to flush game from cover; some will also be expected to retrieve as well. Among the best-known of the retrieving breeds are the Golden Retriever and the Flat-coated Retriever.

Some dogs are bred to help in all aspects of hunting. This is particularly the case in mainland Europe, where such breeds are called hunt, point and retrieve breeds. These dogs include the Weimaraner from Germany, the Large Munsterlander (also from Germany) and the Italian Spinone.

OPPOSITE
A willing, merry dog, the Cocker Spaniel has all the attributes of a well balanced sporting dog. It enjoys plenty of company and exercise and likes carrying things around in its mouth. (Page 148.)

FAR LEFT
The Labrador Retriever is intelligent and soft-mouthed, with a willingness to work and a love of water. Happiest out in the countryside, the dog nevertheless makes an adaptable, devoted family pet and is good with children. (Page 142.)

LEFT
The handsome German Shorthaired Pointer gives a strong impression of alertness and vigour, has a kindly disposition, and is easy to train. (Page 110.)

The Bracco Italiano has a docile, friendly personality, despite its multiple role as hunter, pointer and retriever.

BRACCO ITALIANO

Origins The Bracco Italiano is the result of matings between gundogs and hounds in the 18th century to produce a dog with the best characteristics of both types – in other words, a pointing type of dog with additional stamina. The breed is one of a number of similar multi-purpose dogs which are popular in Europe for hunting, pointing and retrieving.

Appearance A robust, lean and muscular dog with a long and angular head. The skull is broad, and the muzzle is long and deep. The nose is flesh-coloured or chestnut, and the eyes are yellow to brown. The ears are long and pendulous. The short and powerful neck is carried on a deep-chested body with a strong back. Long, well muscled legs terminate in sturdy, oval feet. The medium-length tail may be docked.

Coat Fine, dense and glossy. The colours are orange-and-white, orange roan, chestnut-and-white or chestnut roan.

Size *Height:* 22–27in (56–68.5cm). *Weight:* 55–88lb (25–40kg).

Characteristics and Temperament A powerful and hard-working dog with something of the Bloodhound in its expression, the Bracco Italiano is friendly and docile. The glossy coat is easy to clean.

104

BRITTANY

Origins Originating from France, the Brittany is another hunt, point and retrieve breed. The dog was once known as the Brittany Spaniel, and although this is a true French spaniel, it is really more like a small setter. These good-natured and friendly dogs have gained popularity in America and will likely increase their fan club in Britain, too.

Appearance Compact and square-looking with a medium-length skull and well defined stop. The muzzle is tapered. The expressive eyes are brown, harmonizing with the coat colour. The drop ears are set high and are rather short. The medium-length neck is carried on a deep-chested body with a short, slightly sloping back. The legs are fairly well boned, long and muscular, and the feet are small. These dogs are often born tailless, but when tails are present they are short or docked.

Coat Flat and dense; fine and wavy. Colours are orange-and-white, liver-and-white, black-and-white, tricolour or a roan of any of these colours.

Size *Height:* dog 19–20in (48–51cm); bitch 18–19in (46–48cm). *Weight:* 30–40lb (13.5–18kg).

Characteristics and Temperament This active and energetic dog is keen to please and therefore easy to train. A good worker in the field, being able to hunt, point and retrieve, the Brittany is both intelligent and affectionate.

A vigorous hunter, the Brittany is famous as much for its abilities in the field as it is for its charm. Not surprisingly, it prefers the country life.

ENGLISH SETTER

Origins One of the oldest gundog breeds, and also one of the most stylish and admired, the English Setter shows evidence of a mixed ancestry involving pointers and spaniels. Development of the breed into the animal recognized today began in the mid 19th century, and came largely from stock kept pure for over 35 years. Animals from this line were mixed with others to produce dogs with temperaments better suited for hunting.

Appearance A dog with clean, elegant lines and a smooth movement. The head is long with a moderately broad skull and a moderately deep and square muzzle. The nose should be black or liver, depending on the coat colour. The bright, expressive eyes should be hazel to dark brown. The ears are moderately long and hang in folds. A rather long, muscular neck is carried on a body of moderate length with well rounded ribs. The legs are strong, muscular and well boned. The tail is medium-length and carried with a lively movement.

Coat Wavy, long and silky; shorter on the head, and with a well feathered tail, breeches and fore legs. Colours are black-and-white (known as blue belton), orange-and-white (known as orange belton), lemon-and-white (known as

lemon belton), liver-and-white (known as liver belton) or tricolour (known as blue belton-and-tan, or liver belton-and-tan).

Size *Height:* dog 25.5–27in (65–68.5cm); bitch 24–25.5in (61–65cm). *Weight:* dog 60–66lb (27–30kg); bitch 56–62lb (25–28kg).

Characteristics and Temperament A dog that excels at its task in the field, quartering the ground at speed and then setting rapidly when the quarry is located. This breed also makes a first-rate companion and pet. It is ever-active and ready to play, but may need firm training. As with most long-coated breeds, it takes time to get the dog ready for the house after a day spent out in the fields.

The elegant English Setter is the oldest of the gundogs, and seems to have an innate sense of what is expected of it in the field. As a pet, however, it has a tendency to roam and needs a good deal of exercise.

The handsome German Shorthaired Pointer is the older type and is a versatile all-rounder in the field. They make good pets but are happier when they have plenty of work to do.

GERMAN SHORTHAIRED POINTER

Origins The origins of this breed probably stem from the stock owned by Prince Albert zu Somsbrauenfels – which were worthy but rather slow German gundogs. These were crossed with English Pointer stock. The excellent scenting ability of the German dogs was now combined with more spirited English qualities to produce a highly versatile hunt, point and retrieve gundog.

Appearance A well balanced animal displaying power, endurance and symmetry. The head is lean and clean-cut with a broad skull and a long, strong muzzle. Depending on the coat colour, the nose should be solid brown or black. The brown eyes are medium-sized, with a soft and intelligent expression. The moderately long ears hand down flat. A fairly long neck is carried on a deep-chested body with a firm, short back and slightly arched loins. The legs are strong and well boned. The tail is usually docked to medium length.

Coat Short, dense and flat. Colours are solid black or solid liver, or both coat colours may be spotted or ticked with white.

Size *Height:* dog 23–25in (58.5–63.5cm); bitch 21–23in (53–58.5cm). *Weight:* dog 55–70lb (25–32kg); bitch 45–60lb (20–27kg).

Characteristics and Temperament An aristocratic-looking dog conveying the impression of alertness and energy. These are dual-purpose pointer/retrievers with a keen nose and great perseverance in the field. Rippling with muscular power, this is a dog that needs plenty of regular exercise. They are also loyal, gentle and affectionate, as well as easily trainable.

The Wirehaired German Pointer is a robust hunting dog, happy to work in water and over any terrain. It has a tendency to pick quarrels with other dogs, but is generally good with people and reliable where children are concerned.

Gundogs

GUNDOGS

GERMAN WIREHAIRED POINTER

GERMAN WIREHAIRED POINTER

Origins Created by selectively breeding certain German gundog breeds with the German Shorthair, this attractive and hardy character is a little bigger than its shorthaired cousin. This is another hunt, point and retrieve breed.

Appearance The head is moderately long with a broad skull. The nose is liver or black. The medium-sized oval eyes are hazel or a darker shade. The medium-sized, rounded ears hang down. A strong neck is carried on a deep-chested body with a firm back that falls slightly towards the rear. The legs are strong and muscular. The tail is customarily docked to medium length, and is held horizontally when on the move.

Coat The outercoat is harsh and thick and weather-resistant; the undercoat is dense. Bushy eyebrows and a full beard are desirable features. Colours are liver-and-white, liver, or black-and-white.

Size *Height:* dog 24–26in (61–66cm); bitch 22–24in (56–61cm). *Weight:* dog 55–75lb (25–34kg); bitch 45–64lb (20–29kg).

Characteristics and Temperament A strong, wirehaired hunting breed equally capable of working in water and over ground. An alert, intelligent and steady dog, it is also loyal and affectionate and good in the house. Being essentially a working breed, the dog will require plenty of regular exercise.

GORDON SETTER

Origins As its name implies, the Gordon Setter is of Scottish origins and was bred to perfection by the Duke of Gordon in the late 18th century. Because the breed is somewhat less fashionable than the Irish or English Setters, the Gordon Setter has remained a no-nonsense, steady, working gundog, capable of going all day if necessary.

Appearance A well built, stylish-looking dog with a glossy coat. The head is more deep than broad, with a moderately broad skull and a long, almost square-ended muzzle. The nose is black. The eyes are dark brown and intelligent-looking. The ears are medium-length and pendulous. The neck is long, and carried on a short, deep body with slightly arched loins. Strong, moderately-long, well boned legs terminate in oval feet. The tail is long and tapers to the tip.

Coat The coat should be soft and glossy, straight or slightly wavy. The hair on the ears, under the stomach and chest, back of legs and under the tail is long. Colour is coal-black with tan markings of rich, chestnut-red.

Size *Height:* dog 26in (66cm); bitch 24.5in (62cm). *Weight:* dog 65lb (29kg); bitch 56lb (25kg).

Characteristics and Temperament The Gordon Setter is heavier, and less swift, than the English or Irish Setters. A bold and outgoing dog, the Gordon Setter is capable, trustworthy and intelligent, with an even disposition. The coat needs regular grooming to keep it gleaming.

Because the Gordon Setter has never been as fashionable as the English and the Irish Setter (opposite far right), it has remained true to type. A natural pointer and retriever, it also makes a delightful pet, though it is more reserved with strangers.

Also known as the Hungarian Pointer, as well as being a great swimmer it is also good at jumping and will easily scale a fence if it is not high enough to contain it.

HUNGARIAN VIZSLA

Origins A native of the plains of central Hungary, the Vizsla is sometimes also called the Hungarian Pointer. The breed suffered as a result of wars in 20th-century Europe, but it was brought back from the point of extinction to become a first-class gundog – particularly in water – and to enjoy considerable show success in Britain and America.

Appearance Medium-sized and of distinctive and powerful appearance. The head is lean and muscular. There is a moderately long skull and muzzle. The nose is brown. The slightly oval eyes should tone in colour with the coat. The ears are fairly large, rounded V-shaped and pendulous. The neck is moderately long and muscular. The back is short and well muscled, and the chest is moderately deep. The legs are fairly long and well boned. The tail is fairly thick, and it is customarily docked to two-thirds its length.

Coat Short, smooth, dense and glossy. The colour is rusty gold.

Size *Height:* dog 22.5–25in (57–63.5cm); bitch 21–23.5in (53–60cm). *Weight:* 48.5–66lb (22–30kg).

Characteristics and Temperament A lively and intelligent dog with great stamina, the Hungarian Vizsla is an excellent general-purpose gundog combining a good nose with stable pointing and reliable retrieving skills. The breed also makes a gentle, affectionate and protective pet, adapting to all kinds of homes.

HUNGARIAN WIREHAIRED VIZSLA

Origins A close relative of the smooth-coated Hungarian Vizsla, this breed was produced by crossing the Hungarian Vizsla with rough-coated dogs of German origin. The rough coat affords the dog more protection during the winter, when it is often required to wait in boats and to retrieve game from cold water.

Appearance The head is lean and distinguished-looking, with a moderately wide skull and a tapering, but well squared, muzzle. The soft brown eyes and bushy, bearded face give the dog an appealing expression. The nose is brown. The eyes should be a shade darker than the coat. The fairly low-set ears are a rounded V-shape. The moderately long, muscular neck is carried on a well muscled body with a short back and high withers. The moderately long legs are well boned. The tail is customarily docked to two-thirds its length and is carried horizontally when on the move.

Coat Dense and rough, lying close to the body; shorter on ears, head and legs; a beard and pronounced eyebrows are desirable. Colour russet-gold.

Size *Height:* dog 22.5–25in (57–63.5cm); bitch 21–23.5in (53–60cm). *Weight:* 48.5–66lb (22–30kg).

Characteristics and Temperament A hard-working hunt, point and retrieve breed of striking appearance. Lively, intelligent and easily trained, this dog is also endearingly affectionate and protective towards its owner.

The Hungarian Wirehaired Viszla adapts well to urban living but requires plenty of space. It can be destructive when it is bored.

The good-looking Irish Red-and-White Setter has most of the characteristics of the Irish Setter but with distinctive red-and-white markings. It needs plenty of exercise in order to thrive.

IRISH RED-AND-WHITE SETTER

Origins A close relative of the Irish Setter and arising from similar stock. One of the most famous owners of these dogs was Lord Rossmore of Monaghan, and for this reason the breed is sometimes known as the Rossmore Setter. This dog is similar in build to the Irish Setter but is altogether heavier and with a more powerful and broader head. Now gaining in popularity, the Irish Red-and-White Setter is a striking dog.

Appearance An athletic and powerful-looking dog. The head is broad in proportion to the body, with a well defined stop. The skull is domed and the muzzle is square. The round eyes are hazel to dark brown. The ears are set well back and lie close to the head. The very muscular neck is carried on a strong, muscular body with a deep chest. The legs are strong and well muscled. A well feathered tail is carried level with the back, or slightly below, when on the move.

Coat A fine texture coupled with good feathering are features of this coat. The coat should not be curly, although slight waviness is allowed. The base colour should be white, with solid red patches. Some mottling on face, feet and lower parts of the legs is permitted.

Size *Height:* dog 27in (68.5cm); bitch 23in (58.5cm). *Weight:* dog 70lb (32kg); bitch 60lb (27kg).

Characteristics and Temperament A friendly and obedient dog that proves itself equally well out in the field as in the home.

IRISH SETTER

Origins This is one of the most glamorous of dog breeds, with a striking chestnut coat. The dashing Irish Setter, often called the Red Setter, increased in popularity from the late 1800s on. Little is known about the true origins of the breed, however.

Appearance A sleek and handsome dog with a racy appearance. The head is long and lean, with a fairly narrow, oval skull and a long, almost square muzzle. The nose is dark brown to black. The kindly-looking eyes are dark brown. The ears are of medium length and hang in a neat fold close to the head. The muscular neck is carried on a deep-chested, rather narrow body. The legs are fairly long and strongly boned. The tail should be fairly long and in proportion to the body size; it is carried level with the back, or just below, when on the move.

Coat Of moderate length, flat and free from waviness or curl if possible; short and fine on head, front of legs and ear tips; feathering on upper parts of ears, backs of legs; longer hair on belly and tail. Colour is a rich chestnut red without traces of black.

Size *Height:* dog 27in (68.5cm); bitch 23in (58.5cm). *Weight:* dog 70lb (32kg); bitch 60lb (27kg).

Characteristics and Temperament
Despite the Irish Setter's refined appearance, this is an active, willing and able sporting dog, with a carefree nature. The breed is hugely popular as a pet, too, thanks to its affectionate and playful nature. More training is normally required than for other setters to ensure obedience. The coat needs plenty of attention to keep its sleek appearance.

The Irish Setter is very popular as a pet, being friendly and spirited. But it must not be forgotten that it an active and able working dog and consequently needs plenty of space to run free.

The Italian Spinone is a relative newcomer to the showing world. It has an amiable disposition and as a pet is easy to train.

ITALIAN SPINONE

Origins One of the many Continental hunt, point and retrieve breeds, the Italian Spinone has a very old ancestry made up of native Italian hounds crossed with French Griffons among others. The Spinone is used especially for hunting in woodland and marshy country. The breed only achieved championship status in Britain in 1994, but in a relatively short period of time this dog has achieved well deserved popularity.

Appearance A solid-looking dog with a benign expression. The head is long with a flattish skull and a squarish muzzle. The large eyes are yellow, orange or ochre depending on the coat colour. The triangular ears are pendulous and covered with short, thick hair. The neck is strong and short. The body is short and deep with a broad chest. The legs are long and well boned. The tail is thick but usually docked to half its length.

Coat Thick and close-lying; slightly tough and wiry; pronounced eyebrows, moustache and beard. Colours are white, or white with orange or chestnut patches or spots.

Size *Height:* dog 23.5–27.5in (60–70cm); bitch 23–25.5in (58.5–65cm). *Weight:* dog 70–82lb (32–37kg); bitch 62–71lb (28–32kg).

Characteristics and Temperament A strong, all-purpose gundog with a willing and capable disposition and easy to train. The Italian Spinone also makes a trustworthy and affectionate family dog.

The Dutch Kooikerhondje is an excellent swimmer, used to herd ducks into nets. It is a friendly and energetic little dog.

KOOIKERHONDJE

Origins A small breed from the Netherlands, the Kooikerhondje is used for helping to trap swimming ducks in nets. The dog is fairly new to the international show scene.

Appearance An attractive, medium-sized dog with a flowing coat. The moderate-sized skull and muzzle are approximately equal in length, and the nose is black. The eyes are dark brown and should have an alert expression. The medium-sized ears are pendulous with long feathering. A short, muscular neck is carried on a strong body with a level back and a deep chest. The legs are strong and partly feathered and terminate in hare-shaped feet. The tail is well feathered and carried level with the back, or slightly higher, when on the move.

Coat Medium-length and slightly wavy or straight; close-fitting with a well developed undercoat. The colour consists of red-orange patches on a white background; a white blaze is desirable.

Size *Height:* 14–16in (35.5–40.5cm). *Weight:* 20–24lb (9–11kg).

Characteristics and Temperament A compact dog with a happy, friendly and energetic disposition.

LARGE MÜNSTERLANDER

Origins The Large Münsterlander originates from Münster in Germany, and was developed after the First World War from the same stock that was used to create the similar-looking Small Münsterlander.

Appearance A distinguished and muscular dog with an alert expression. The head is lean, the skull is moderately-broad, and the muzzle is long. The nose is black. The eyes are dark brown with an intelligent expression. The ears hang flat, and the hair on them should extend beyond the tips. The neck is strong and muscular and sits on a body which has a strong back and a wide chest. The back is slightly higher at the shoulders. The legs are well muscled. The tail tapers towards the tip and is rarely docked these days.

Coat Long and thick but shorter on the head; well feathered on fore legs, hind legs and tail. The head should be solid black in colour, but a white blaze or star is allowed; the body is white with large black patches, flecks or ticking.

Size *Height:* dog 23.5–25.5in (60–65cm); bitch 23–25in (58.5–63.5cm). *Weight:* dog 55–65lb (25–29kg); bitch 55lb (25kg).

Characteristics and Temperament
Easily trained and a good worker with an energetic, easy movement, the Large Münsterlander is adaptable to all kinds of terrain including water. The breed also makes an ideal family companion, being loyal, affectionate and good with children.

The Large Münsterlander is equally at home working over rough terrain and water as it is as a family pet. An attractive dog, it is both intelligent and loyal.

NOVA SCOTIA DUCK-TOLLING RETRIEVER

Origins The Nova Scotia Duck-Tolling Retriever originates from Canada. The first examples of this breed arrived in Britain in 1988. The dog has been bred selectively to enhance the trait of intelligence. In the field, the dog waves its profuse, white-tipped tail to attract ducks and other waterfowl within range of the hunters' guns and then retrieves the kills.

Appearance A richly-coloured dog of compact and powerful appearance. The skull is wedge-shaped, broad and slightly rounded, and the muzzle tapers from stop to nose. The nose may be black or flesh-coloured. The medium-sized eyes are brown or amber. The triangular-shaped ears are held slightly erect at their base. The neck is of moderate length and well muscled. The deep-chested body has a short back and strong, muscular loins. The legs are strong and muscular and terminate in round, strongly webbed feet – an adaptation for swimming. The tail is well feathered and curled over the back when alert.

Coat A medium-length, double coat with a softer undercoat. The hair is straight and water-repellent. There is feathering on the throat, behind the ears, at the back of the thighs and on the fore legs. Colour may be any shade of orange or red, with lighter tail feathering; white tips to the tail, feet and chest are permitted.

Size *Height:* dog 19–20in (48–51cm); bitch 18–19in (46–48cm). *Weight:* 37.5–51lb (17–23kg).

Characteristics and Temperament A powerful swimmer and tracker, the Nova Scotia Duck-Tolling Retriever, or Duck-Toller as it is often known, also makes a playful and friendly pet.

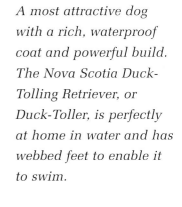

A most attractive dog with a rich, waterproof coat and powerful build. The Nova Scotia Duck-Tolling Retriever, or Duck-Toller, is perfectly at home in water and has webbed feet to enable it to swim.

These versatile, athletic dogs are excellent all-rounders, able to perform all the duties required of a gundog in the field. However, they are as well behaved in the home and are excellent watchdogs.

POINTER

Origins The Pointer is thought to have originated in Spain, but was used in Britain from the mid 17th century to indicate, by pointing, where game was lying up. In the early 18th century, when guns came into more general use, the Pointer was bred further to improve its ability as a gundog. Excellent scenting powers, a speedy action over the ground and a steadiness when pointing, are all traits shown by the modern-day Pointer.

Appearance The breed should give the impression of compact power, agility and alertness. The head is aristocratic-looking with a moderately-broad skull and a long muzzle with a concave nose bridge. The eyes, which should have a kindly expression, are brown or hazel, according to the coat colour. The ears are medium length and hang down. The neck is long, round and strong. The body is short and fairly broad with a deep chest and carried on moderately-long, strongly boned legs. The tail is medium length and swings from side to side when on the move.

Coat Short, fine and hard with a sheen. Colours are lemon-and-white, orange-and-white, liver-and-white and black-and-white. Solid colours and tricolours are also allowed.

Size *Height:* dog 25–27in (63.5–68.5cm); bitch 24–26in (61–66cm). *Weight:* dog 65lb (29.5kg); bitch 57.5lb (26kg).

Characteristics and Temperament An enthusiastic and able worker with great powers of speed and endurance. The Pointer also fits in well with family life, being docile, intelligent and affectionate.

CHESAPEAKE BAY RETRIEVER

Origins During the early part of the 19th century two puppies, reported as Newfoundland in type, were rescued from a shipwreck off the coast of Maryland, USA. These dogs were mated with local retrievers; the crossings were the start of the breed known as the Chesapeake Bay Retriever. The dog was used to retrieve ducks in the cold waters of Chesapeake Bay, and it is suitably adapted for this purpose by virtue of its thick, oily, waterproof coat. A layer of subcutaneous fat also helps to keep out the cold and adds to the impression of solidity.

Appearance A strong, muscular dog with a distinctive coat. The skull is broad with a shortish, relatively broad muzzle. The nose colour should harmonize with the coat. The eyes should be yellow or amber. The small ears hang loosely at the side of the head. The muscular neck tapers from the head to the shoulders. The body is of medium length with a deep chest. The strong, medium-length legs terminate in webbed hare-feet. The tail is heavy and strong and should be straight or slightly curved.

Coat Short and thick with a dense, woolly undercoat. The coat should be oily and able to resist water. Any colour ranging from dark brown to faded tan or the colour of dead grass.

Size *Height:* dog 23–26in (58.5–66cm); bitch 21–24in (53–61cm). *Weight:* dog 65–80lb (29–36kg); bitch 55–70lb (25–32kg).

Characteristics and Temperament Essentially a duck dog, and in its element when in the water, the Chesapeake Bay Retriever is willing, courageous and independent. It also makes a good guardian and companion – albeit one with a hearty appetite.

This is a hardy outdoor type and probably the most talented of the duck dogs. It has the uncanny ability to remember where each duck falls and to retrieve it swiftly.

CURLY-COATED RETRIEVER

Origins This breed arose as the result of crossings between water spaniels, various sorts of retrievers and, possibly, pointers. The tight, curly coat was probably enhanced by adding poodle stock to the breeding programme. The breed reached the peak of its popularity in the latter half of the 19th century, when many were taken to Australia and New Zealand to be used for hunting birds. The unique coat is well adapted for work in the water and soon dries.

Appearance A strong, elegant-looking dog with a dark, curly coat. The head is long and wedge-shaped with a fairly broad skull and longish muzzle. The nose is black in dogs with black fur and brown in brown-furred dogs. The eyes are large and, again, should harmonize with the coat colour. The pendulous ears are rather small and lie close to the head. The strong neck is carried on a broad body with a deep chest. The legs are strong and muscular and terminate in round feet. The tail is long.

Coat The coat is a mass of small, tight curls extending over most of the body except for the face and skull. Colours are black or liver.

Size *Height:* dog 27in (68.5cm); bitch 25in (63.5cm). *Weight:* 70–80lb (32–36kg).

Characteristics and Temperament In the field, the Curly-coated Retriever is adept at marking where fallen game is lying and retrieving it. An intelligent dog with great stamina and confidence, the breed is happiest when leading an active life in the open – preferably around water. Nevertheless, it is a friendly and loyal dog.

The Curly-coated Retriever is the result of crossing water spaniels, retrievers and poodles to give the dog its distinctive curly coat. They are most happy doing the job for which they were bred and love water.

The Flat-coated Retriever is also a keen swimmer. It is naturally playful and retains its puppy-like behaviour long into adulthood, being correspondingly late to mature.

FLAT-COATED RETRIEVER

Origins A blend of the St John's Newfoundland (a smaller version of the Newfoundland) and spaniels, setters and sheepdogs. The breed was first shown in Britain in 1859. Less popular than other types of gundog for some years, there is now growing interest in the Flat-coated Retriever. This has the lightest built of all the retrievers.

Appearance A medium-sized dog with an intelligent expression and an active nature. The head is long, with a medium-broad skull and a longish muzzle. The eyes are dark brown to hazel. The ears are small and close-fitting to the side of the head. The body has a rather broad, deep chest. Moderately-long, strongly boned legs terminate in rounded feet with thick soles. The tail is fairly short and carried jauntily, but seldom above the level of the back.

Coat The coat is dense, of fine to medium texture and should be as flat as possible. Colours are black or liver.

Size *Height:* dog 23–24in (58.5–61cm); bitch 22–23in (56–58.5cm). *Weight:* dog 60–80lb (27–36kg); bitch 55–70lb (25–32kg).

Characteristics and Temperament The Flat-coated Retriever matures slowly, retaining its puppy-like nature for years. This is a cheerful and playful extrovert that enjoys the companionship of humans, yet makes a good guard dog when needed. In the field, the dog works effectively and is a capable and willing swimmer.

GOLDEN RETRIEVER

Origins The Golden Retriever is thought to have originated from first crossing a yellow wavy-coated retriever with a spaniel, and then mating on with setters and other retrievers. These dogs were first known as Retrievers (Golden or Yellow), but in 1920 they took their present name of Golden Retriever. One of the most versatile of breeds, and also one of the most popular, the Golden Retriever is used to retrieve game in the field, for detecting drugs and explosives, as a tracker and guide dog – and last but not least as a favourite family dog.

Appearance The head has a broad skull with a powerful, wide, deep muzzle. The nose should be black. The eyes are dark brown and have a kindly expression. The ears are moderately large and hang flat. A clean, muscular neck is carried on a shortish body with deep ribs. The legs are moderately-long and well boned, and the feet are round and cat-like. The muscular tail is carried level with the back; it is used for steering when swimming.

Coat The coat should be flat or wavy and well feathered; the undercoat is dense and water-resistant. Colour may be any shade of cream or gold.

Size *Height:* dog 22–24in (56–61cm); bitch 20–22in (51–56cm). *Weight:* dog 70–80lb (32–36kg); bitch 60–70lb (27–32kg).

Characteristics and Temperament An intelligent dog with natural ability, the Golden Retriever is easy to train. The breed possesses a confident, friendly and patient temperament and makes an enthusiastic pet – using its tail profusely to express its pleasure.

Its even temperament makes the Golden Retriever one of the most versatile of dogs, used to retrieve game in the field, for detecting drugs and explosives, as a tracker and guide dog – and last but not least – as a favourite family dog.

LABRADOR RETRIEVER

Origins The Labrador Retriever is believed to have its origins in Greenland, where similar dogs were once used by fishermen to retrieve fish. It was introduced into Britain in the late 1800s and made its reputation in field trials. The breed club for these dogs was started comparatively recently, in 1916, with the Yellow Labrador club being formed in 1925. One the best-known and popular breeds in the world today, the dog is a great all-rounder, being employed for a variety of working roles as well as a companion.

Appearance Instantly recognizable, the overall impression is of a strongly built, active dog. The head has a broad skull with a broad, medium-length muzzle. The eyes are brown or hazel, and should express intelligence and good nature. The ears are set fairly far back on the head and hang flat. The strong neck is carried on a body with a broad, deep chest. The legs are well developed. The tail is thick and broad and covered in short, dense fur, giving it a rounded appearance.

Coat The distinctive coat is short and dense and feels fairly hard to the touch; the undercoat is waterproof. Colours may be solid black, yellow or liver.

Size *Height:* dog 22–22.5in (56–57cm); bitch 21.5–22in (54.5–56cm). *Weight:* dog 60–75lb (27–34kg); bitch 55–70lb (25–32kg).

Characteristics and Temperament An intelligent, soft-mouthed retriever with a willingness to work and a love of water. Happiest out in the countryside, the dog nevertheless makes an adaptable, devoted family pet and is good with children.

These are capable and energetic dogs, eager to work and play with vigour and enthusiasm. Beware of overfeeding, however, as it is an easy matter for them to become lazy and obese.

AMERICAN COCKER SPANIEL

Origins This attractive-looking dog was bred in America in the 19th century from Cocker Spaniels imported from Britain. Its main job was to retrieve gamebirds such as quail. The smallest of the gundog group, the American Cocker Spaniel is a sound and willing worker. Today, this long-coated breed is more often seen in the show ring or family home than working in the field.

Appearance A distinctive, smallish, neat dog with a full coat on the legs and abdomen. The head is shortish and refined, with a rounded skull and a deep, broad muzzle. The nose should be black in black-and-tans and brown or black in dogs of other colours. The eyes are full and round, with a forward-looking gaze; the expression should be alert and appealing. The ears are long and lobe-shaped and should be covered with long fur. The neck is long and muscular. The body is short and compact with a deep chest; the back slopes slightly from withers to tail. The legs are strong and muscular. The tail is usually docked by three-fifths of its length.

Coat The medium-length coat is silky and flat or slightly wavy; shorter on the head. The dog comes in various colours including solid black and black-and-tan.

Size *Height:* dog 14.5–15.5in (37–39.5cm); bitch 13.5–14.5in (34–37cm). *Weight:* 24–28.5lb (11–13kg).

Characteristics and Temperament A keen and happy dog with a friendly and confident manner, the breed makes an excellent family pet. The profuse coat needs regular grooming, however.

Derived from the same stock as its English cousin, the American Cocker Spaniel has evolved so differently that it is now recognized as a separate breed. It is the smallest of the gundog breeds, used to retrieve gamebirds. Now, however, it is more often seen as an appealing family pet.

145

The Clumber Spaniel is best suited to life in the country and is highly valued as a retriever.

CLUMBER SPANIEL

Origins The Clumber Spaniel is believed to have originated by crossing a type of spaniel with a Basset. The breed was brought to Britain by a French duke at the beginning of the French Revolution and thereafter remained safely at the Duke of Newcastle's seat of Clumber Park – from whence the breed name now comes. The breed was being shown by the late 1850s. Today, the dog is a highly-valued retriever.

Appearance A distinctive, massively-built dog with a thoughtful expression. It moves with the rolling gait characteristic of the breed. The head is massive with a fairly broad skull and a heavy, square muzzle with well developed flews. The eyes should be dark amber, slightly sunk and showing a moderate amount of haw. The ears are described as vine-leaf-shaped and hang slightly forward. The neck is thick and powerful. The body is long, heavy and deep, and close to the ground; the loins are muscular. The legs are short and well developed. The tail is low-set and carried level with the back on the move.

Coat The abundant coat is close, silky and straight. The legs, chest and tail are well feathered. The colour is plain-white with lemon (preferably) or orange patches.

Size *Height:* 16.5–18in (42–46cm). *Weight:* dog 55–70lb (25–32kg); bitch 45–60lb (20–27kg).

Characteristics and Temperament A steady and intelligent dog with a good nose, the Clumber Spaniel makes a dignified companion – especially for a country-dweller.

The Cocker is full of charm matched with good looks and a lively personality. It needs all the exercise you can give it, but be careful to remove tangles after a walk in the woods.

ENGLISH COCKER SPANIEL

Origins One of the oldest spaniel breeds, the dog's original name of Cocking Spaniel derived from it being used to flush woodcocks from cover in woods and marshes. Soon after the Kennel Club formed in 1873, Cocker Spaniels were recognized as a separate breed from Springer Spaniels and Field Spaniels. Cockers used for work are less sturdy and less heavy than their counterparts seen in the show ring. This is the most popular of the spaniel breeds.

Appearance The overall impression is of a merry, compact, well balanced sporting dog. The skull should not be too broad or long, and the muzzle should be square with a distinct stop. The eyes are dark brown or lighter brown or hazel, toning

with the coat; the expression is intelligent, alert and gentle. The ears are lobe-shaped, thin and pendulous. A muscular, moderate-length neck is carried on a strong, compact body with a well developed chest. The dog has short, strongly boned legs and cat-feet. The tail is usually docked, but never so short that it impedes its non-stop action on the move.

Coat Flat and silky; well feathered fore legs, hind legs (above hocks) and body. Various colours are available; self-colours should only have white on the chest.

Size *Height:* dog 15.5–16in (39.5–41cm); bitch 15–15.5in (38–39.5cm). *Weight:* 28–32lb (13–14.5kg).

Characteristics and Temperament A willing and happy dog if ever there was one. The Cocker Spaniel is quick to adapt to its surroundings and is equally at home sniffing around in the countryside as it is playing indoors with its family. The breed enjoys exercise and company and delights in carrying things about in its mouth.

ENGLISH SPRINGER SPANIEL

Origins Formerly known as the Norfolk Spaniel, this pure and ancient breed was awarded official status in 1902. The breed gets the name 'springer' from the fact that this type of spaniel was used to flush birds into the air from cover so that they would spring upwards and thus be bagged by the shooters.

Appearance A compact, racy dog of symmetrical build that stands high on the leg. The medium-length skull is fairly broad, and the muzzle is rather broad and deep. The almond-shaped eyes, of hazel coloration, have a kind and alert expression. The ears are lobe-shaped, fairly long, and hang flat. The neck is rather long, strong and muscular. The body is strong with a deep chest and is carried on well developed legs. The tail, customarily docked, is well feathered and has a lively action.

Coat Long, dense and soft but also tough and weather-resistant; feathering on ears, fore legs, belly and hindquarters. Colours are black-and-white, liver-and-white, or these colours with tan markings.

Size *Height:* 20in (51cm). *Weight:* 47lb (21kg).

Characteristics and Temperament A friendly and extrovert gundog, willing to search for, flush, and retrieve game – even in icy water. An affectionate family dog, too, but one that likes plenty of exercise.

Formerly known as the Norfolk Spaniel, the Springer is an ancient breed. It excels in the field, flushing out game, but needs plenty of space to run and swim, without which it may become lazy and obese.

The Field Spaniel is a working dog through and through, as its name suggests. It likes nothing better than to be out in the countryside, and could never be entirely happy as a town-dweller.

FIELD SPANIEL

Origins This breed arose through crossings between the Sussex Spaniel and the Cocker Spaniel. The Field Spaniel has enjoyed mixed fortunes; the breed almost disappeared in the early 1900s and again in the 1950s. At one time, its numbers were so small that the Kennel Club would not allow it championship status. However, determined efforts by enthusiasts and breeders reversed this decision in the 1960s.

Appearance A dog built for activity and endurance and one with a noble character. The head has a broad, long skull and a lean muzzle. The almond-shaped eyes are dark hazel in colour and have a gentle expression. The moderately-long ears are set low and are well feathered. The neck is long and muscular. The body has a level and strong back and a deep chest. The moderate-length legs terminate in round feet. The tail is docked by one-third and should not be carried higher than the back.

Coat Flat, glossy and silky; weatherproof and dense; well feathered chest, underbody and behind legs. Colours are black, liver, golden-liver, mahogany or roan; any of these colours with tan markings are permissible. White or roan is permissible on the chest of solid-coloured dogs.

Size *Height:* 18in (46cm). *Weight:* 40–55lb (18–25kg).

Characteristics and Temperament An active gundog, but also placid, obedient and intelligent. Not a breed recommended for the town-dweller, however, since the Field Spaniel really belongs where its name suggests – out in the open countryside.

The Irish Water Spaniel is excellent at retrieving and even better where water in involved, hence its name. They are loyal to their owners, but that curly coat requires regular attention.

IRISH WATER SPANIEL

Origins This is a very ancient breed, but there is some disagreement among experts as to its true ancestry. What is undeniable, however, is that the Water Spaniel makes a versatile worker in the field as well as a good companion. This is the tallest of the spaniel breeds.

Appearance A large and purposeful-looking spaniel with a distinctive curly coat. The skull is high-domed and fairly broad and long, and the muzzle is long and strong. The nose is dark liver in colour. The eyes have an alert expression and are amber to dark brown. The long ears are oval-shaped and pendulous. The neck is powerful and arching and is carried on a short, deep body. The legs are long and strongly boned and terminate in large feet. The tail is fairly long and tapers to a point.

Coat Composed of dense, crisp, tight ringlets and with a natural oiliness which aids the dog's ability to retrieve from water; the coat is shorter on the muzzle, throat and lower part of the tail. Colour is a rich, dark liver.

Size *Height:* dog 21–23in (53–58.5cm); bitch 20–22in (51–56cm). *Weight:* dog 55–65lb (25–29kg); bitch 45–58lb (20–26kg).

Characteristics and Temperament A useful gundog, especially where retrieving from water is required. Although sometimes described as reserved, the breed is affectionate and faithful. Fans talk of the dog's great sense of humour. Proper grooming is required for this breed.

The Sussex Spaniel is a rare sight these days. It is a powerful dog with a strange rolling action when on the move. It is also unusual in that it is highly vocal. It is docile and friendly.

SUSSEX SPANIEL

Origins The Sussex Spaniel, like the Field Spaniel, is a rarely-seen variety today. This is a heavily-built dog with a characteristic rolling gait when on the move; it seems to be less fashionable than the more lightly-built breeds of spaniel. The breed first arose in Sussex, England, over 120 years ago.

Appearance A massive and powerfully-built dog with a heavy-browed expression. The head is medium long with a broad skull and a long, square muzzle. The nose is liver. The large hazel eyes have a gentle expression. The ears are thick and lobular and hang flat. The neck is long and strong and is carried on a deep and muscular body. The well boned legs are rather short. The tail is usually docked and has a lively action.

Coat An abundant, flat coat with good feathering on the forequarters and hindquarters. Colour is golden-liver.

Size *Height:* 15–16in (38–41cm). *Weight:* 39.5–51lb (18–23kg).

Characteristics and Temperament The Sussex Spaniel has a characteristic rolling gait when on the move. It is also unusual among spaniels in being quite vocal when working. Despite its heavy appearance, the breed is energetic as well as docile and friendly.

The attractively marked Welsh Springer Spaniel is slighter and smaller than its English counterpart, making it extremely agile and good at fast work without tiring.

WELSH SPRINGER SPANIEL

Origins Red-and-white spaniels closely resembling the Welsh have existed for many years. The Welsh Springer Spaniel was recognized by the Kennel Club in 1902. Slightly lighter in build than the English Springer, the Welsh was used extensively for hunting but nowadays is seen increasingly at shows.

Appearance A compact and attractively marked dog, similar to, but slightly smaller than the English Springer. The head has a moderate length, slightly domed skull and a medium-length muzzle. The nose is flesh-coloured or darker. The eyes are hazel or dark brown with a kindly expression. The ears are fairly small and hang flat. The neck is long and muscular. The body is not long but is strong and muscular. Medium-length, well-boned legs terminate in round, cat-like feet. The tail is usually docked and has a lively action.

Coat Straight, thick and silky; feathering occurs on the fore legs, hind legs above the hocks, ears and tail. Colour is rich red-and-white.

Size *Height:* dog 19in (48cm); bitch 18in (46cm). *Weight:* 34–45lb (15–20kg).

Characteristics and Temperament A dog built to work hard and without tiring, being fast and active. The Welsh Springer Spaniel also makes an obedient and friendly house pet.

The tall, sophisticated Weimaraner has a short glossy coat with a silvery sheen. It is a confident and assertive dog that requires firm handling.

WEIMARANER

Origins The Weimaraner gets its name from the German court of Weimar, where the dog was very popular. Dogs of similar appearance, albeit more houndlike, appear in paintings from the early 1600s by Van Dyck. The dog has proved effective for hunt, point and retrieve duties. Originally it was used to hunt boar and deer, but today it usually accompanies hunters looking for smaller game. The most commonly seen version of this dog is the shorthaired variety, although there is also a longhaired form.

Appearance A tall, elegant and purposeful-looking dog with an unusual coloration. The head is fairly long and aristocratic with a long muzzle. The nose is grey. The eyes are round and vary in colour from amber to blue-grey. The ears are long, taper to a point, and are slightly folded. A moderately-long neck is carried on a rather long body with a deep chest, and the legs are strong and well boned. The tail is docked.

Coat Short and sleek. In the longhaired variety, the fur is 1–2in (2.5–5cm) long, with feathering on the tail and back of the limbs. Colour is silver grey, mouse grey or roe grey with a metallic sheen.

Size *Height:* dog 24–27in (61–68.5cm); bitch 22–25in (56–63.5cm). *Weight:* dog 59.5lb (27kg); bitch 49.5lb (22.5kg).

Characteristics and Temperament An able multi-role hunting dog which is fearless but friendly and obedient. Increasingly, the breed is finding favour as a companion, too.

TERRIERS

The word 'terrier' comes from *terra*, the Latin word for earth, and aptly describes the part of the landscape in which these dogs were originally employed – being bred to drive badgers, foxes, rabbits and other quarry from their underground retreats. On occasions, when the terrier could not reach into the burrow or earth, it would still indicate the presence of the quarry to the hunter, who would then unearth it by other means.

Because of the qualities required to perform these underground tasks, most terriers are small to medium-sized dogs, often with short legs, great digging skills and powerful jaws – but always with huge amounts of courage and tenacity. In time, the name terrier came to be applied to all dogs that were also kept for despatching vermin such as rats and mice.

Because different sorts of terriers were required for working over many varied kinds of terrain, cross-breeding with other types of dogs became common practice. Thus breeds of terrier required to keep up with huntsmen on horseback might be bred with hounds to improve the stamina and increase the length of the legs. Terriers used for fighting would be bred with mastiffs and other large, powerful dogs to improve their skills in combat. Many of these

new terrier breeds arose because of local needs, and often bear the name of the region from which they originated. The Manchester Terrier, the Skye Terrier and the Australian Terrier, for example, leave no doubt as to their origins.

The rise in the popularity of terriers began in the latter part of the 19th century when dog shows brought many of these animals to a wider audience. This was also the period when many of the breed standards were set. As with many other dog breeds, shows today tend to concentrate on appearance, and terriers have been among the top award winners around the world.

Terriers range in size from the largest, the Airedale Terrier (which is 24in /61cm at the shoulder), to the much smaller Norfolk Terrier (which stands only 10in/25.5cm high). Despite these great differences in size, terriers usually show many shared characteristics. They are naturally alert

RIGHT
The Airedale is the largest of the terriers, originally developed to hunt otters, badgers and wolves. It is a lively and adaptable dog which should be handled firmly but kindly, while at the same time learning who is in charge. (Page 164.)

FAR LEFT
Norwich Terriers are tough, active little dogs and are among the smallest of the working terriers. They can be distinguished from the almost identical Norfolk Terrier in that they have pricked ears rather than drop ears. (Page 194.)

LEFT
This Lakeland Terrier puppy is endearingly cheerful and mischievous – even its naughty ways are soon forgiven. (Page 190.)

and curious dogs, being sharp in movement, and their ancestry means that they like nothing better than to explore underground at any opportunity. They also have a great propensity for digging – much to the alarm and consternation of owners with well kept gardens.

On the whole, terriers are robust dogs, and less sensitive than many other pedigree breeds. For this reason, they make good pets for a young growing family. They are usually easy for young

children to pick up and cuddle, are always ready for action and for joining in games, and don't take it too personally when scolded for doing wrong. They can, however, be a little too ready to pick a fight with any other dogs they may encounter, on occasions tending to charge straight in without warning.

About two-thirds of the world's terrier breeds originated in Britain. Some breeds of terrier are not classed in the main terrier group, but in other groups

such as the toy dogs or the utility dog group. Furthermore, the so-called Tibetan Terrier is not a terrier at all, being related to the working dogs. The coats of some of the terrier breeds require regular clipping or trimming – often referred to as stripping – to retain their classic, strong-lined appearance. This is usually carried out professionally twice-yearly, although for show purposes more detailed preparation is usually needed.

The Airedale is the largest of the terrier group. It has an excellent sense of smell and is nowadays used for tracking, drug detection, and searching for victims trapped in collapsed buildings. They are incorrigible diggers, so watch your flower beds!

AIREDALE TERRIER

Origins This breed, the largest by far of all the terriers (and sometimes called the King of Terriers for this reason), originates from Yorkshire, England. The dog reflects both terrier and hound ancestry in its makeup and behaviour, although it is too big to go underground in the traditional way of terriers. The Airedale Terrier's imposing size means that it is used on occasions as a guard dog, among other duties.

Appearance A muscular, cobby and active-looking dog. The head is long and flat, and not too broad between the ears, and the nose is black. The dark eyes should have a lively expression. The V-shaped ears are small, folded and placed high at the sides of the head. The neck is muscular and is carried on a body with a short, strong and level back; the chest is deep. The legs are long and well boned. The tail is strong and carried high; it is customarily docked.

Coat The texture is hard, wiry and dense; undercoat is softer. Colour is tan, with black or grizzle saddle, top of neck and top of tail.

Size *Height:* dog 23–24in (58.5–61cm); bitch 22–23in (56–58.5cm). *Weight:* 45lb (20.5kg).

Characteristics and Temperament The dog's remarkable scenting powers mean that it is used for tracking, for detecting victims in collapsed buildings, and for game hunting. The Airedale also comes into its own as an intelligent and courageous guard dog. Nevertheless, the breed makes a devoted and protective family dog, always ready to join in the next game or simply go wherever its owners are going. Not a huge eater, despite its size, it is nevertheless a dog with a healthy appetite.

The Australian Terrier's talents as a rat and snake catcher may no longer be to the fore, but it still retains all the characteristic pluckiness associated with the working terrier.

AUSTRALIAN TERRIER

Origins Thought to have been bred from British terriers imported into Australia by early settlers, the Australian Terrier achieved show recognition in Britain in 1936. This is one of very few terrier breeds to have originated outside Britain.

Appearance A low-set, longish dog with a rough coat and a 'ready-for-action' look about it. The head is long with a flat skull and a longish muzzle. The nose is black. The dark-brown eyes are small and have a keen expression. The small ears are pricked and free from long hair. The neck is long and slightly arched. The body is quite long in proportion to the dog's height, and it is fairly deep-chested. The legs are quite short, and the tail is docked.

Coat Long, straight and hard to the touch. There are two colours: the coat may be blue, steel blue or dark blue-grey with tan on the face, ears, underbody, lower legs and feet; topknot is blue or silver. Alternatively the coat may be sandy or red, with the topknot a lighter shade.

Size *Height:* 10in (25.5cm). *Weight:* 14lb (6.3kg).

Characteristics and Temperament A bright, lively little dog with a hardy character. The breed likes both exercise and play and makes a cheerful and affectionate pet, being anxious to please.

BEDLINGTON TERRIER

Origins A dog with one of the longest traceable pedigrees of any terrier, the Bedlington hails from Rothbury in north-east England – indeed, its original name was the Rothbury Terrier. The high-arched back suggests some Whippet blood in its ancestry, among other breeds. Originally a dog bred with the intention of catching food, such as rabbits for the pot, the breed remains a tough and spirited performer despite its lamb-like appearance.

Appearance A graceful and muscular dog with a large, wedge-shaped head. The skull is narrow, deep and rounded. The eyes are small, bright and triangular; colours vary with the coat colour. The ears are moderately long and hang flat to the cheeks. The neck is long and tapering, and is carried on a long, muscular body with a deep chest and arched back and loins. The legs are moderately long and end in hare-feet. The tail is long and tapering, and is never held over the back.

Coat Thick and with a characteristic texture described as 'linty', and with a tendency to twist on the head and face. Usually trimmed to produce the appearance so distinctive of the breed.

Colours are blue, blue-and-tan, liver or sandy.

Size *Height:* 16in (41cm). *Weight:* 18–23lb (8–10.5kg).

Characteristics and Temperament The gentle and unusual appearance of this dog belies its true terrier nature. It is capable of fast movement, when its characteristic mincing gait can be seen during slower speeds. Confident and intelligent but also good-natured and affectionate.

Despite its unusual appearance, the Bedlington is far from lamb-like and retains all the qualities of a champion ratter.

BORDER TERRIER

Origins The Border Terrier originated in the border region between England and Scotland, although the name is probably a reference to the fact that the dog worked with the Border Foxhounds. The present name was adopted in the early part of the 19th century, but the breed was not recognized by the Kennel Club until 1920. A true worker, the dog was bred to enter fox lairs to flush out the occupants and also needed to be able to keep up with riders on horseback.

Appearance A tough, no-nonsense little dog with typical terrier attributes. The head is shaped like that of an otter but with a broad skull and a short, strong muzzle. The nose is black, liver or flesh-coloured. The dark eyes have an alert expression. The ears are small, V-shaped, and folded. The strong neck is carried on a deep, narrow and fairly long body. The legs are moderately long. The tail is fairly short and carried high, although not over the back.

Coat Thick and harsh with a dense undercoat. Colours are red, wheaten, tan-and-grizzle, or tan-and-blue.

Size *Height:* dog 12in (30.5cm); bitch 11in (28cm). *Weight:* dog 13–15.5lb (6–7kg); bitch 11–14lb (5–6.5kg).

Characteristics and Temperament This dog is as it looks; a strong, well boned and active little terrier whose job is to go to ground to flush out foxes. Its legs are sufficiently long for it to keep up with riders on horseback, yet the dog is small enough to pick up when necessary. It needs strong jaws and a chest narrow enough to allow it to move in and out of lairs. Despite these workmanlike qualities, the Border Terrier is a kindly and adaptable family dog, too.

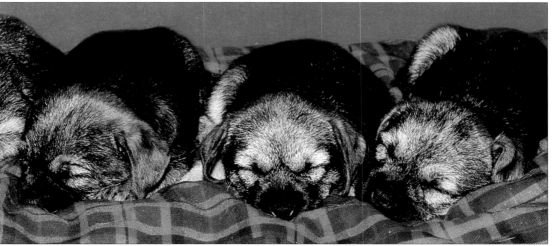

The workmanlike Border Terrier has a happy-go-lucky nature and, despite its innate qualities as a hunter, can still happily adapt to family life.

The Bull Terrier has always been prized for its courage, tenacity and speed. A ferocious fighter, the Bull Terrier is more of a danger to other dogs than it is to people. Nevertheless, to make it a sweet-natured, gentle and playful pet, it needs firm and careful handling right from the very start.

BULL TERRIER

Origins The Bull Terrier was first bred in Birmingham, England, by crossing dogs with Bulldog and terrier blood with English White Terriers. Standardization of the breed is accredited to James Hinks, and the Bull Terrier Club was formed in 1887. The breed has a unique appearance, but unfortunately has also gained a reputation for its pugnacious behaviour. Today, however, breeders have succeeded in producing an animal with a more sociable attitude towards other dogs. A miniature Bull Terrier also exists; this is almost identical in appearance to the standard Bull Terrier, but is only 14in (35.5cm) in height.

Appearance A muscular, stocky dog with a characteristic egg-shaped head. The long, strong head has powerful jaws and a gently sloping profile from the top of the head down to the nose tip. The nose is black. The eyes are narrow, triangular and slanting. The ears are small and pricked. The neck is long and muscular. The body has a very broad chest when viewed from the front and a short, strong back. The legs are moderately long with strong bones. The tail is short and carried horizontally.

Coat Short, flat and harsh and with a gloss. Colours are either pure white, or coloured – black, brindle, fawn, red or tricolour.

Size *Height:* 18in (46cm). *Weight:* 72lb (33kg).

Characteristics and Temperament
Despite this dog's rather intimidating appearance – it stands four-square in a manner not unlike a bull, from which its name is partly derived – it is in fact well disposed towards human beings. Bull Terriers sometimes need firm handling to ensure a peaceful coexistence with other dogs, however. They can also be rather obstinate on occasions.

The Cairn has contributed elements of its alert and vibrant personality to other terriers through cross-breeding. As a pet, it is delightful and fun-loving and needs only moderate exercise to keep it happy and healthy.

CAIRN TERRIER

Origins The Highlands of Scotland and the Isle of Skye are the original home of the Cairn Terrier, where it was bred for hunting otters, badgers and foxes. No longer required for these duties, the breed nevertheless remains a popular dog for the house. The breed was first shown in 1909, although dogs of this type can be traced back over 500 years.

Appearance A game little dog with a wiry, slightly unkempt look. The head is small with a broad skull and a powerful muzzle. The nose is black. The hazel eyes are deep-set and offset by shaggy eyebrows. The small, pointed ears are

pricked. The compact body is strong, with a deep chest and a level back. The legs are short and strongly boned. The tail is short and well covered with hair.

Coat A thick, harsh outercoat with a short, close undercoat. Colours are cream, red, wheaten, grey or nearly black – all of these colours may be brindled. The ears and muzzle may be darker.

Size *Height:* 11–12in (28–30.5cm). *Weight:* 14–16lb (6–7.5kg).

Characteristics and Temperament An alert and endearingly mischievous-looking dog, the Cairn Terrier is fearless and ready for anything. The dog also makes an affectionate companion, delighted to be out and about with its owner – whether romping in the country or just walking in town.

The Cesky Terrier is a tough short-legged little dog, bred to work under ground. They are fairly rare outside the Czech Republic where they originated.

CESKY TERRIER

Origins The Cesky Terrier was bred in the Czech Republic for work under ground. So far, the breed is relatively rare outside its country of origin and was only registered in Britain in 1990.

Appearance A short-legged dog, rather long in the body compared with its height. The head is fairly long and has a slightly arched skull. The nose is black in blue-grey dogs or liver in brown dogs. The eyes are black or brown depending on the coat colour. The ears are triangular and hang down. The powerful, medium-length neck is arched. The body is long with a level back, and there is a slight rise over the loins. The legs are short but muscular. The tail is long and is carried slightly upwards when on the move.

Coat The wavy coat has a silken sheen and is usually clipped, except on the upper part of the head, legs and underbody. Colours are blue-grey or light brown.

Size *Height:* 11–14in (28–35.5cm). *Weight:* dog 17.5lb (8kg); bitch 15.5lb (7kg).

Characteristics and Temperament Tough, hardy and agile, the Cesky Terrier is a somewhat wary, yet nevertheless friendly dog.

DANDIE DINMONT TERRIER

Origins The fictional character Dandie Dinmont from the novel *Guy Mannering* by Sir Walter Scott is the inspiration for the name of this breed, although dogs of this type existed in the region between England and Scotland long before the story was penned. The dog was originally developed for hunting otters and badgers.

Appearance A dog with a ferret-like body, short legs, and a large, distinctive head. The head has a large, almost square skull and a deep muzzle. The nose is black. The dark hazel eyes are large and expressive. The ears are pendulous. The strong and muscular neck is carried on a long, deep body with well arched loins. The legs are short and heavy-boned, with the hind legs a little longer than the fore legs. The tail is short.

Coat A double coat with a soft undercoat and a hard, crisp, top coat; fore legs are feathered; head is covered with soft, silky fur. Colours are pepper or mustard.

Size *Height:* 8–11in (20–28cm). *Weight:* 18–24lb (8–11kg).

Characteristics and Temperament The Dandie Dinmont can do its work well, but it still makes a devoted and affectionate pet – albeit a rather wilful one on occasions.

Although bred to work hard, the Dandy Dinmont is a devoted and affectionate pet though, being a terrier, it can still be wilful on occasions.

SMOOTH-HAIRED FOX TERRIER

Origins This is one of the most popular and well established of all terriers. It originated in Britain and has an ancestry that is probably linked to Bull Terriers and Manchester Terriers. The standard for the breed was drawn up in the 1870s. This terrier is a valuable addition to the foxhound pack, being small enough to chase foxes from cover which is too inaccessible to be reached by larger dogs. Although fashionable in the show ring, the breed has remained true to the original type.

Appearance A compact and purposeful-looking dog. The skull is flat and rather narrow, and the muzzle is long and strong. The nose is black. The eyes are small and dark with an alert, intelligent expression. The breed has small, V-shaped drop ears. The neck is moderately long, lean and muscular. The body has a deep chest and a short, level back. The legs are quite long and strong. The tail is docked and carried merrily.

Coat Smooth, short, hard and dense. Preferred colours are all-white, black-and-white, or tan-and-white.

Size *Height:* dog 15.5in (39.5cm); bitch proportionately smaller. *Weight:* dog 16–18lb (7–8kg); bitch 15–17lb (7–7.5kg).

Characteristics and Temperament Big enough to cope with foxes and strong enough to run with a hunt, the Smooth-haired Fox Terrier is lively and eager. The breed needs a firm hand but rewards a caring owner with devotion and affection. Not usually one to start an argument with other dogs, this breed will nevertheless give a good account of itself if provoked.

The charming Smooth-haired Fox Terrier is bred to run with the hunt and flush out foxes from areas too small for larger dogs. It is a lively little dog which requires a firm hand, but it can be a rewarding pet.

The Wirehaired Fox Terrier is at his happiest in a family household. He will expect to be included in every game and has boundless energy. He will also guard against intruders.

WIREHAIRED FOX TERRIER

Origins It is likely that the Wirehaired Fox Terrier was developed before its smooth-haired counterpart, although it was the latter that appeared first in the show ring. The Wirehaired was originally called the Rough-haired Terrier. A popular family dog, the breed appears at its best when trimmed into the classic shape.

Appearance A compact and well balanced dog. The skull is flat, rather narrow, and slightly sloping. The muzzle is long and strong, and the nose is black. The eyes are small and dark with an alert, intelligent expression. The small drop ears are V-shaped and moderately thick. The neck is fairly long, lean and muscular. The body has a deep chest and a short, level back. The legs are strong and muscular. The tail is docked and carried erect.

Coat Wiry and dense with an undercoat of shorter, softer hair. Colour is mainly white with black, tan, or black-and-tan markings.

Size *Height:* dog 15.5in (39.5cm); bitch proportionately smaller. *Weight:* dog 16–18lb (7–8kg); bitch 15–17lb (7–7.5kg).

Characteristics and Temperament Bred for sporting pursuits, this is another big-hearted terrier. Fearless and ever-ready, the breed also makes an excellent family pet, expecting to join in every game and always on guard in case of intruders.

GLEN OF IMAAL TERRIER

Origins This breed gets its name from a glen in the Wicklow Mountains, Ireland. The Glen of Imaal Terrier only achieved recognition in 1930. The breed was developed for digging into fox and badger setts, where its bowed front legs were considered an ideal adaptation. This is not a common breed, but its good nature and characterful expression may increase its appeal.

Appearance A tough-looking little dog, longish in the body and short of leg. The head has a fairly broad skull and a tapering muzzle. The nose is black. The brown eyes are quite wide-set and have an intelligent expression. The small rose ears are half pricked when alert but are held back when resting. The strong neck is carried on a long body with a broad chest. The legs are short and strongly boned; the front legs may be slightly bowed. The tail is often docked.

Coat Medium-length and coarse but with a soft undercoat. Colours are blue, wheaten and brindle.

Size *Height:* 14in (35.5cm). *Weight:* 35lb (16kg).

Characteristics and Temperament This terrier, like most, is alert and active. It also likes water. With people, the dog is gentle and affectionate.

The Glen of Imaal Terrier originated in the Wicklow Mountains of Ireland, where it was used for digging out foxes and badger setts. Like most terriers, it is full of life and good with people.

IRISH TERRIER

Origins The Irish Terrier, or Irish Red Terrier as it was once called, was first shown in Ireland in the 1870s, although it had been used by sportsmen for many years before that – and indeed still is. This was the first Irish dog breed to be recognized by the Kennel Club.

Appearance A wiry, racy-looking dog with an attractive reddish coat.The head is long with a flat, fairly narrow skull. The nose is black. The eyes are dark and full of life. The drop ears are small and V-shaped. The neck is of fair length and is carried by a moderately-long body with a straight, strong back; the loins are muscular and slightly arched. The legs are quite long with plenty of muscle and bone. The tail is usually docked to about three-quarters of its length.

Coat Hard and wiry, with a broken appearance. Colours are red, red-wheaten or yellow-and-red.

Size *Height:* dog 19in (48cm); bitch 18in (46cm). *Weight:* dog 27lb (12kg); bitch 25lb (11.5kg).

Characteristics and Temperament The breed has a reputation for being a bit of a daredevil – rushing into action without fear of the consequences. It can also be intolerant of other dogs. However, with its human companions it is the very model of devotion, sensitivity, affection and good nature.

The Irish Terrier can be rather impetuous and wilful and as a result can land itself in hot water! It does, however, enjoy family life, and given a firm hand makes an affectionate pet.

KERRY BLUE TERRIER

Origins The Kerry Blue Terrier is believed to have originated in Kerry, Ireland. There it was used originally by farmers for hunting foxes, otters and badgers. Nowadays, however, with careful trimming to achieve the classic Kerry shape, it has been transformed into a successful show dog. In the 1920s, when the breed reached its peak, there were four clubs in Ireland devoted to the Kerry Blue.

Appearance A well proportioned, muscular and upstanding dog. The long, lean head has strong, deep jaws and a fairly long muzzle. The nose is black. The eyes are small and dark and convey a typically keen terrier expression. The V-shaped, drop ears are small. The neck is long and is carried on a short, deep-chested body. The legs are long and powerful and end in small feet. The tail, customarily docked, is carried erect.

Coat Profuse, soft and wavy. The colour may be any shade of blue. Puppies are born black, and the colour may take up to 18 months to develop.

Size *Height:* dog 18–19in (46–48cm); bitch slightly less. *Weight:* dog 33–37lb (15–17kg); bitch 35lb (16kg).

Characteristics and Temperament This is an extrovert and determined dog, bred for an outdoor life. It shows many of the characteristics typical of terriers. Bold and game, the breed is also a good pet and house guard. Regular trimming is required to maintain the typical 'look'.

This is a determined and extrovert dog, like most of the terriers. The Kerry shape must be carefully maintained if you decide to show it.

The Lakeland Terrier was originally bred to run with the hunt, but in recent years has excelled itself in the show ring. It requires regular grooming to maintain its classic appearance.

LAKELAND TERRIER

Origins The Lakeland Terrier was developed in the Lake District of England, its role being to run with the fox hunts. The Kennel Club formerly recognized the breed in 1921. A popular show dog, one Lakeland Terrier achieved Best in Show at Crufts in 1967 and then went on to become Best in Show the following year at the American Westminster show. Regular grooming is needed to maintain the dog's classic appearance.

Appearance An attractive, compact and purposeful-looking dog. The head features a flat skull and a broad, moderately-long muzzle. The nose is black, except in liver-coloured dogs when the nose is also liver. The eyes are hazel or a darker shade. The ears are V-shaped and folded. The neck is slightly arched and carried on a shortish body with a strong back. The legs are long and powerful. The tail is customarily docked and carried high, but never over the back.

Coat Dense, hard and weatherproof. Colours are black-and-tan, blue-and-tan, wheaten, red, red-grey, liver, blue or black.

Size *Height:* 14.5in (37cm). *Weight:* dog 17lb (7.5kg); bitch 15lb (7kg).

Characteristics and Temperament Although small, the Lakeland Terrier is a tough, fearless and active dog, ever-alert and ready to work all day if necessary. The breed is also endearingly cheerful and affectionate – even its sometimes naughty ways are soon forgiven.

MANCHESTER TERRIER

Origins Around the mid 1850s, rat-catching contests were extremely popular in Britain, with heavy wagers being placed on the outcome. This breed was developed for just such activities and soon gained the name of Manchester Terrier. The breed combined all the qualities required of such a sporting dog – terrier instincts, a great turn of speed (there is a suggestion of Whippet in its ancestry) and a clean and easy manner in a household.

Appearance An attractive, clean-looking and smooth-coated dog. The head is long and wedge-shaped with a long, flat skull. The small, almond-shaped eyes have a sparkle about them. The small, V-shaped ears are carried above the topline of the head. The longish neck is carried on a short, narrow body with slightly arched loins. Long and muscular legs end in semi-hare-feet. The tail is fairly short and tapering.

Coat Short, close and glossy. The colour is jet black and rich mahogany tan; the breed standard calls for very precise placement of the tan markings.

Size *Height:* dog 16in (40.5cm); bitch 15in (38cm). *Weight:* dog 18lb (8kg); bitch 17lb (7.5kg).

Characteristics and Temperament A graceful and elegant breed, the Manchester Terrier is a highly efficient rodent catcher and general sporting dog. The breed also makes a devoted family companion, capable of fitting into a town or country home, and is the ideal choice for any owner wanting a breed with a bit of a difference.

A graceful and elegant breed, the Manchester Terrier is a sporting all-rounder, but has proven itself more than capable of adapting to family life.

The Norfolk and Norwich Terriers are almost identical, except that the drop-eared version is called the Norfolk (opposite), while the Norwich is prick-eared. A small, compact breed, they are fun-loving pets, love exploring, and are great at digging.

NORFOLK TERRIER AND NORWICH TERRIER

Origins The Norfolk Terrier, and the almost identical Norwich Terrier, take their names from the English county (in the case of the Norfolk) and city (in the case of the Norwich). The breeds came about by crossing small red terriers with other terriers. Originally, there was no distinction between the Norfolk and the Norwich, but in 1964 it was decided that dogs with drop ears would be called Norfolk Terriers and dogs with prick ears would be classed as Norwich Terriers. The descriptions which follow apply to both breeds, with the exception of the style of ears already described.

Appearance A small, compact and keen-looking dog. The head has a broad, slightly-rounded skull. The muzzle is wedge-shaped with a well defined stop. The oval eyes are deep-set and either black or dark brown; they should have a keen and alert expression. The ears are medium-sized and pointed; in the Norfolk Terrier they are folded, and in the Norwich Terrier the ears are erect. A strong, medium-length neck is carried on a short, compact body. The legs are shortish but strong. The tail may be docked, but this is optional.

Coat The hard, straight and wiry coat is slightly longer on the neck and shoulders; hair on head and ears is shorter and smoother. Colours are red, wheaten, grizzle or black-and-tan.

Size *Height:* 10in (25.5cm). *Weight:* 10–12lb (4.5–5.5kg).

Characteristics and Temperament These tough, active little dogs have occasionally been used to hunt badgers, foxes and rats. They love to dig and to explore any holes large enough to enter. Although fearless, they make lovable, friendly pets.

The Jack Russell Terrier may be small but it will take on any challenge, so always keep on a leash when other dogs are around. Playful and intelligent, it can be destructive if left to its own devices.

PARSON JACK RUSSELL TERRIER

Origins The Parson Jack Russell Terrier gets its name from a Devonshire parson, the Reverend Jack Russell. He was a keen huntsman who bred a small, active terrier using, among others, Fox Terriers. The dog has now achieved show status and comes in either smooth-coated or rough-coated forms. Only a few kennel clubs recognize the Jack Russell, and thus there are no official breed standards. The Parson Jack Russell described here is a longer-legged animal than the short-legged version so commonly seen in farmyards and family homes.

varieties. Colours are all-white, or white with tan, lemon or black markings.

Size *Height:* dog 13–14in (33–35.5cm); bitch 13in (33cm). *Weight:* 14lb (6.5kg).

Characteristics and Temperament A tough, active little worker, bred for pace and endurance. A playful and intelligent rascal with sharp eyes and sharp wits, the Parson Jack Russell makes a good house pet but can be destructive if left long enough to become bored.

Appearance A no-nonsense dog resembling a shorter-legged Fox Terrier. The head has a moderately broad and flat skull. The nose is black. Keen, almond-shaped eyes give the dog an alert expression. The ears are V-shaped and folded. The neck is medium-length and muscular and is carried on a body with a strong, straight back. The legs are strong and muscular. The tail is straight, and is usually docked.

Coat Hard, dense and close in both smooth-coated and rough-coated

The Scottish Terrier can be a loyal companion, but is inclined to be stubborn and needs careful handling from an early age to prevent it from dominating the household. It is capable of a good turn of speed, when the mood takes it, and is an excellent watchdog.

SCOTTISH TERRIER

Origins A breed which hails from the Highlands of Scotland, the dog was originally used to destroy rodents and foxes. The standard for the breed was drawn up in 1880, and the Scottish Terrier Club was formed in 1882. Although still fairly popular, the Scottish Terrier is less commonly seen than it was about 50 years ago.

Appearance A sturdy, short-legged and thick-set dog. The head gives the impression of being large in comparison to the body size. The head is long with a flat skull. The dark brown eyes are deeply set beneath long eyebrows. The ears are finely pointed and pricked. A muscular neck is carried on a body with a deep chest and a short, muscular back. Short, strong legs terminate in good-sized feet. The tail is of moderate length and tapers at the tip.

Coat The outercoat is hard, dense and wiry, and the undercoat is short, soft and dense. Colours are black, wheaten or brindle.

Size *Height:* 10–11in (25.5–28cm). *Weight:* 19–23lb (8.5–10.5kg).

Characteristics and Temperament Somewhat reserved at times, the

'Scottie' is a vigilant and loyal companion. When ready for a game, the Scottish Terrier can move remarkably swiftly in pursuit of a toy such as a ball.

The Sealyham was an experiment to produce the perfect terrier and it remains a versatile little dog that will adapt itself to any situation, be it town or country.

SEALYHAM TERRIER

Origins The Sealyham Terrier came about as the result of an obsession to produce 'the perfect terrier'. The person responsible for this undertaking was Captain John Edwardes of Haverfordwest in Pembrokeshire, Wales. Over 150 years ago, he crossed a variety of terriers including Bull Terriers and West Highland Whites with Welsh Corgis to produce what became known as the Sealyham Terrier. The Sealyham was designed for hunting rats, foxes and badgers. The breed of today is somewhat different from the one envisaged by its original creator, but it remains a versatile and active dog.

Appearance A mobile, well balanced dog of substance. The head has a broad, slightly-arched skull and a long, square muzzle. The nose is black. The round eyes are of medium size. The ears are fairly large and folded. A long, thick and muscular neck is carried on a medium-length body with a deep, broad chest. The legs are short and strong and terminate in cat-feet. The tail is short and customarily docked and is carried erect.

Coat The outercoat is hard and wiry, with a weather-resistant undercoat. Colours are all-white, or white with brown, lemon, blue or pied markings on ears and head.

Size *Height:* 12in (30.5cm). *Weight:* dog 20lb (9kg); bitch 18lb (8kg).

Characteristics and Temperament A faithful and intelligent little dog, the Sealyham Terrier makes the perfect companion for the town- or the country-dweller. Always ready for play, this dog can usually find some way to amuse itself during times when its owner is busy.

The Skye Terrier can be wary of strangers, a quality which makes it a good watchdog. They are very loyal and form a strong and lasting bond with their owners.

SKYE TERRIER

Origins Originally called the Terrier of the Western Isles, the Skye Terrier gets its name from the Isle of Skye in Scotland. The dog was bred to hunt animals such as foxes, polecats, martens, otters and badgers. Most Skye Terriers have prick ears, but there is also a variety which has drop ears.

Appearance A low, long dog with a very full coat. The head is long with a strong muzzle and a black nose. The eyes are close-set and dark brown to hazel in colour. The ears may be prick or drop and are fringed with hair. The long neck is carried on a long, low body. The legs are short. The tail is long and gracefully feathered.

Coat The highly characteristic outercoat is long, hard and straight, and the undercoat is woolly and soft. Colours are black, grey, cream or fawn, all with black points.

Size *Height:* 10in (25.5cm). *Weight:* 25lb (11kg).

Characteristics and Temperament This breed will often become extremely bonded and faithful to its owner, but can be wary of strangers. The Skye Terrier makes a good watchdog despite its size. The coat needs regular grooming to keep it free from mud.

SOFT-COATED WHEATEN TERRIER

Origins An old breed of Irish terrier, the Soft-coated Wheaten Terrier is very similar to the Kerry Blue in appearance and temperament. Indeed, the Soft-coated Wheaten and the Kerry Blue were both bred to carry out similar duties – hunting foxes, rats or badgers. The coat may either be trimmed or left natural. The breed was registered with the Kennel Club in Britain in 1943, and with the American Kennel Club in 1973.

Appearance A medium-sized, compact terrier with a soft, wheaten-coloured coat. The head is fairly long with a flat-topped skull and there is a well defined stop. The nose is black. The eyes are dark hazel with dark rims. The drop ears are V-shaped. The neck is moderately long, arched and muscular. A short and compact body is carried on strong, moderately-long legs. The tail, customarily docked, is carried merrily but never arched over the back.

Coat Soft and silky; curled or loosely waved. The coat is especially profuse on the head and legs. Colour should be clear wheaten.

Size *Height:* dog 18–19.5in (46–49.5cm); bitch slightly less. *Weight:* dog 35–45lb (16–20.5kg); bitch slightly less.

Characteristics and Temperament A natural sort of terrier with an extrovert and playful disposition, the Soft-coated Wheaten is ready for action at any time. With patient training, the breed makes an excellent pet, being particularly good with children.

The Soft-coated Wheaten Terrier is now rare in Ireland where it is thought to have originated. It can get along with moderate exercise as long as it is regular.

The Staffordshire Bull Terrier was bred to fight and can be aggressive with other dogs. Consequently, careful training and firm control are most important. However, they do make good family pets and are patient with children.

STAFFORDSHIRE BULL TERRIER

Origins The result of crossings between Bulldog and terrier, the Staffordshire Bull Terrier was bred as a fighting dog – being used especially to bait bulls and bears in the 19th century. When this cruel pastime was abolished, the dogs were pitted against each other instead. The name 'Staffordshire' comes from the breed's association with the Black Country area of England where it was originated. Only recognized as a true breed in the 1930s, the dog is popular in the show ring today.

Appearance A smooth-coated dog of muscular build and with a low centre of gravity. The head is short and deep with a broad skull and prominent cheek muscles. The nose is black. The round, medium-sized eyes are usually of a dark colour, but this may vary according to coat tone. The ears are rose or half-pricked. A short, muscular neck is carried on a body with a broad chest and strong shoulders. The legs are well boned and set wide apart. The tail is of medium length and carried rather low.

Coat Short, smooth and close-lying. Colours are red, fawn, white, black or blue, or any of these colours with white; also brindle or brindle-and-white.

Size *Height:* 14–16in (35.5–40.5cm). *Weight:* dog 28–38lb (13–17kg); bitch 24–34lb (11–15kg).

Characteristics and Temperament The breed's reputation as a pugnacious fighter means that it needs careful training and firm handling when near other dogs. With humans, however, the Staffordshire Bull Terrier is affectionate and calm, and good with children. The dog is naturally brave, strong and fiercely tenacious but also has a lively intelligence.

The Welsh Terrier is a lively and cheerful dog, reminiscent of the Airedale. It makes a charming companion and will happily live in the house.

WELSH TERRIER

Origins The Welsh Terrier was originally used for hunting badgers, foxes and otters. Its devotees say that it resembles a smaller version of the Airedale Terrier (which it certainly looks like colour-wise), although it is

more likely that it shares a common ancestry with the Lakeland Terrier. It was introduced to America in the 1880s.

Appearance A squarely-built, workmanlike dog with a smart appearance. The head has a flat, moderately-narrow skull and a longish muzzle. The nose is black. The eyes are small and dark and have a courageous expression. The drop ears are small and triangular. The neck is long and slightly arched and is carried on a short body with strong loins. The legs are moderately long and well boned. The tail is docked and carried jauntily.

Coat Profuse, dense and wiry; a double coat is preferred. The preferred colours are black-and-tan, although black, grizzle-and-tan is allowed.

Size *Height:* 15.5in (39.5cm). *Weight:* 20–21lb (9–9.5kg).

Characteristics and Temperament The Welsh has that typical terrier-like 'tip-toe' stance suggesting an alert, ever-ready nature. A good worker, the breed also makes a clever and happy companion for the house. It is not shy, always affectionate, and usually obedient.

The West Highland White has held its place as one of the most popular breeds for many years. It has a cheeky little face and will never refuse the opportunity for a game.

WEST HIGHLAND WHITE TERRIER

Origins The breed is thought to have originated in Poltallock, Scotland, where the Malcolm family bred these white terriers for several generations. In fact, the dogs were originally called Poltallock Terriers. These smart little sporting dogs are also much admired in the show ring and as companions.

Appearance An eager, squarely-built little terrier with a characteristic white coat. The head has a slightly arched skull with a tapering muzzle and a black nose. The medium-sized eyes are set wide apart; the colour should be as dark as possible and should impart a keen expression. The ears are small, erect and pointed. The body is compact, with a deep chest and broad, strong loins. The legs are short and strong. The tail should be as straight as possible and is carried jauntily.

Coat Outercoat is harsh, long and free from curl; undercoat is short, soft and close. Colour should be pure white.

Size *Height:* 11in (28cm). *Weight:* dog 19lb (8.5kg); bitch 16.5lb (7.5kg).

Characteristics and Temperament The 'Westie' is a deservedly popular little dog. Possessing a lively and outgoing personality, the dog is always ready for a game and seems to be full of boundless energy. A sharp bark to warn off strangers also makes the dog a useful guard.

UTILITY DOGS

RIGHT
The Leonberger never seems to be in a hurry, happy to amble along at its own speed. An easy-going, friendly dog, it can nevertheless give a good account of itself as a guard dog (Page 236.)

The utility, or non-sporting, group includes dogs of many different shapes and sizes and which perform a variety of tasks. The group ranges from the large breeds such as the Japanese Akita and the Leonberger, to the much smaller oriental breeds like the Shih Tzu. The group is sometimes said to include all of the breeds that do not satisfactorily fit into any of the other main groups such as gundogs and terriers. However, a more useful classificatory criterion might be to say that within the utility group are to be found dogs that are appreciated first and foremost for their companionship qualities but which may also undertake other useful roles such as guarding property. (This does not mean, however, that dogs from some of the other groups are not efficient guards or do not make good companions.)

However, all of the breeds found within the utility group seem to have an hereditary aptitude for defending and guarding. Some, like the Bulldog and the Japanese Akita, were originally bred as fighting dogs, and these aggressive qualities also stood them in good stead when required to stand guard. Even among the breeds which did not display these gladiatorial skills, there is a propensity to give voice in no uncertain manner at the arrival of strangers to the door, making such animals ideal

watchdogs. This is a virtue no less important today than in the past, for it is a well known fact that a property guarded by a loudly barking dog is a much less attractive proposition for a would-be burglar than one in which the arrival of a stranger is greeted by silence. Although the modern-day utility dog is not usually pugnacious by nature, most will be prepared to respond appropriately if there is a real threat to the family or home that they think they are guarding.

Among the diverse shapes and sizes to be found within the utility group, there is one group of dogs that is fairly uniform in type and appearance. These are the spitz breeds. Spitz dogs are of Arctic origin, and these hardy animals were bred to work in the harsh and inhospitable conditions of the frozen north. They all have compact, muscular bodies and loud voices. Among the adaptations designed to help reduce heat loss from the body are a thick, insulating coat, hooded ears and a tail that is usually held curled over the back, close to the body. Spitz dogs were, and in some places still are, expected to carry out a wide range of tasks. These include guarding duties for domestic herds, working as watchdogs, hunting, and acting as draft dogs – pulling sleds or carrying tents and other equipment on

Poodles are intelligent creatures, once highly prized as performing animals in circuses and stage shows due to their ability to quickly learn new tricks. The Toy and the Miniature are the most suited to a life in town, whereas the Standard is a real country dog at heart. (Page 242.)

their backs. They probably also served a useful function by being something warm to sleep next to at night.

Another group of utility dogs, the schnauzers, are sometimes called German terriers. They do not bark with the frequency that characterizes spitz dogs, but they are generally considered to be more intelligent. The larger versions of schnauzers, in particular, can be rather wilful unless trained correctly to bring out their best qualities and character. They also need to be handled

properly to prevent them from trying to get the upper hand.

Some of the other dogs within the utility group can also be trained to perform useful tasks over and above those of guard or companion. The Dalmatian, a keen and powerful runner, can be trained for hunting and retrieving. Poodles, too, have considerable retrieving skills and are particularly adept at gathering from the water. Poodles are also sometimes used to sniff out truffles from below the ground.

The Boston Terrier is an attractive little dog and one of the most popular American breeds. It can be strong-willed and will benefit from training, but its useful size and cheerful disposition makes it an admirable companion.

BOSTON TERRIER

Origins The ancestors of this American breed include Bulldogs and Bull Terriers. Derived from pit fighting dogs, the first of the breed appeared in the 1890s around Boston. The animal is striking to look at, and is often regarded as the national dog of America. In America, and to a lesser extent in Britain, it is a popular show dog and companion.

Appearance A muscular dog with distinctive, erect ears and a striking coat. The head is square-shaped with a short, wide muzzle. The nose is black. The large, round eyes are set wide apart and have an alert expression. The ears are carried erect. The slightly arched neck is carried on a short, deep-chested body. The legs are strong and muscular. The tail is short and tapering; it may be straight or screw.

Coat Short and glossy. Brindle-and-white are the preferred colours, but black-and-white is also permissible.

Size *Height:* 15–17in (38–43cm). *Weight:* Not to exceed 25lb (11.5kg). Divided into classes as follows: under 15lb (7kg); 15–20lb (7–9kg); and 20–25lb (9–11.5kg).

Characteristics and Temperament A dapper-looking, small to medium-sized dog. The Boston Terrier is quite strong-willed and determined, but nevertheless makes an amiable and intelligent housedog.

The Bulldog is synonymous with quiet determination and is said to have an indomitable spirit. It has a totally reliable temperament, making it good with children and it will see off any intruder.

BULLDOG

Origins One of the most instantly recognizable dogs, the Bulldog is the national dog of Britain and is known the world over as a symbol of indomitable spirit and determination. The history of the Bulldog probably goes back to at least the 1600s, when it was used for bull-baiting and dog fights. (The shape of its jaws meant that it could grab bulls' noses and hang on.) Fortunately this, and similar barbaric pursuits, were abolished in the 19th century. Instead, the dog then became a show dog and companion, the ferocity of earlier individuals being bred out.

Appearance A massively-built, low and sturdy dog. The head is massive and deep with a broad, square skull and a short, broad muzzle with an upturned lower jaw. The nose is black. The eyes are round, set wide apart, and have a quizzical and appealing look. The rose ears are small. The neck is very thick, deep and powerful. The body is short, broad in front and narrow towards the rear; the chest is deep and broad. The fore legs are stout and placed far apart; they can appear slightly bowed, although the bones themselves are actually straight; the hind legs are longer. The tail is rather short and tapers to a fine point.

Coat Fine, close and short. Colours are whole or smut (in other words, whole colour with a black muzzle or mask), brindles, reds plus shades such as fawn, white and pied (in other words, white with any of the aforementioned colours).

Size *Height:* 12–14in (30.5–36cm). *Weight:* dog 55lb (25kg); bitch 50lb (22.5kg).

Characteristics and Temperament The Bulldog's pugilistic appearance belies an affectionate nature. Somewhat stubborn and tenacious on occasions, the breed is nevertheless good with children and makes a protective watchdog when required. The Bulldog can also be humorous – even comical – which adds to its charm. Would-be owners should note that, although the Bulldog can show a good turn of speed when needed, it usually prefers to proceed at a more leisurely pace. It can become short of breath, due to the shape of its breathing apparatus, if overexerted.

The Canaan is an attractive, medium-sized dog, rare outside the Middle East. It tends to be wary of strangers and is an effective guard dog.

CANAAN DOG

Origins This is the national dog of Israel. It was selectively bred from pariah dogs, the feral or semi-wild dogs that are common in parts of North Africa and countries of the Middle East. This is a comparatively rare breed outside its native land.

Appearance A medium-sized, well balanced dog. The wedge-shaped head has a fairly flat skull and a moderately-broad muzzle. The nose is black. The almond-shaped eyes are dark. The prominent ears are erect and broad at the base. The body is square, with a level back and muscular loins. The legs are long and strong and end in round, cat-like feet. The tail is long and bushy, and is held curled over the back when on the move.

Coat Straight, hard and of medium length. Colours are sandy to tan, black, white or spotted; white markings are permissible in all colours.

Size *Height:* 20–24in (51–61cm). *Weight:* 40–55lb (18–25kg).

Characteristics and Temperament Alert and intelligent, the Canaan Dog can be rather aloof with strangers but makes a good watchdog.

The Chow Chow is a rather sedate dog and generally wary of strangers. But they are loyal to their owners and are gradually becoming more popular. They are unsuited to hot climates due to the thickness of their coats.

CHOW CHOW

Origins The Chow Chow is a spitz-type dog that has been known in China for about 2,000 years. However, because China was closed to outsiders for long periods in its history, the breed did not appear in other countries until the 1800s. In China, the dog was used as a guard, a companion and for hunting – it was even used as a source of food! There are two versions of the Chow Chow: a smooth-coated variety and a rough-coated variety.

Appearance A heavy-looking, woolly-coated dog with a lion-like appearance. The head has a heavy, broad skull and a medium-length, broad muzzle. The nose is black. The gums, roof of the mouth and tongue are blue-black. The eyes are dark and oval-shaped. The ears are small and pricked. A strong neck is carried on a short, broad, deep-chested body. The legs are heavily-boned and muscular. The tail is carried curled over the back.

Coat Rough-coated dogs have a coat which is thick and abundant; the outercoat is somewhat coarse and the undercoat is soft and woolly; it is especially thick around the neck and behind the legs. In smooth-coated dogs the coat is short, dense, straight and plush. Colours are solid black, red, blue, cream, fawn or white.

Size *Height:* dog 19–22in (48–56cm); bitch 18–20in (46–51cm). *Weight:* 55lb (25kg).

Characteristics and Temperament The Chow Chow does not generally take readily to strangers, although it is loyal towards its owner. Rather independent, and seldom moving at great speed, this is a quiet dog that may not appeal to all.

DALMATIAN

Origins Another breed that is recognizable by almost anyone with a passing interest in dogs, the Dalmatian was highly popular in Britain during the Regency period. Then it was also known as the 'carriage dog', since it used to run alongside, or even underneath, all kinds of carriages. In both Britain and America it also used to run in front of horse-drawn fire engines. The ability to run in such a way was possible because of the great stamina and endurance possessed by the breed. Today, the Dalmatian is a popular, friendly and long-lived pet.

Appearance A clean-looking, elegant and athletic dog with a distinctive coat pattern. The head is fairly long, with a broad skull and a long, strong muzzle. The nose is black in black-spotted varieties and brown in liver-spotted individuals. The eyes are dark or amber, according to the coat colour; they should look bright and express intelligence. The ears are fairly large and pendulous. A long, well arched neck is carried on a deep-chested body with a powerful back. The legs are long and muscular. The tail is long and carried with a slight upward curve when on the move.

Coat Short, dense, glossy and sleek. The ground colour is pure white, evenly covered with either black or liver spots.

Size *Height:* dog 23–24in (58.5–61cm); bitch 22–23in (56–58.5cm). *Weight:* dog 55lb (25kg); bitch 49.5lb (22kg).

Characteristics and Temperament The Dalmatian has great freedom of movement, using a long-striding, rhythmic action. A good sporting dog if required – with boundless energy and enthusiasm – the breed is also the perfect housedog and companion for an active owner.

The Dalmation is the ideal pet for anyone with an active lifestyle. It has abundant energy and is a rewarding pet for owners who have time to exercise and train it.

This sturdy little dog, like other bulldog types, can be a little restricted in its breathing and likes to take things at its own pace. However, it can be active enough when it has a mind to be.

FRENCH BULLDOG

Origins Lace-makers from England working in France in the 1850s took their small Bulldogs with them, and it is thought that these bred with local French dogs to produce the French Bulldog. The French Bulldog was introduced to Britain in the early part of the 20th century.

Appearance A small, sturdy and compact dog with characteristic 'bat' ears. The head is square, with a broad, short skull and muzzle. The nose is black. The eyes are round and set forward, and give an expression of trust. The bat ears are wide at the base and held upright and parallel. The powerful neck is carried on a short and muscular body with a deep chest. The legs are short and powerful, the hind legs being longer than the front legs. The tail is short and thick at the root.

Coat Short, close, glossy and smooth. Colours are brindle, pied or fawn.

Size *Height:* 12–12.5in (30.5–32cm). *Weight:* dog 28lb (13kg); bitch 24lb (11kg).

Characteristics and Temperament Like the British Bulldog, breathing can be somewhat restricted in the French Bulldog, therefore it may be inclined to take things at its own pace from time to time – although it can rush about well enough when the need arises. This is a jolly, affectionate and endearing breed which is quiet in the house and only too happy to curl up with family and friends.

The German Spitz makes a fine pet and has a cheerful personality. However, it will require careful grooming to enhance its beautiful coat.

GERMAN SPITZ

Origins In Germany, there are five different varieties of spitz dogs, ranging in size from the large Wolfspitz to the small Pomeranian. The two varieties described here are the *klein* (small) and the *mittel* (medium) varieties. Apart from the difference in size, they are identical.

Appearance A compact, full-coated dog with erect ears. The head has a broad, flattish skull with the muzzle narrowing to a wedge. The nose is either black or a colour harmonizing with the coat colour. The eyes are dark; either black or a tone harmonizing with the coat colour. The small ears are held completely erect. The body is short, with well developed loins. The legs are well boned and terminate in cat-feet. The tail is curled and held up over the back.

Coat A double coat consisting of a long, hard, straight outercoat and a soft, woolly undercoat. The fur is very thick around the neck and forequarters. All colours are acceptable, such as chocolate, white and fawn.

Size *Height:* small 9–11.5in (23–29cm); medium 12–15in (30–38cm). *Weight:* small 17.5–22lb (8–10kg); medium 23–25lb (10.5–11.5kg).

Characteristics and Temperament Cheerful and friendly with an undemanding appetite, the German Spitz enjoys joining in all the family games. Its long coat will keep it warm in the coldest weather, but requires regular and thorough grooming.

The Japanese Akita is Japan's best-known breed. Though brave and affectionate, the dog has a will to dominate and must be kept firmly under control.

JAPANESE AKITA

Origins Also known as the Akita Inu, meaning 'large dog', the Akita is Japan's largest and best-known breed. Its origins can be traced back to the polar regions, from where spitz-type dogs reached northern Japan. Similar dogs were depicted on reliefs dating back to 2000BC, and the history of the Akita itself can be traced back for 300 years. Originally used for fighting, as well as hunting bears and wild boar, the breed is mainly used today as a guard and army dog.

Appearance An immensely powerful and striking dog with a bear-like face. The head has a fairly broad skull and a medium-length, strong muzzle. The nose is black. The small, almond-shaped eyes are brown. The hooded ears are fairly small, triangular and set wide apart; they are held firmly erect. A thick, muscular neck is carried on a body with a deep, wide chest and a level back. The legs are well boned, strong and muscular. The tail is large, and carried curled over the back.

Coat A double coat consisting of a coarse, straight outercoat and a soft undercoat. The coat may be of any colour, such as white, brindle or grey, but should be brilliant and clear; a contrasting mask is often present.

Size *Height:* dog 26–28in (66–71cm); bitch 24–26in (61–66cm). *Weight:* 110lb (50kg).

Characteristics and Temperament A dog of impressive appearance and with a character to match. This is not a typical family dog by any means. The Japanese Akita is reserved and protective but clearly likes to dominate; the dog requires firm controlling by its owner to remind it who is in charge.

The Japanese Shiba Inu is a spitz-type dog, similar in looks to the Japanese Akita, though somewhat smaller. It is very boisterous as a puppy but will eventually calm down to be a good pet, given the correct training.

JAPANESE SHIBA INU

Origins Shiba Inu means 'small dog', and this breed resembles a small Japanese Akita. The Shiba Inu comes from Japan's mountainous inland regions, where it is sometimes used to hunt game. The breed is popular in its native country and is slowly becoming more available elsewhere.

Appearance A sturdy spitz-type dog. The head appears triangular viewed from above; it has a broad skull and a short muzzle. The nose is usually black but may be flesh-coloured in white-coated dogs. The small, almond-shaped eyes are brown. The hooded ears are fairly small, triangular and inclined slightly forward; they are held firmly erect. A thick, muscular neck is carried on a body with a deep, wide chest. The legs are moderately long and muscular and end in cat-feet. The tail is large, and carried curled over the back.

Coat A double coat consisting of a coarse, straight outercoat and a soft undercoat. Colours are red, black, black-and-tan, brindle, or white with a grey or red tinge.

Size *Height:* dog 15.5in (39.5cm); bitch 14.5in (37cm). *Weight:* 18–22lb (8–10kg).

Characteristics and Temperament A much better choice as a family pet than the larger but similar-looking Japanese Akita. The Shiba Inu is a good, but not over-noisy, watchdog with a lively and playful personality.

The Japanese Spitz makes a good family pet. It is fairly small, good-natured and requires moderate amounts of food and exercise to keep it happy. However, its thick coat requires regular grooming to keep it in good condition.

JAPANESE SPITZ

Origins This small breed originates from Nordic spitz stock. Early in the 20th century, dogs were brought to Japan and bred to reduce their size. From Japan, the dogs were exported to Sweden and other countries.

Appearance A small, spitz-type dog with a profuse, bushy coat. The head has a moderately-broad skull and a pointed muzzle. The nose is black. The eyes are dark and oval-shaped. The small triangular ears are held slightly forward and erect. The neck is strong and is carried on a deep-chested body with a short, straight back. The legs terminate in cat-feet. The tail is of moderate length and is held curled over the back.

Coat The outercoat is straight and stand-off, and there is a short, thick, soft undercoat. The coat colour is pure white.

Size *Height:* dog 12–14in (30.5–35.5cm); bitch slightly smaller. *Weight:* 11–13lb (5–6kg).

Characteristics and Temperament A nimble and active little dog with an attractive, friendly nature and good guarding instincts. The breed does not require excessive amounts of exercise or food, but the coat will need regular attention to keep it clean and tidy.

The Keeshound, also known as the Dutch Bargedog, is an amiable breed and alert to every sound, making it an excellent watchdog. Like all spitz types, it requires careful grooming.

KEESHOND

Origins The Keeshond takes its name from the Dutch patriot Cornelius de Gyselaer, whose nickname was 'Kees'. The dog was adopted as the mascot in the years before the French Revolution, although it already had long associations as a watchdog for Dutch bargemen and is still known as the Dutch bargedog. The dog's popularity declined somewhat in the years leading up to 1920, but was revived through the efforts of Baroness von Hardenbroek, who bred some fine examples. Today, the breed's excellent guarding instincts are still employed, and the dog is also a popular family companion.

Appearance A compact, spitz-type dog with a bushy coat. The fox-like head has a moderately broad skull and a narrowing muzzle. The nose is black. The eyes are dark and almond-shaped. The small triangular ears are held erect. The neck is moderately long and arched, and is carried on a short and compact body. The legs are strongly muscled and terminate in cat-feet. The tail is of moderate length and is held curled tightly over the back.

Coat The outercoat is harsh, straight and stand-off, and there is a short, thick, soft undercoat. The coat forms a dense ruff as well as giving good feathering on the legs

above the hocks. The coat colour is a mixture of black and grey.

Size *Height:* dog 18in (46cm); bitch 17in (43cm). *Weight:* 43lb (19.5kg).

Characteristics and Temperament This is a delightful, trusting and cheerful breed, good with children and always ready for exercise. Alert to every sound, the breed makes an excellent watchdog. The thick coat means that the Keeshond is happy to be out in even the coldest weather. Thorough grooming should be carried out regularly.

The Leonberger is an easy-going dog, but its huge size does not make it the ideal dog for everyone. However, they make good guard dogs and are excellent swimmers.

LEONBERGER

Origins This very substantial dog, the result of crossing St Bernards with Newfoundlands, comes from Leonberg in Germany where in 1840 the mayor decided to create a new breed in honour of the town. An even-tempered and intelligent dog, the breed was nonetheless in serious decline after both the First World War and the Second World War. However, in due course, the few remaining specimens were used to re-establish the breed.

Appearance A large, purposeful-looking dog with a medium-length coat. The head has a fairly wide skull and a broad, square muzzle. The dark eyes have a friendly, intelligent expression. The pendulous ears are well feathered and have rounded tips. The strong neck is carried on a deep-chested body. The legs are well boned, strong and muscular and end in webbed feet. The tail is long and carried 'at half mast'.

Coat The coat is medium-length, and varies in texture from fairly soft to hard; it may be wavy but should not be curly. Colours are yellow or golden to red-brown, preferably with a black mask.

Size *Height:* dog 28–32in (71–81cm); bitch 26–30in (66–76cm). *Weight:* 75–110lb (34–50kg).

Characteristics and Temperament The Leonberger never seems to be in a hurry, happy to amble along at its own speed. An easy-going, friendly dog, it can nevertheless give a good account of itself when called upon to guard the household. The breed likes the outdoor life and is a keen swimmer, as suggested by its webbed feet. Being such a large dog, the Leonberger has a hearty appetite.

The Lhasa Apso originated from Tibet, hence the dense longhaired coat enabling it to survive in cold mountain conditions. Should be considered only if you particularly like grooming dogs, and remember that it is neither a toy nor a lapdog.

LHASA APSO

Origins This little dog originated in Tibet, where it was used mainly as a house watchdog. Many of these dogs live at high altitudes in the mountainous countryside, and the breed's long coat and warm undercoat, together with the generous covering of hair over the face, help keep it warm. Apsos first appeared in Britain in the 1920s. They are also popular in other Western countries, including America.

Appearance A solid dog with a long coat. The head has a medium to narrow skull and a blunt muzzle. The nose is black. The oval eyes are dark brown. The pendulous ears have a very generous covering of hair. A long neck is carried on a long, deep-chested body. The legs are short and terminate in cat-feet. The tail is carried curled over the back.

Coat The outercoat is long, straight and hard; the undercoat is dense. Colours range from golden, sandy, honey, grizzle, slate, smoke, parti-colour, black, white and brown.

Size *Height:* dog 10in (25.5cm); bitch slightly smaller. *Weight:* 13–15.5lb (6–7kg).

Characteristics and Temperament The Lhasa Apso is alert and watchful. Strangers are likely to be greeted with fierce barking – which explains the dog's popularity as a watchdog. However, with its family and friends the Lhasa Apso is affectionate and cheerful, and hardy enough to go for long walks. The coat needs regular careful grooming to avoid it becoming matted.

The Lhasa Apso is a hardy little dog, more than able to cope with long walks. Daily grooming is vital to prevent its long luxurious coat from matting.

MINIATURE SCHNAUZER

Origins This bright and lively German dog is believed to have originated through crossing a Schnauzer with the Affenpinscher. The Miniature Schnauzer has very much of the terrier in its appearance and character – and indeed, in America, it is placed within that group. Schnauzers come in two other sizes in addition to the one described here.

Appearance A sturdy, alert-looking dog of nearly square proportions. The head is long with a flat skull and strong muzzle. The nose is black. The dark eyes are oval and set forward in the skull. The V-shaped ears are usually folded forward, although in some countries they are cropped. The arched, moderately-long neck is carried on a short body with a fairly deep chest. The legs are well boned and muscular. The tail is usually docked.

Coat Rough and wiry, with a bushy beard and eyebrows. Colours are pure black, black-and-silver, or all pepper-and-salt (dark grey) colours.

Size *Height:* dog 14in (35.5cm); bitch 13in (33cm). *Weight:* dog 20lb (9kg); bitch 16.5lb (7.5kg).

Characteristics and Temperament Alert and quick moving, the Miniature Schnauzer makes the ideal companion – whether it be for an active family looking for a dog to join in the fun or an older person wanting a trusting and loyal friend. One of the most adaptable dogs in the utility group.

The Miniature Schnauzer is a sturdy, well proportioned little dog with a definite look of the terrier about it. In fact, in America, it is categorized as such. The ears are sometimes cropped, which is illegal in some parts of the world, such as Britain.

Considered by many to be the most intelligent of the breeds, the Poodle also has a sensitive nature and may become jealous of children in the family; however, it seldom becomes aggressive. It is said that once you own a Poodle you will never look at another dog again.

POODLE

Origins The Poodle, one of the most well known breeds, comes in three sizes: Toy, Miniature and Standard. It is usually also one of the most recognizable of breeds, due mainly to the fact that its fur is often clipped into a very distinctive shape. Despite the somewhat unlikely appearance of some show poodles, the breed was originally used as a truffle hunter and as a retriever, being especially adept at gathering from water. Although considered to be a French dog, it is more likely that the breed actually originated in Germany and was later taken to France. In some countries the Toy Poodle is placed in the toy group.

Appearance An elegant-looking and balanced dog with a distinctive coat. The head is long with a moderately-broad skull and a strong muzzle. The almond-shaped eyes are black or dark brown, and express intelligence and verve. The ears are long and hang close to the face. The neck is strong and carries the head with dignity. The body is broad and deep-chested, with powerful loins. The legs are long and well boned. The tail is usually docked and is carried away from the body at a slight angle.

Coat Dense and profuse with a harsh texture; the coat does not moult; it is often clipped into patterns such as the lion clip or the less fussy Dutch clip.

All solid colours are allowed.

Size *Height:* Toy under 11in (28cm); Miniature 11–15in (28–38cm); Standard over 15in (38cm). *Weight:* Toy 10lb (4.5kg); Miniature 13lb (6kg); Standard 66–75lb (30–34kg).

Characteristics and Temperament Poodles are intelligent dogs, once highly prized as performing animals for circuses and stage shows due to their ability to learn quickly. The two smaller breeds are the most suited to a life in town, whereas the Standard is a real country dog at heart. However, all Poodles are friendly, high-spirited dogs, and make good pets.

SCHNAUZER

Origins The Schnauzer, also known as the Standard Schnauzer in America, is the middle-sized of the three Schnauzers. A German breed with a long history, the dog was used to catch vermin, herd livestock, pull carts and guard property.

Appearance A robust, almost square dog with an alert manner. The head has a rather broad skull and a fairly long, strong muzzle. The nose is black. The eyes are oval and dark. The V-shaped ears usually drop forward but are cropped in some countries. The neck is strong and slightly arched and is carried on a short body with a moderately-deep chest. The legs are muscular and well developed and end in cat-feet. The tail is usually docked.

Coat Wiry, harsh and short with a dense undercoat; prominent moustache, whiskers and eyebrows. Colours are either pure black or pepper-and-salt (shades of grey).

Size *Height:* dog 19in (48cm); bitch 18in (46cm). *Weight:* dog 39.5lb (18kg); bitch 35lb (16kg).

Characteristics and Temperament An outgoing and lively dog with a trustworthy nature, the Schnauzer actually looks fiercer than it is, although this stands it in good stead when called upon to guard property. Fond of children and always ready for work or play, the Schnauzer makes an ideal companion.

The Schnauzer is a sturdy, well built dog, the name referring to its distinctive moustache. However, it has a tendency to be aggressive with people it doesn't know.

The unusual Shar Pei has a suggestion of the Mastiff in its ancestry. Be aware, however, that it needs a lot of attention to guard against skin problems. While its unusual looks are not to everyone's tastes, it nevertheless has many enthusiastic fans.

SHAR PEI

Origins A Chinese breed, the Shar Pei was originally bred for use as a guard, hunter and herding dog. This is a most unusual-looking dog, with a suggestion of Mastiff in its ancestry. Early examples in the West were short in the leg and unfortunately tended to suffer from a condition known as entropion (inward rolling of the eyelid), but the breed has been improved greatly in recent years. Devotees of the breed will not hear a word said against it, although others will find its looks not to their liking.

246

Appearance A squarely-built dog with a characteristically wrinkled skin and frowning expression. The head is rather large and rectangular, and the muzzle is long, broad and padded. The nose is preferably black, but any colour harmonizing with the coat colour is allowed. The eyes are almond-shaped and may be dark or light, depending on the coat colour. The ears are small, triangular and folded. The neck is short and strong. The body is short and deep and slightly raised under the loins. The legs are muscular and strong. The tail tapers at the tip and may be carried high and curved or curled over the back.

Coat Bristly, short and hard and standing off from the body. Colours are solid black, red, cream or fawn.

Size *Height:* 18–20in (46–51cm). *Weight:* 35–44lb (16–20kg).

Characteristics and Temperament This is a vigorous and active dog. Early exports were reported to have some problems with their temperament, but over the last ten or fifteen years the breed has improved.

The Shih Tzu is a fun-loving little dog and despite its small size has a confident and dignified air. Regular grooming is a necessity, however, and ears must be examined regularly for signs of infection to which it has a tendency.

SHIH TZU

Origins The Shih Tzu comes originally from Tibet, although it was developed in China and found favour in the royal courts of the imperial palaces. Records dating back to AD624 show dogs very similar to the Shih Tzu being given as tributes to the Tang Emperor. The name Shih Tzu translates as 'lion dog', and is believed to be a reference to the dog's brave character rather than to its appearance. The first examples of this breed to be seen in Britain occurred in 1931. In America, the breed is placed in the toy group.

Appearance A long-coated little dog with a very proud carriage. The head is broad and round with a short, square muzzle. The nose is usually black but may be liver-coloured in liver or liver-marked dogs. The eyes are large, round and dark and have a friendly expression. The ears are large and pendulous. The body is long with a deep chest. The legs are short, muscular and well boned. The well-plumed tail is carried curled over the back.

Coat Long, straight and dense, with a dense undercoat; a slight wave is permitted in the coat, but not a curl; the hair should form a good beard and whiskers, and hair growing upwards over the nose bridge should create the familiar 'chrysanthemum' look. All colours are allowed.

Size *Height:* dog 10.5in (27cm); bitch 9in (23cm). *Weight:* 10–16lb (4.5–7kg).

Characteristics and Temperament An outgoing, enthusiastic little dog, the Shih Tzu is also intelligent and friendly and makes a good family addition. Moderate exercise is all that the dog requires, but regular grooming is needed to keep the coat glossy and tangle-free.

TIBETAN SPANIEL

Origins Bred in the border valleys between Tibet and China, this was one of the first of the Tibetan breeds to reach Britain, arriving in about 1900. In its native lands, it was popular among members of the royal courts as well as monasteries.

Appearance A neat and tidy little dog, the head is slightly small in proportion to the body and has a slightly domed skull and a shortish muzzle. The nose is usually black. The dark brown, oval eyes are of medium size and set wide apart but forward-looking. The medium-sized ears are pendulous. The neck is short and strong and is carried on a longish body with a good chest and a level back.

The legs are moderately boned with the fore legs slightly bowed; the legs terminate in hare-feet. The well-plumed tail is carried curled over the back.

Coat Outercoat silky; smooth on face and front of the legs; undercoat dense and fine. All colours are allowed.

Size *Height:* 10in (25.5cm). *Weight:* 9–15lb (4–7kg).

Characteristics and Temperament
Another of the small oriental breeds with a dignified air to it, the Tibetan Spaniel is nevertheless quite happy to have mad sessions racing around the garden. Somewhat aloof with strangers, the dog is intelligent and loyal and makes a good companion and watchdog.

It may be small, but the Tibetan Spaniel carries itself with pride. But don't be fooled: it also has an exuberant side to its nature and loves to play. Loyal but aloof with strangers, it makes an ideal watchdog.

The Tibetan Terrier is the largest of the Tibetan breeds, where it is associated with good luck. It is bursting with energy, and requires regular play sessions to maintain its zest for life.

TIBETAN TERRIER

Origins The Tibetan Terrier has a history going back over 2,000 years, and in its native lands the breed was thought to bring luck to its owner as well as having religious associations. In fact, the Tibetan Terrier is also known as the Holy Dog. Although they are called terriers, they are in fact herding dogs, and were often used to accompany traders travelling to and from China.

Appearance A well built, long-coated dog reminiscent of a small Old English Sheepdog. The head has a medium-length skull and a strong muzzle. The nose is black. The round, dark brown eyes are large and set wide apart. The V-shaped ears are pendent and heavily feathered. The neck is of medium length and is carried on a compact and well muscled body. The legs are well boned and terminate in large, round feet. The well plumed tail is carried curled over the back.

Coat Outercoat is profuse, fine and long; it may be straight or waved, but not curled; the undercoat is fine and woolly. Colours are white, cream, golden, smoke, grey, black, parti-colour or tricolour.

Size *Height:* dog 14–16in (35.5–40.5cm); bitch slightly smaller. *Weight:* 18–31lb (8–14kg).

Characteristics and Temperament This is the largest of the Tibetan breeds in the utility dog group. An energetic and enthusiastic dog, the Tibetan Terrier is friendly to those it knows, loyal and full of character. The dog makes a good pet and will guard the house and family if required.

WORKING DOGS

Keen, alert, responsive, hard-working and intelligent – these are some of the attributes that have made the Border Collie such a successful working dog. (Page 274.)

This group of dogs includes more breeds than any other. In some countries, this large group is split into two smaller ones – working dogs and herding dogs. The working dogs group features breeds that, between them, do a variety of work – guarding, herding, carrying loads or pulling sleds and other vehicles, law enforcement duties and rescue work, for example. Some are bred to carry out more than one task. Thus,

for example, the Alaskan Malamute is a powerful sled-pulling dog, but its huge size and loud bark mean that it also performs an important role as a guard dog. In addition to these roles, many of the dogs in this group are among the most popular of pets.

The working dog group has within it animals of hugely differing shapes and dimensions. They range in size from the small Welsh Corgi, standing only

10–12in (25.5–30.5cm) high, to the giant of the group – the Anatolian Shepherd Dog at 32in (81cm). But although this huge dog is the tallest of the group, it is not the heaviest. The Mastiff can weigh up to 190lb (86kg). Despite any differences in vital statistics, what these dogs all have in common is generation upon generation of breeding that has brought them to the peak of perfection. Each dog, whatever its size, is ideally suited to the task expected of it. Many are indispensable servants of mankind. Most also share common traits of intelligence and obedience and an inbuilt desire to do the job for which they were bred.

The history of herding dogs goes back thousands of years. Nomadic shepherd tribes adopted mountain dogs to act as guards, both to protect the herd from marauding wolves, bears and other predators, and to act as watchdogs against thieves and other enemies of the tribesmen. Thus the dogs had to be big, strong and courageous. Interestingly, light-coloured or even white dogs were favoured, since at night they could be more easily distinguished from attackers by the shepherds. The majority of these mountain dogs carried mastiff blood, which no doubt gave them the fighting qualities so necessary for them to do their work. Among the best-known

examples of these tough mountain dogs are the Estrela Mountain Dog, the Hungarian Kuvasz and the Pyrenean Mountain Dog.

Later, as some of these mountain tribes began to settle in the fertile valleys and lowlands, the need for such large and often cumbersome dogs began to diminish. The requirement now was for smaller, faster and more mobile dogs that could keep large flocks of domestic animals together. Many of these dogs became the ancestors of modern-day sheepdogs such as the various types of collies, as well as the quick-moving Australian Cattle Dog and the Lancashire Heeler. Some of the world's working sheepdogs are hardly ever seen outside their native countries. The qualities that suit them for a life spent working with livestock do not always translate into suitable attributes for the show ring or even family life.

The qualities required of a herding dog include the ability to control large flocks of cattle, sheep, goats or other livestock and to quickly and obediently respond to the commands of the shepherd. It is also vital that the dogs are instinctively protective towards their owner and the animals they are looking after. These traits, together with a high degree of intelligence and willingness to be trained, mean that dogs of this type

also make excellent guard dogs. This is not to say that training is always a simple task, however. Many of these breeds are strong-minded – and strong-bodied – dogs that need some initial convincing that their owner's bidding is the best course of action for them!

Among the working dogs whose role was primarily to guard property and people are included the Boxer, the Bullmastiff, the Dobermann and the German Shepherd Dog (often more commonly known as the Alsatian). These are all strong, active dogs with highly developed protective instincts. Although this quality is one of their main virtues, it must not be allowed to develop to the extent that the dog becomes overprotective and aggressive. Difficult behaviour in such large and potentially dangerous dogs can be a real problem, and ownership of such breeds must be considered carefully and correct training and handling adhered to at all times. It is vital that dogs such as these are fully aware of their place in the 'pack' and respond quickly and consistently to commands from their owner.

The intelligent German Shepherd Dog is one of several working dogs that is so versatile that it can be employed in a variety of different roles. As its name suggests, the breed was initially bred as

a watchful herding dog, but it has found favour the world over in roles that include police dog, sniffer dog (for drugs, explosives and people buried under collapsed buildings), guard dog and guide dog for the blind. It is also used by the military. Moreover, it is one of the most popular pet dogs of all time.

The Newfoundland. No other breed has such a natural affinity with water or has such an outstanding number of rescues to its credit. (Page 319.)

The Alaskan Malamute is not the first dog to spring to mind when looking for a pet. However, it is a handsome and friendly dog with a huge amount of stamina, which means that it requires a lot of exercise.

ALASKAN MALAMUTE

Origins This large dog originating in Alaska is named after a local Inuit tribe. The Alaskan Malamute was bred for pulling sleds for long distances over the frozen terrain of Alaska and northern Canada. In fact, it is the largest of all the sled dogs. The breed was brought to the polar regions with the first peoples to settle the land. It was first shown outside its native country in the 1920s.

Appearance A powerfully-built, handsome dog. The head is broad, with a skull that narrows towards the eyes. The muzzle is large and the nose is usually black, although in red-and-white examples it is brown. The almond-shaped eyes are usually brown; darker shades are preferred, except in red-and-white dogs when they may be lighter. The ears are small and triangular and are normally held erect but may also be held close to the skull. The strong neck is carried on a deep-chested and powerfully-built body with strong loins. The legs are well muscled and strong. The tail may hang down at rest but is usually carried curled loosely over the back when working.

Coat Thick, coarse, outercoat; dense, oily and woolly undercoat. Colours range from solid white, grey through to black, and from gold through red shades to liver; the underbody, legs, feet and mask are always white.

Size *Height:* dog 25–28in (63.5–71cm); bitch 23–26in (58.5–66cm). *Weight:* 85–125lb (38.5–56.5kg).

Characteristics and Temperament Although this strong dog is not especially fast, it needs plenty of exercise and has the power to pull enormous weights for long distances – therefore it can also take some stopping if it has a mind not to. Quite a friendly animal, although not necessarily with other dogs, the Alaskan Malamute should receive careful training from an early age to ensure it is always under control. The dog makes an excellent guard.

ANATOLIAN SHEPHERD DOG

Origins This is a large herding and guard dog much prized by Anatolian shepherds in Turkey. Over many centuries, the breed was developed from mastiffs that had long existed in the Middle East and the Babylonian Empire. The dog is also known as the Karabash – a reference to its most familiar markings of cream and fawn with a black mask and ears.

Appearance A tall, powerfully-built dog of the mastiff type. The head has a large, broad skull and a strong muzzle, square in outline. The nose is black. The rather small eyes are golden or brown and are set well apart. The triangular ears are also rather small compared with the size of the head and are pendent. A powerful, moderate-length neck is carried on a long body with a deep chest and a level back. The legs are long and well boned. The long tail is carried low and slightly curled when at rest, but is carried curled over the back when the dog is alert.

Coat Close-lying and flat; short and dense with a thick undercoat; the hair on the neck, shoulders and tail is slightly thicker. All colours from cream to fawn are acceptable, with a black mask and ears.

Size *Height:* dog 29–32in (73.5–81.5cm); bitch 28–31in (71–79cm). *Weight:* dog 110–141lb (50–64kg); bitch 90.5–130lb (41–59kg).

Characteristics and Temperament A very big, active, alert and intelligent dog, the Anatolian Shepherd Dog was bred to guard, and that is what it does best. The breed is extremely hardy but needs a large amount of food to keep its great bulk satisfied. It likes exercise, but is more inclined to move at a leisurely pace.

The Anatolian Shepherd Dog comes from Turkey where it was highly prized for guarding flocks; it still retains this protective instinct. It is a large dog which requires a firm hand, a good deal of feeding, and plenty of exercise.

The Australian Cattle Dog was initially bred to guide cattle over long distances to auction. As a result, they have incredible stamina and are able to work all day. They can be kept as a pet, though they require plenty of exercise.

AUSTRALIAN CATTLE DOG

Origins A tough breed developed to control cattle on the long journeys to market, the Australian Cattle Dog is also known by other names, including the Blue Heeler and the Australian Heeler – 'Heeler' being a reference to the dog's habit of nipping the heels of cattle when manoeuvring them. The breed was developed initially by crossings involving sheepdogs, the Dingo, the Kelpie, the Dalmatian and the Bulldog. The breed, which has been pure since the 1890s, is a fairly recent arrival in Britain and America.

Appearance A compact, tough and symmetrical-looking dog with a typical sheep-herding dog's head. The head is wedge-shaped with a broad skull and a medium-length muzzle. The nose is black. The brown eyes are alert and intelligent. The ears are broad at the base, pricked and pointed. The neck is very strong and muscular. The body has a deep, broad chest and is carried on strong legs. The tail resembles a fox's.

Coat Hard, straight, weather-resistant outercoat; undercoat is short and dense. Colours are blue, blue-mottled or blue-speckled with tan, blue or black markings; or red-speckled with red markings.

Size *Height:* dog 18–20in (46–51cm); bitch 17–19in (43–48cm). *Weight:* 35–44lb (16–20kg).

Characteristics and Temperament Watchful and intelligent, the Australian Cattle Dog loves to work. It is tireless and capable of fast movements. Loyal and easy to tame, the breed is wary of strangers.

260

The Australian Shepherd is most likely of Spanish origin, brought to Australia and America by Basque shepherds to accompany their flocks of Merino sheep and crossed with Collies. It has not long been recognized as a separate breed.

AUSTRALIAN SHEPHERD DOG

Origins Despite its name, the Australian Shepherd Dog did not in fact originate in Australia. Its roots lie in the sheepdogs of the Basque region of Spain, and when Basque shepherds emigrated to Australia with their herds in the 19th century they took some of their dogs with them. Later, these people and their dogs moved again, this time to America. It was in America that the dogs got their name.

Appearance A long-bodied, well-balanced dog. The head has a squarish and slightly domed skull and the muzzle is slightly tapering towards the nose. The nose is variously coloured; it is black in blacks and blue merles and liver or brown in reds and red merles. The oval-shaped, moderately-sized eyes are blue, amber or brown, or a combination with flecks and marbling. The triangular ears are set high on the head. The neck is of moderate length and is carried on a strong, deep-chested body with a level back. The legs are of medium length. The tail is straight and may be docked.

Coat Straight or wavy and of medium length and texture; the undercoat is weatherproof. Colours are black, blue merle, red or red merle; all these colours may have tan points.

Size *Height:* dog 20–23in (51–58.5cm); bitch 18–21in (46–53.5cm). *Weight:* 35–70.5lb (16–32kg).

Characteristics and Temperament An agile, sure-footed dog with well developed herding and guarding instincts. The Australian Shepherd Dog is nevertheless friendly – although sometimes reserved initially – and quick to learn.

BEARDED COLLIE

Origins It is possible that the origins of the Bearded Collie go back to the 16th century, when Polish Lowland Sheepdogs brought to Scotland by visiting sailors were bred with local herding dogs. Today, the Bearded Collie is one of the most popular and instantly recognizable of all breeds, with a strong following both within the farming community as well as with people who simply appreciate the dog's rascally good looks and appealing nature.

Appearance A long-coated, lean and active dog. The head has a broad, flat skull and a fairly long muzzle. The nose is usually black, but may be of a colour to harmonize with the coat in blues or browns. The eyes also harmonize with the coat colour, and should be large, expressive and friendly. The ears are moderately large and hang down. The slightly arched neck is carried on a deep-chested body with strong loins. The legs are well boned and muscular. The long tail is normally carried low, with a slight upward curl at the end, but extends when on the move.

Coat Outercoat is flat, strong and shaggy; the undercoat is soft and close; the coat should be long enough to enhance the shape of the dog and to form the characteristic beard. Colours are slate-grey, reddish-fawn, black, all shades of grey, brown and sand, with or without white markings.

Size *Height:* dog 21–22in (53.5–56cm); bitch 20–21in (51–53.5cm). *Weight:* 39.5–59.5lb (18–27kg).

Characteristics and Temperament An active, self-confident and fun-loving dog with an endearing expression, the Bearded Collie is many people's idea of the perfect pet – although it also makes a highly capable working dog. It is blessed with plenty of stamina and enjoys nothing more than a romp in the open air. The long coat is likely to pick up plenty of the countryside, however, so a thorough grooming is needed to keep it in good condition.

The Bearded Collie is a hardy breed with few genetic weaknesses. It needs daily grooming to keep matting and moulting hairs at bay, but most think the extra care is well worth the trouble.

The Beauceron is France's most popular sheepdog, but makes an excellent family pet. As with all herding dogs, it requires plenty of exercise.

BEAUCERON

Origins This is a breed of French origin. In fact, it is one of the best-known sheepdogs in France. It was originally used for hunting wild boar, but was later used for sheep- herding and guarding. The Beauceron is also known by its alternative names of Bas Rouge (meaning 'red stocking' – a reference to the tan markings on the legs) and Berger de Beauce.

Appearance A lean and muscular dog with a resemblance to the Dobermann. The head is long, the slightly-domed skull and long muzzle being approximately equal in length. The nose is black. The eyes are dark, and should tone with the colour of the coat. The ears may be cropped, or if natural are folded and hang down. The neck is moderately-long. The body is long and deep-chested. The legs are strong and of medium length; the hind legs have double dew claws. The tail is long – an immediate difference compared with the docked tail of a Dobermann.

Coat The coat is smooth and flat, with fringes on the flanks, legs and tail. Colours are black, black-and-tan, fawn, fawn with dark tips, grey or grey with black spots.

Size *Height:* dog 28in (71cm); bitch 25.5in (65cm). *Weight:* 66–85lb (30–38.5kg).

Characteristics and Temperament This intelligent and attractive dog is a good worker and is also good-natured, making it a suitable breed for the family home. As expected from a dog with a long history of herding behind it, the Beauceron is also loyal and protective. It welcomes plenty of exercise.

266

The Belgian Shepherd's handsome exterior conceals a reliable and adaptable animal, fiercely loyal and protective of its family. However, thorough training is essential.

BELGIAN SHEPHERD DOG

Origins The Belgian Shepherd Dog has a history stretching back to the Middle Ages, but in the 1890s the breed was differentiated into three separate coat types and four coat-colour patterns. The basic body shape of each of these types remains the same, however. Each of the four types of Belgian Shepherd is named after a region in Belgium. These are the Groenendael; the Tervueren; the Malinois and the Laekenois. All of these dogs are sheepdogs and guards, but they are increasingly seen as pet dogs, too.

Appearance A medium to large, well balanced and square dog, carrying itself elegantly and proudly; some types are slightly reminiscent of the German Shepherd. The head is fairly long, the skull and muzzle being almost equal in length; the muzzle tapers towards the nose. The nose is black. The brown eyes are almond-shaped, of medium size and have a direct, quizzical look. The ears are triangular, stiff and erect. The neck is well muscled and broad at the shoulders. The body is deep-chested and powerful; the rump slopes slightly. The legs are well boned and muscular. The tail is long.

Coat *Groenendael:* Outercoat long, straight and abundant and fairly harsh; undercoat dense; hair particularly long around neck forming a ruff; fringe of long hair on back of fore legs; hair also long on tail and hindquarters; hair longer on dogs than on bitches. Colour is black, or black with small amounts of

white on chest and parts of feet.
Tervueren: Coat similar to that of the Groenendael in length and texture. Colours are red, fawn or grey, with black tipping – this feature especially apparent on shoulders, back and ribs.
Malinois: Coat thick and close; undercoat woolly; hair especially short on head, ears and lower legs; short on rest of body but thicker on tail and around neck; fringing on parts of legs. Colours are similar to that of the Tervueren.
Laekenois: Coat is hard and wiry but not actually curled; about 2.5in (6cm) in length. Colour is reddish-fawn with black shading, especially on the muzzle and tail.

Size *Height:* dog 24–26in (61–66cm); bitch 22–24in (56–61cm). *Weight:* 60.5–63lb (27.5–28.5kg).

Characteristics and Temperament An intelligent and alert breed that is also graceful and dignified. Loyal and obedient, the Belgian Shepherd is protective of its owner and property. These dogs require plenty of exercise.

The Bergamasco originates from the mountains of northern Italy, where it was bred to protect sheep from wolves. It has an unusual corded coat which requires a good deal of attention to maintain it in good condition.

BERGAMASCO

Origins This herding and guard dog hails from Italy, where for centuries it has been used to guard livestock in the mountains in the north of the country. Its distinctive cord-like coat may have helped to protect it against wolves. The breed became more well known generally following its success at dog shows in the late 1940s.

Appearance A heavily- and uniquely-coated sheepdog of medium size. The head has a broad skull, which is slightly convex between the ears; the muzzle tapers slightly towards the nose. The eyes are large and oval; usually chestnut, they impart an alert but calm expression. The ears are triangular in shape and semi-drooping. The neck is strong and is carried on a body with a broad, straight back. The legs are well muscled. The tail is carried high when on the move but held low and slightly curled at the tip at other times.

Coat Gives the appearance of long, matted strands; the long and abundant coat is hard at the front of the body but softer on the head and legs; the undercoat is thick and oily. Colours are solid grey or all shades of grey up to black.

Size *Height:* dog 23–25in (58.5–63.5cm); bitch 21–23in (53.5–58.5cm). *Weight:* dog 70–84lb (32–38kg); bitch 56–70lb (25.5–32kg).

Characteristics and Temperament A solid and strong dog with a highly protective instinct. Fairly cautious by nature, the Bergamasco is also intelligent and vigilant. The coat needs careful grooming.

BERNESE MOUNTAIN DOG

Origins It is likely that the foundations for this large, affable dog arose from crossings of local Swiss herding dogs and a type of guard dog brought by invading Roman armies into what is now Switzerland about 2,000 years ago. A powerful animal, the Bernese Mountain Dog has long been used to pull small carts loaded with produce to market. The dog gets its name from the Swiss canton of Berne. A popular dog in Europe, the breed is less common elsewhere, although its friendly nature will always win it admirers.

Appearance A stocky, well balanced dog with an attractive coat. The head has a broad skull and a medium-sized muzzle. The almond-shaped eyes are dark brown and convey a kindly expression. The ears are medium-sized and triangular. A strong and muscular neck is carried on a compact body with a deep chest and a strong, level back. The legs are strongly-boned and well muscled. The bushy tail is raised when on the move.

Coat Long, soft and silky; a slight wave is allowed, but the coat should not be curly. The colour is jet black with russet-brown or tan markings, a white blaze is present on the head and a white cross on the chest; white paws and a white tail tip are desirable.

Size *Height:* dog 25–27.5in (63.5–70cm); bitch 23–26in (58.5–66cm). *Weight:* 87–90lb (39.5–41kg).

Characteristics and Temperament A delightful and well mannered character, full of good humour and responsive to training. It makes the perfect companion for a country-dwelling owner. The Bernese Mountain Dog has an easy-going view on life and should be encouraged to exercise regularly to avoid becoming overweight.

The handsome Bernese Mountain Dog is the perfect pet for the country-dweller as it likes nothing better than to ramble across hill and dale. Plenty of living space is also required for this very large dog.

BORDER COLLIE

Origins Recognized the world over as one of the finest and most intelligent of all sheepdogs, the Border Collie was formerly used in the border regions between England, Scotland and Wales, but is now found far and wide. The breed was well established by the mid 19th century, and a comprehensive stud book and registration system has been in operation in Britain for many years. However, the breed was only registered by the Kennel Club in 1976, since when the dog has featured widely in the show ring as well as in obedience trials. This agile and clever dog has also been used to great effect in rescue work and as a sniffer dog.

Appearance A graceful, balanced dog with a low-slung body. The head has a fairly broad skull and a fairly short, straight muzzle tapering to the nose. The nose is usually black but may be brown, chocolate or slate to harmonize with other coat colours. The oval eyes are brown, but in merles one or both may be blue; the eyes have an alert and intelligent expression. The ears are medium-sized and are carried semi-erect or erect. The strong, slightly-arched neck is carried on a long, athletic-looking body with a deep chest. The

medium-length legs are strong and muscular. The tail is moderately long and raised when on the move, but never carried over the back.

Coat Moderately-long; the outercoat is dense and medium-textured, and the undercoat is soft and dense. Various colours are possible, including black, black-and-white, and tan-and-white.

Size *Height:* dog 21in (53.5cm); bitch 20in (51cm). *Weight:* dog 52lb (23.5kg); bitch 42lb (19kg).

Characteristics and Temperament
Keen, alert, responsive, hard-working and intelligent – these are among the qualities that have made the Border Collie such a successful farm dog. The breed is also loyal and faithful and responds well to commands. However, these attributes mean that pet dogs of this breed can become destructive and difficult if they do not receive adequate exercise for both their bodies and their brains.

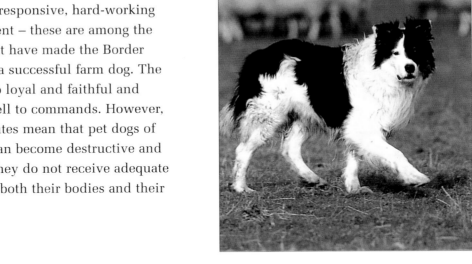

The Border Collie is ever-alert and ready for anything. It is an intelligent, active dog with boundless energy, and requires a corresponding amount of exercise and mental stimulation.

The Bouvier des Flandres is good-natured despite its slightly forbidding appearance. Given a moderate amount of exercise and plenty of attention, it will adapt well to its role as family pet.

BOUVIER DES FLANDRES

Origins The Bouvier des Flandres was originally bred for herding and protecting cattle in Belgium and also France. In fact, the name translates as 'Flanders Ox-driver'. After the First World War, during which the dog was also used as an ambulance dog and messenger, the breed was rescued from near-extinction by a Belgian army vet who saved one dog. Today, this big, amiable breed has also found favour as a house pet as well as being used for police work.

Appearance A strongly-built and powerful dog with a large head and a compact body. The head has a flat, wide skull and a broad, powerful muzzle. The nose is black. The oval eyes should be as dark as possible and impart an intelligent expression. The ears are triangular. The neck is strong and thickens towards the shoulders. The body is short, deep and strong. The legs are strong, well muscled and of medium length. The tail is usually docked.

Coat A coarse, rugged and thick coat about 2.5in (6cm) long; undercoat dense; the hair around the mouth should form a thick beard, and with the prominent eyebrows, gives the dog a somewhat fearsome expression. Colours range from fawn to black, including brindle; there may be a white star on the chest.

Size *Height:* dog 25–27in (63.5–68.5cm); bitch 23–25.5in (58.5–65cm). *Weight:* dog 77–88lb (35–40kg); bitch 59–77lb (27–35kg).

Characteristics and Temperament
Although this big dog can have a rather forbidding appearance, it is in fact good-natured, calm and trustworthy. Nevertheless, the Bouvier des Flandres makes an alert and effective guard dog. Moderate exercise only is required, and the dog settles well into family life.

BOXER

Origins The likely ancestors of the Boxer are the Bulldog and the Great Dane. A German breed, the Boxer has existed in the form seen today for over 100 years. The breed became unpopular during the First World War, but its popularity was later restored – no doubt mainly due to its virtues as a guard dog and active companion. In America and Germany, Boxers have cropped ears, but in Britain they are left uncropped.

Appearance Clean and hard in appearance, the Boxer is a squarely-built and active dog. The head is short and square, with the skin forming wrinkles. The muzzle is broad and deep, with the lower jaw undershot and curving slightly upward. The nose is black. The dark brown eyes face well forward and impart a lively and alert expression. The ears are set wide apart at the top of the skull and lie flat to the cheeks when resting but fall forward when alert; ears may be cropped and erect in some countries. The neck is round and strong. The body is short and deep-chested with a strong, slightly-sloping, straight back. The muscular legs are moderately long and terminate in cat-feet. The tail is usually docked.

Coat Short, hard and glossy. Colours are shades of fawn or brindle, with white.

Size *Height:* dog 22.5–25in (57–63.5cm); bitch 21–23in (53.5–58.5cm). *Weight:* dog 66–70lb (30–32kg); bitch 55–60lb (25–27kg).

Characteristics and Temperament An extrovert by nature, the Boxer is fearless and confident. Although loyal to family and friends, it can be wary of strangers and therefore makes an efficient guard dog. The Boxer needs firm handling by its owner to remind it who is in charge – especially when in the presence of other dogs with whom it tends to become rather unfriendly.

The Boxer needs firm handling and an energetic owner. However, it will guard your property with its life, as well as your children.

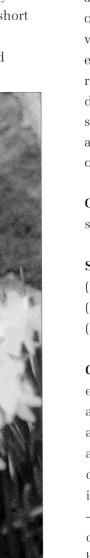

A long history of association with human beings as shepherds and pack dogs has made this gentle giant reliable and good-natured. The Briard is fond of boisterous games and is good with children.

BRIARD

Origins There is a legend that a type of dog similar in appearance to the modern Briard helped to trace the murderer of the nobleman Aubry de Montdidier, and hence the breed became called 'Chien d'Aubry'. A more likely explanation may be that the breed hails from the province of Brie, in France. Undoubtedly, the Briard has long been used all over France for sheep herding and guard duties. It has also found employment as a pack dog for the army. Nowadays, the dog is also kept as a rumbustious but friendly pet.

Appearance Muscular and well proportioned with a long, flowing coat. The head has a slightly-rounded skull and a square, strong muzzle. The nose is black. The large, dark brown eyes have a gentle and intelligent expression. The ears are fairly short and should not hang too close to the head. The neck is moderately long and arched. The deep-chested body has a firm and level back and is carried on strongly-boned, well muscled legs. The tail is long with an upward curl at the tip.

Coat Long and slightly wavy with a dense undercoat; the head sports a beard, moustache, and eyebrows that form a veil over the eyes. Colours are black, slate-grey or various shades of fawn.

Size *Height:* dog 24–27in (61–68.5cm); bitch 23–25.5in (58.5–65cm). *Weight:* dog 85lb (38.5kg); bitch 75lb (34kg).

Characteristics and Temperament The Briard has an effortless gait and seems to

glide over the ground. A friendly and extrovert dog, and good with children, the Briard can on occasions get a little over-boisterous during play. This is a dog that likes to exercise.

BULLMASTIFF

Origins The Bullmastiff came about through crossings between the Bulldog and the Old English Mastiff. The dog was used as a very effective guard dog and gamekeeper's dog – in fact, it was often known as 'the gamekeeper's dog'. A strong animal, but highly amenable to training and correct handling, the Bullmastiff was officially recognized as a breed in 1924, although it had been in existence well before that date.

Appearance A powerful and symmetrical dog with a smooth coat. The head has a square skull and a deep, strong muzzle. The skin on the head becomes wrinkled when the dog is aroused. The eyes are hazel or darker in colour and of medium size. Ears are V-shaped and folded, and help to accentuate the impression of squareness to the skull. The neck is very muscular and almost as wide as the skull. The body is short with a broad chest and a straight back and carried on moderate-length, powerful legs. The tail is long and tapering.

Coat Short and hard and lying flat to the body. Colours may be any shade of brindle, fawn or red.

Size *Height:* dog 25–27in (63.5–68.5cm); bitch 24–26in (61–66cm). *Weight:* dog 110–130lb (50–59kg); bitch 90–110lb (41–50kg).

Characteristics and Temperament A powerful and purposeful dog with an independent nature, the Bullmastiff is not recommended for the novice dog owner. It is reliable, faithful and affectionate, however, and makes an excellent guard dog. The Bullmastiff can also cover the ground with remarkable speed and agility for a dog of such commanding size and build.

The Bullmastiff is a large and powerful animal, unsuitable for the novice dog handler. However, it is faithful and affectionate and is an effective guard dog.

ROUGH COLLIE

Origins Basically the same breed as the Smooth Collie, the Rough Collie originated from the dark-coated herding dogs of Scotland. These in turn may have had their origins when dogs brought to Scotland by the Romans were mated with local dogs. The Rough Collie achieved royal recognition when Queen Victoria kept the breed at Balmoral Castle in Scotland. Although this form of the breed is today more likely to be seen in the show ring than working on the hills with sheep, it nevertheless retains many of its herding instincts. The breed found immortal fame in the guise of Lassie, the famous film star dog.

Appearance An attractively-coated, well proportioned dog. The wedge-shaped head has a flat and fairly wide skull and a long muzzle. The nose is black. The eyes are medium-sized and almond-shaped and should impart a gentle expression; the colour is dark brown, except in blue merle-coated dogs when they are blue or blue-flecked. The ears are held back when resting, but when the dog is alert they are brought forward and held semi-erect. The neck is powerful and arched, and is carried on a rather long body with a deep chest. The legs are strongly-boned and terminate in oval feet. The long tail is held low at rest but raised on the move, although never over the back.

Coat Very dense, with the outercoat straight and harsh; undercoat soft and close; mane and frill very abundant. Colours are sable-and-white, tricolour, or blue merle; all colours also include white.

Size *Height:* dog 22–24in (56–61cm); bitch 20–22in (51–56cm). *Weight:* dog 45–65lb (20.5–29.5kg); bitch 40–55lb (18–25kg).

Characteristics and Temperament This elegant and beautifully-coated dog makes an ideal pet, being friendly and loyal, especially towards its owner. The coat needs plenty of grooming to retain its luxurious condition.

The Rough Collie or 'Lassie' dog has been popular as a pet for a good many years. However, its spectacular coat must never be neglected so that mats are allowed to form.

SMOOTH COLLIE

Origins This breed is essentially a short-coated version of the Rough Collie, and it also comes from Scotland. The same colour varieties are available. Many consider this breed to be the more attractive and practical of the two.

Appearance A dog of dignified appearance, giving the impression of ability in the field. The wedge-shaped head has a flat and fairly wide skull and a long muzzle. The nose is black. The eyes are medium-sized and almond-shaped and should impart a gentle expression; the colour is dark brown, except in blue merle-coated dogs when they are blue or blue-flecked. The ears are held back when resting, but when the dog is alert they are brought forward and held semi-erect. The neck is powerful and arched, and is carried on a rather long body with a deep chest. The legs are strongly-boned and terminate in oval feet. The long tail is held low at rest but raised on the move, although never over the back.

Coat The outercoat is short, flat and harsh; the undercoat is dense. Colours are sable-and-white, tricolour, or blue merle; all colours may also include white.

Size *Height:* dog 22–24in (56–61cm); bitch 20–22in (51–56cm). *Weight:* dog 45–65lb (20.5–29.5kg); bitch 40–55lb (18–25kg).

Characteristics and Temperament This elegant dog makes an ideal pet, being friendly and loyal, especially towards its owner. More of a working dog than its close relative, the Rough Collie, this breed expects more exercise.

The handsome Smooth Collie is more of a workdog than its rough-coated relative. However, it makes a loyal and friendly pet that requires plenty of regular exercise.

The Dobermann is an elegant breed, combining a muscular frame with a glossy short coat. It has acquired a bad image in the past, no doubt from the common perception that it is a fierce guard dog. However, with early and careful training they can make good pets.

DOBERMANN

Origins The breed takes its name from Herr Louis Dobermann, a German tax collector who bred the dog in the 1870s. He crossed a variety of dogs, including German Shepherd, Pinscher, Rottweiler and Manchester Terrier to produce an animal capable of protecting him – and also of encouraging recalcitrant debtors to pay up! Given its pedigree, it is not surprising that the Dobermann reflects many virtues including speed, strength and intelligence. In America, where the breed is extremely popular, it is usually referred to as the Dobermann Pinscher.

Appearance Muscular and elegant with a smooth, glossy coat. The head has a fairly narrow, flat skull with a rather long, deep muzzle. The nose is solid black in black dogs, dark brown in brown dogs, dark grey in blue individuals and light brown in fawn dogs. The eyes are fairly deep-set and should convey a lively and intelligent expression. The neat ears may be erect or dropped; in some countries they are docked. A long and lean neck is carried on a deep-chested body with a short, firm back. The legs are long and well boned and terminate in cat-feet. The tail is usually docked.

Coat Smooth, short and close-lying. Colours are black, blue, brown or fawn, with tan markings above the eyes, on the muzzle, throat, chest, legs, feet and tail.

Size *Height:* dog 27in (68.5cm); bitch 25.5in (65cm). *Weight:* dog 83lb (37.5kg); bitch 73lb (33kg).

Characteristics and Temperament
Unfortunately, the Dobermann has suffered an image problem in the past, being seen primarily as a rather fierce guard dog. However, the breed can make a highly intelligent, loyal and delightful pet for owners willing to train it carefully from puppyhood and to be firm and consistent in handling the dog, so that it knows who is in charge. Careful selection has largely reduced the propensity for wayward and bad-tempered behaviour often seen previously. The dog requires plenty of exercise but is easy to groom after a romp in the countryside.

With its boundless energy and huge appetite, the Eskimo Dog is not the ideal pet for everyone. However, it is good-natured, intelligent and enjoys the company of human beings.

ESKIMO DOG

Origins This tough dog originates from Greenland, although it is often described as coming from Canada, because Canadians were instrumental in the breed's development. Similar in appearance to both the Siberian Husky and the Alaskan Malamute, the Eskimo Dog was bred to haul loads across the frozen northern wastes for the local Inuit peoples as well as for Arctic exploration teams before mechanized transport took over. Ability was always more important than temperament with this dog, and unlike many other breeds, the Eskimo Dog has not had a long history of life spent in households among people. Ownership of such a dog – lively, characterful and affectionate though it may be – should therefore not be considered lightly.

Appearance A powerful husky-type dog. The head is broad and wedge-shaped with a flat skull and a medium-length, gently tapering muzzle. The nose may be black or brown. The eyes are dark brown or tawny and set rather obliquely, and convey a fearless expression. The short ears are set well apart and held erect. The neck is short and muscular. The strong, well muscled body has a deep chest and a level back and is carried on heavily-boned legs.

The big, bushy tail is carried curled over the back.

Coat The breed has a thick, double coat. The undercoat is about 1–2-in (2.5–5-cm) thick and covers the whole body uniformly; an oute coat of coarse, longer hairs protrude and is longest on the neck, withers, breeches and underside of the tail; fur between the toes helps to protect the feet.

Size *Height:* dog 23–27in (58.5–68.5cm); bitch 20–24in (51–61cm).

Weight: dog 75–104lb (34–47kg); bitch 59.5–90.5lb (27–41kg).

Characteristics and Temperament This breed is fairly wary by nature, and socialization with other dogs is essential early on. The Eskimo Dog is also likely to display many of the other characteristics for which it was so highly prized in its homeland, particularly an inexhaustible level of energy and the desire to pull something along – more often than not its owner. It also has a voracious appetite. On the plus side, the breed is generally good-natured, intelligent and enjoys company.

ESTRELA MOUNTAIN DOG

Origins The huge Estrela Mountain Dog comes from the Estrela region of central Portugal where it has long been used for both guarding and herding livestock. A relatively rare breed in many places outside its native homeland, the dog's good-natured character should see it winning over plenty of converts. The breed exists in two distinct coat types – a long-coated and a short-coated form.

Appearance A sturdy, mastiff-type dog. The head is long and strong with a broad, slightly-domed skull. The muzzle is slightly tapering, and the nose is black. Medium-sized, amber, oval eyes convey an impression of calmness. The ears are smallish, triangular and carried at the sides of the head. The neck is short and thick and is carried on a body with a broad, muscular back, a deep chest and slightly-arched loins. The legs are well boned and well muscled. The tail is long and well furred.

Coat *Long-coated:* Outercoat thick, close-lying and fairly harsh; it may be flat or slightly wavy; the undercoat is dense. *Short-coated:* Thick, short, fairly harsh and straight with a short, dense undercoat. Colours are fawn, brindle, or wolf-grey.

Size *Height:* dog 25.5–28.5in (65–72.5cm); bitch 24.5–27in (62–68.5cm). *Weight:* 66–110lb (30–50kg).

Characteristics and Temperament This large dog is remarkably well disposed towards its friends and family, although it can be rather stubborn on occasions. Easy to groom and undemanding in its eating habits, the Estrela Mountain Dog makes a good companion and guard dog for an active family.

The Estrela Mountain Dog is a sociable animal and enjoys the company of its human family. However, it can be obstinate on occasions.

FINNISH LAPHUND

Origins A spitz-type dog from the Nordic countries, the Finnish Laphund was bred to herd reindeer – a task this dog still undertakes, in addition to working with sheep and other livestock.

Appearance A handsome, medium-sized dog with a full coat. The head has a moderately-broad skull and a medium-long, wedge-shaped muzzle. The nose is black. The eyes are dark brown, with a confident, intelligent expression. The ears are of medium size and held erect. A strong neck is carried on a long body with a straight, broad back. Strong, medium-length legs terminate in well arched, oval feet. The tail is carried curled over the back when on the move.

Coat Outercoat is long and coarse; undercoat dense, woolly and soft. All colours are allowed, with shades differing from the main one appearing on the head, neck, chest, legs and tail tip.

Size *Height:* dog 18–20.5in (46–52cm); bitch 16–18.5in (40.5–47cm). *Weight:* 44–46lb (20–21kg).

Characteristics and Temperament This is an attractive dog, not too big for the average household and with a responsive nature. The profuse coat needs regular grooming, but the dog is not demanding in terms of feeding or exercise.

The Finnish Laphund makes a good household pet as it isn't too large and requires only moderate feeding and exercise.

It seems as though the versatile German Shepherd can be trained to do almost any job, and do it well. In the wrong hands, however, these intelligent dogs have a tendency to aggression. Therefore, they need to form a lasting relationship with a strong adult who will handle them firmly and consistently.

GERMAN SHEPHERD DOG

Origins One of the most popular and instantly recognizable dogs anywhere, the German Shepherd is a byword for excellence and versatility throughout the canine world. Bred to the standard we know today in the later part of the 19th century by German army officer Max von Stephanitz, the breed was originally used as a sheep-herding dog. Later, however, it found favour as a police and military dog. Indeed, during the First World War nearly 50,000 were used by the German army. By 1926 it was the most popular dog in Britain, where it was often called the Alsatian Wolf Dog. The term 'Alsatian' is still often used to describe the breed. Poor breeding and thoughtless handling – coupled with the dog's widespread use as a guard dog – unfortunately resulted in it gaining a reputation for aggressive and unpredictable behaviour. The best examples of the breed, however, are dogs which cannot be praised too highly. Today, the German Shepherd excels in its various roles, including police and military work, tracking, leading the blind, guarding, drug detection, and of course being a perfect companion for an owner prepared to offer the kind of life this intelligent dog deserves.

Appearance An alert, long-bodied, purposeful-looking dog. The head has a moderately-broad skull and a long muzzle. The eyes are almond-shaped, usually brown, and should convey intelligence and confidence. The ears are medium-sized, broad at the base, and carried erect. The neck is long, strong and muscular. The deep-chested body is long with a straight back that slopes towards the hindquarters; the body-length should be slightly greater than the dog's height. The legs are strong and muscular. The tail is long and bushy and hangs in a curve at rest.

Coat Outercoat close, straight, hard and weather-resistant; undercoat thick, woolly and close. Colours include black, black-and-tan, and sable; occasionally white or cream dogs appear. Sometimes, long-coated varieties still appear, but these are not generally accepted for show purposes.

Size *Height:* dog 25in (63.5cm); bitch 23in (58.5cm). *Weight:* dog 80.5lb (36.5kg); bitch 65lb (29.5kg).

Characteristics and Temperament A good-quality German Shepherd Dog will make a highly trainable, tireless, intelligent and loyal companion. The dog is also excellent in a variety of working roles. It has supple movements, using a long-reaching gait. The dog needs plenty of exercise to keep body and mind occupied, although some have a tendency to be a little lazy if given the chance.

As its name suggests, the Giant Schnauzer is the largest of the Schnauzer family, the others being the Standard and the Miniature. It is a powerful dog with an amiable personality and makes an imposing guard dog.

GIANT SCHNAUZER

Origins This is the biggest of the three Schnauzer breeds. It was used in Bavaria in Germany as long ago as the 15th century for herding duties. It started to become redundant in this role when railways became a more economical option for moving cattle about. However, the Giant Schnauzer's impressive size and appearance meant that it soon found favour in the cities of Germany as a guard dog. For a time, it was known as the Munich Schnauzer. The breed is now popular both as a guarding companion dog and as a police dog.

Appearance A powerful, long-legged and almost square dog. The head has a fairly broad skull and a long, strong muzzle. The nose is black. The eyes are oval and dark. The V-shaped ears drop forward to the temple. The strong neck is slightly arched and is carried on a body with a broad, deep chest and a strong, straight back. The legs are long and well boned. The tail is customarily docked.

Coat The outercoat is hard and wiry, and there should be a good undercoat; there are prominent beard, moustache and eyebrows. Colours are pure-black or pepper-and-salt.

Size *Height:* dog 25.5–27.5in (65–70cm); bitch 23.5–25.5in (60–65cm). *Weight:* dog 100lb (45.5kg); bitch 90lb (41kg).

Characteristics and Temperament
Intelligent, strong and active, the Giant Schnauzer is also friendly and reliable. However, its size and boldness mean that it can also make a very effective deterrent to a would-be burglar. The coat needs stripping twice-yearly.

GREAT DANE

Origins Despite its name, the Great Dane is of German origin and not Danish. In fact, it has been the national dog of Germany since 1876. Originally used to hunt wild boar, the breed was initially classed as a hound, and it undoubtedly has hound blood – possibly Greyhound – in its makeup. Another misconception is that the Great Dane is an aggressive dog, for this is the archetypal gentle giant.

Appearance Muscular, elegant and of imposing appearance. The head has a flattish skull and a deep, broad muzzle. The eyes are round, medium-sized and dark in colour; in harlequins odd, or wall eyes are permissible. The ears are triangular and folded forward; in some countries, such as America, the ears are docked. The neck is long and arched, and held well up. The body is deep, with slightly-arched loins. The legs are long and muscular and terminate in cat-feet. The long tail tapers towards the tip.

Coat Short, dense and glossy. Colours are brindles, fawns, blues, black, or harlequin (pure white background with black patches or blue patches appearing ragged).

Size *Height:* dog 30in (76cm); bitch 28in (71cm) – these are minimum height requirements. *Weight:* dog 119lb (54kg); bitch 101.5lb (46kg).

Characteristics and Temperament A majestic-looking dog with a dignified and friendly nature, the Great Dane is really only suitable for those with space to house this huge dog and the budget to keep up with its appetite. Devoted to its family, the Great Dane is an endearing character but sadly has a relatively short lifespan.

The majestic Great Dane, despite its great size, is the archetypal gentle giant. However, its great size may exclude it as a pet, which is a pity, as it is patient, loyal and affectionate.

Hovawarts are playful dogs and enjoy family life. However, they can be difficult with other dogs and need to be ruled with a firm hand.

HOVAWART

Origins This is a breed originating from the Black Forest region of Bavaria in Germany. The name Hovawart means 'farmyard warden', and dogs of this type were known to guard farms as far back as the 1200s. Only seen in Britain since about the mid 1970s and in America since the 1980s, the breed was first recognized by the German Kennel Club in 1936.

Appearance A medium-sized dog with a strong physique. The head is fairly long with a broad skull and a gently-tapering muzzle. The nose colour should match the coat. The eyes are oval and have an alert expression; they should be as dark as possible. The ears are triangular and pendent. The neck is of medium length and carried on a moderately-long body. The legs are strong and muscular. The tail is long and bushy and carried high when on the move.

Coat Medium-length, but shorter on the face and front legs; undercoat fine and light. Colours are black-and-gold, blond, or black.

Size *Height:* dog 24–27.5in (61–70cm); bitch 23–25.5in (58.5–65cm).

Weight: dog 66–88lb (30–40kg); bitch 55–77lb (25–35kg).

Characteristics and Temperament A playful dog and quite devoted to its family, the Hovawart can nevertheless be a domineering character where other dogs are concerned. Easy to feed and groom, and with a good nose for hunting, the Hovawart is a good choice for an all-round companion dog.

The large Hungarian Kuvasz has been bred predominantly as a guard dog. However, it finds it difficult to forget the fact and may take the task too seriously. Though gentle and loyal with those it knows, it is not the ideal pet.

HUNGARIAN KUVASZ

Origins Used by Hungarian tribesmen for guarding duties, the Hungarian Kuvasz probably arrived in about 1200, via Turkey. It bears a resemblance to both the Maremma Sheepdog and also to the Pyrenean Mountain Dog, with which it may have a common ancestry. The Kuvasz is quite popular in America.

Appearance Large, sturdy and powerful. The head has a long, slightly-arched skull and a broad, slightly-tapering muzzle. The eyes are almond-shaped, dark brown and set wide apart. The ears are V-shaped and folded. The neck is long and muscular and is carried on a fairly long, deep body. The dog stands on powerful legs, and the hind feet are longer than the fore. The tail is carried level with the loins when on the move, with a slight upward curve at the tip.

Coat Slightly wavy, the outercoat being medium coarse; the undercoat is woolly and fine. The coat colour is pure white.

Size *Height:* dog 28–29in (71–73.5cm); bitch 26–27.5in (66–70cm). *Weight:* dog 88–114lb (40–52kg); bitch 66–92lb (30–43kg).

Characteristics and Temperament This is an attractive dog, but by no means one of the easiest to keep as a pet. Although the Kuvasz is gentle and loyal with those it knows, it is a dog that was bred to guard, and still considers guarding an important part of its life. It is therefore wary of strangers and likes to have somewhere it can patrol and guard. The dog is also big and burly and has a demanding appetite.

HUNGARIAN PULI

Origins The origins of the Hungarian Puli are not entirely clear, but it is thought that the dog may have come from Asia in the 9th century. This highly distinctive-looking dog is a herder of sheep, and its unusual corded coat is designed to keep out wet and cold weather.

Appearance A sturdy and wiry dog, whose body is obscured by a long corded coat. The head has a round skull and a short muzzle. The nose is black. The dark-brown eyes have a lively expression. The ears are V-shaped and pendent but are scarcely discernible beneath the hair on the head. The medium-length neck is carried on a body with a broad, deep chest. The legs are strong and muscular. The tail is curled tightly over the rump.

Coat The thick, long coat forms into cords as the dog matures; coat is usually longest on the hindquarters; in some individuals the coat reaches the ground. Colours are black, rusty-black, white, grey or apricot.

Size *Height:* dog 16–17.5in (40.5–44.5cm); bitch 14.5–16in (37–40.5cm). *Weight:* dog 28.5–33lb (13–15kg); bitch 22–28.5lb (10–13kg).

Characteristics and Temperament A lively, alert and highly active dog. The Puli is affectionate but naturally wary of strangers – who are normally greeted with an animated bout of barking. Despite its appearance, the coat requires plenty of regular attention to keep it in good condition.

As a sheep herder, the Puli's distinctive coat was designed to keep out wind and rain, which, despite its scruffy appearance, requires a good deal of attention to keep it in good condition.

The Kelpie is a tireless worker on the vast sheep stations of Australia. Therefore, extreme toughness is required, and a waterproof coat to enable it to function in all weathers.

KELPIE

Origins This Australian breed came about in the latter half of the 19th century, when imported English collies were mated with local breeds. The dog was first shown in 1908. The Kelpie is used on the vast Australian sheep stations.

Appearance A tough and muscular little sheepdog with a fox-like face. The head has a flat skull and a slightly-tapering muzzle. The brown eyes convey a lively and intelligent expression. The ears are large, wide at the base and held erect. The powerful neck is carried on a body slightly longer than the height of the dog; the chest is broad. The strong legs are of medium length and end in cat-feet. The bushy tail is usually carried low.

Coat Short and smooth, with a harsh, shiny outercoat. Colours are black, black-and-tan, red, red-and-tan, fawn, smoke-blue or chocolate.

Size *Height:* dog 18–20in (46–51cm); bitch 17–19in (43–48cm). *Weight:* 25–45lb (11.5–20.5kg).

Characteristics and Temperament The Kelpie is a tireless worker in its native country, where its tough constitution, weatherproof coat, and keen senses make it a highly-regarded sheepdog.

The Komondor is an imposing guard dog with powerful jaws, and not entirely suited to family life. Its thick coat also requires a good deal of attention, despite its scruffy appearance.

KOMONDOR

Origins Another of the cord-coated breeds, this guarding dog resembles the Hungarian Puli although it is bigger. Long known in its native Hungary, the Komondor was probably introduced into the country by wandering Magyar peoples. The coat helps the dog blend in with the flocks of sheep it guards.

Appearance A big, muscular dog with a corded coat. The head has a broad, arched skull and a broad, deep muzzle. The nose is black. The eyes should be as dark as possible and not too deeply set. The ears are medium-sized, U-shaped and pendent. The strong neck is carried on a body with a deep, muscular chest. The legs are strongly boned and muscular. The tail is slightly curved at the tip and is raised to the horizontal position when the dog is excited.

Coat Long, coarse outercoat and a soft undercoat; hair forms tassels giving a corded appearance; it may take two years for the coat to grow to full length. The colour is always white.

Size *Height:* 26–32in (66–81cm). *Weight:* 80–135lb (36–61kg).

Characteristics and Temperament Despite its unusual and disreputable-looking coat, the Komondor is an imposing and effective guard dog with powerful jaws. This is an animal bred for living in the countryside and as such is not really suitable for town life. The Komondor makes a devoted companion, but constant care of the coat is extremely demanding.

The Maremma, despite its large size, is very agile, making it capable of moving easily over rough ground. It is not aggressive and its intelligence and bravery make it an ideal guard dog.

MAREMMA SHEEPDOG

Origins The Maremma Sheepdog is used to guard flocks and property in its native Italy. The breed's exact origins are unknown, but it is possible that the dog is a descendant of those owned by the wandering Magyar peoples. The temperament of examples seen outside Italy are reported to have improved considerably over the years.

Appearance A large, muscular dog with a thick white coat. The skull is wide between the ears but narrows towards the eyes, and the muzzle is fairly long and tapers slightly towards the nose – the whole head being slightly conical in shape. The nose is black. The eyes are almond-shaped and dark brown in colour. The V-shaped ears hang flat by the side of the head but move forward when the dog is alert. A strong neck is carried on a fairly long, broad body with a deep chest. The medium-length, large-boned legs end in large, almost round feet. The long tail is carried almost level with the back when on the move.

Coat Thick, long and harsh with a thick undercoat; the coat is sometimes slightly wavy. The colour is all-white, but there may be slight fawn or ivory shades present.

Size *Height:* dog 25.5–28.5in (65–72.5cm); bitch 23.5–26.5in (60–67.5cm). *Weight:* dog 77–99lb (35–45kg); bitch 66–88lb (30–40kg).

Characteristics and Temperament Despite its size, the Maremma Sheepdog is capable of moving easily over rough terrain and of turning quickly. Intelligent and brave, although not aggressive, the breed is rather aloof and naturally wary of strangers but makes a good guarding companion when properly trained.

MASTIFF

Origins This huge breed is one of the oldest in Britain. Dogs similar in appearance to the modern Mastiff were to be found in Britain at the time of the Roman invasion. They fought alongside their masters as they tried to repel the invaders. Later, recognizing the breed's great strength, courage and presence, the Romans took Mastiffs back to Rome to take part in gladiatorial contests against animals such as bulls, lions and bears. The dog's popularity went into decline in Britain after the Second World War but was revived using imported stock. The Mastiff is also known as the Old English Mastiff.

Appearance A massive, powerfully-built dog with a large, heavily-jowled head. The head has a square skull, a short, broad muzzle and a marked stop. The small eyes are set wide apart, are brown in colour and convey an expression of calmness and strength. The ears are small and thin and hang down by the side of the head. The neck is highly muscular. The body has a deep, wide chest and a very muscular back and loins. The legs are large-boned and muscular. The tail tapers at the tip and is held slightly curved when on the move.

Coat The coat is short. Colours are apricot-fawn, silver-fawn, fawn or fawn brindle.

Size *Height:* 27.5–30in (70–76cm). *Weight:* 174–190lb (79–86g).

Characteristics and Temperament

Fortunately, this large and impressive dog is docile and good-natured, but it still makes an admirable guard dog. It is affectionate and loyal and needs plenty of human company and reasonable amounts of exercise. The Mastiff also has a prodigious appetite – as befits a dog of this size – and this should be taken into account when ownership is being considered.

Despite its imposing size, the Mastiff is a quiet and docile animal and thrives on human company and regular exercise. They also have a voracious appetite which must be taken into account when considering it as a pet.

The Neapolitan Mastiff is an ancient breed with ancestors dating back to Roman times. It is bred to be a guard dog, but is only aggressive on command. Not for the novice dog-handler.

NEAPOLITAN MASTIFF

Origins The Neapolitan Mastiff is another very old breed. It is thought to be a descendant of the Molossus breed of Ancient Roman times. Because of its huge strength and size, the dog was once used for fighting, although it also found favour as a guard dog and for pulling carts. The painter Piero Scanziani established a kennel for the breed and is credited with its revival and promotion; the dog was first shown in 1946. In its native Italy, the Neapolitan Mastiff is sometimes seen with cropped ears.

Appearance A muscular, powerfully-built dog with a massive-looking head. The head has a wide skull and a short, square and deep muzzle. The fairly large, chestnut-brown or black eyes have a penetrating expression. The ears are short with triangular tips and usually hang down, although in some countries they are cropped. The neck is short and massive. The body has a broad, muscular chest and is fairly short and deep. The legs are powerful and well boned. The tail tapers towards the tip; it may be docked by one-third of its length

Coat Short, dense and fine, with a glossy sheen. Colours are black (preferably), blue, grey and browns.

Size *Height:* 26–29in (66–73.5cm).
Weight: 110–154lb (50–70kg).

Characteristics and Temperament The dog's gait can be described as bear-like – moving along with slow trots or longer steps, it rarely runs at a gallop. Reliable, obedient and not aggressive unless provoked or commanded to attack, the breed is nevertheless not one for the inexperienced owner. The breed's loose jowls and pendulous lips mean that it is somewhat inclined to slobber and dribble.

The Newfoundland and water go hand-in-hand, and for centuries they were used as fishermen's companions. They are powerful swimmers and renowned for saving lives.

NEWFOUNDLAND

Origins The exact origins of the Newfoundland are somewhat obscure, but it is possible that the breed developed from a type of dog that was brought by nomadic peoples into the northern polar regions and not actually from Newfoundland itself. From there, the breed was taken by sailors and traders to England, where it became very popular.

Appearance A big-boned, strong-looking dog. The head is broad and massive with a short, square muzzle. The dark-brown eyes are small and deep set. The ears are also small and fall close to the side of the head. A strong neck is carried on a deep-chested body with muscular loins. The legs are of moderate length and strongly boned, and terminate in webbed feet – an invaluable aid to swimming. The tail is of medium length.

Coat An oily, waterproof, double coat; the coat is flat and dense. Colours are black, brown (chocolate or bronze), or landseer – this last colour, named after the painter Sir Edwin Landseer who illustrated the breed on many occasions, is white with black markings.

Size *Height:* dog 28in (71cm); bitch 26in (66cm). *Weight:* dog 140–150lb (63.5–68kg); bitch 110–120lb (50–54.5kg).

Characteristics and Temperament When one thinks of dogs and water, the name Newfoundland invariably springs to mind. No other breed has such a natural affinity with water. Used for centuries to help fishermen retrieve their nets, the Newfoundland also has a deserved reputation as a powerful swimmer and life-saver. On land, the nautical theme is continued, for the dog moves along with a slightly rolling gait. Looking like a cuddly bear, especially in puppyhood, the Newfoundland grows into a delightful character – affectionate, docile and willing to please, but also capable of guarding family and home.

NORWEGIAN BUHUND

Origins A spitz breed, the Norwegian Buhund is a herding and guard dog. The word Buhund means 'the dog found on the homestead'. The Buhund was only officially recognized in the early part of the 20th century.

Appearance A lightly-built, compact, spitz dog. The head is wedge-shaped, with a flat skull and a tapering muzzle. The nose is black. The eyes are dark brown, with an alert and fearless expression. The tall ears are held erect and are very mobile. A medium-length neck is carried on a short, strong body with a deep chest. The medium-length legs are lean and strong. The tail is short and thick and carried curled over the back in typical spitz fashion.

Coat The outercoat is hard and smooth; the undercoat is soft and woolly. Colours are wheaten, red, black, or wolf-sable.

Size *Height:* 16–18in (40.5–46cm). *Weight:* 53–57lb (24–26kg).

Characteristics and Temperament Lively and alert, the Norwegian Buhund is a little reserved with strangers but friendly towards its family. The dog does not have a big appetite and has a coat which is easy to keep clean.

The Norwegian Buhund is a relatively new breed. It makes a good family pet, though can be a little wary of strangers.

OLD ENGLISH SHEEPDOG

Origins Another of the almost universally recognized breeds of dog, the Old English Sheepdog, or Bobtail as it is also known, probably originated from crossings between European sheepdogs and British sheepdogs over 150 years ago. The breed's coat is its most distinctive feature – indeed, there is little else of the actual dog to be seen unless the coat has been clipped. The Old English Sheepdog has moved from working dog to highly popular pet and advertising icon, perhaps to the detriment of the breed's original type.

Appearance A strong, symmetrical, square dog. The head has a rather square skull and a strong, square muzzle. The nose is black. The eyes may be dark or wall-eyed; sometimes the eyes are blue. The ears are small and carried close to the side of the head. The neck is fairly long and arched. The short, compact body with muscular loins is carried on long, strongly-boned legs. The tail is usually completely docked.

Coat Hard-textured and profuse, the coat should be free from curl but shaggy; the undercoat should be waterproof. Colours are grey, grizzle or blue in any shade; the head, neck, forequarters and under-belly should be white, with or without markings.

Size *Height:* dog 24in (61cm) minimum; bitch 22in (56cm) minimum. *Weight:* dog 80.5lb (36.5kg); bitch 65lb (29.5kg).

Characteristics and Temperament Cheerful and extroverted, the Old English Sheepdog is always ready to join in any activity. The breed needs plenty of exercise, and careful, regular grooming is required to avoid the coat from becoming hopelessly matted and tangled. The dog walks with a bear-like gait but moves freely and effortlessly at speed.

You need to have plenty of time and patience if you have an Old English Sheepdog as a pet. Its coarse, longhaired coat needs very regular attention, while the dog itself, having been bred for hard work, needs a good deal of exercise. However, you will be amply rewarded for your trouble.

PINSCHER

Origins This is a clean-looking, medium-sized dog of German origin, with an appearance reminiscent of a small Dobermann. The German Kennel Club recognized the breed in 1879. The dog is also known as the Standard Pinscher. The word Pinscher means 'terrier', but this dog is too long-legged to go to earth like other terriers. Instead, it is used mainly for tasks such as watchdog.

Appearance A smooth-coated, elegant dog. The head has a moderately wide skull and a deep muzzle. The nose is black. The eyes are oval, dark and of medium size and have a lively expression. The ears are V-shaped and usually folded, although sometimes they are cropped. The neck is elegant and well muscled. The body has a deep chest and is carried on strong, medium-length legs. The tail is usually docked.

Coat Short, dense and glossy. Solid colours from fawn to red, or black and blue with red or tan markings, are most commonly seen.

Size *Height:* 17–19in (43–48cm). *Weight:* 25–35lb (11.5–16kg).

Characteristics and Temperament A neat and nimble dog, the Pinscher is easy to groom and inexpensive to feed. Obedient, lively and friendly with those it knows, its wariness of strangers makes it a useful guard.

The German Pinscher was one of the breeds Louis Dobermann used to develop the powerful and imposing Dobermann. The Pinscher itself is somewhat smaller, is nimble and attractive, and makes a charming pet.

The Polish Lowland Sheepdog is full of exuberance and energy and has a fondness for children. However, it requires plenty of exercise and regular grooming.

POLISH LOWLAND SHEEPDOG

Origins With an ancestry that is believed to include the Hungarian Puli and long-coated herding dogs, the Polish Lowland Sheepdog has been in existence since the 16th century at least. Polish sailors visiting British seaports in the 16th century are thought to have exchanged these dogs for native ones, and so helped the breed to spread. The Polish Lowland Sheepdog almost became extinct after the Second World War, but was saved by the efforts of a Polish vet who bred from some of the few remaining animals.

Appearance A chunky, muscular, long-coated breed reminiscent of the Bearded Collie. The head has a fairly broad, slightly arched skull with a muzzle equal in length to the skull. The nose should be as dark as possible. The eyes are hazel or brown and have an alert expression. The moderately large drop ears are heart-shaped. The neck is muscular and strong. The body is rectangular in side view with a level back and muscular loins and is carried on well muscled legs. The tail is usually docked, although some dogs are born tailless.

Coat Long, thick and shaggy with a hard texture; undercoat is soft; the eyes are covered by long hair. Any colours are acceptable.

Size *Height:* dog 17–20in (43–51cm); bitch 16–18.5in (40.5–47cm). *Weight:* 43lb (19.5kg).

Characteristics and Temperament This is a lively, intelligent and friendly dog that seems particularly fond of playing with children. The Polish Lowland Sheepdog needs plenty of exercise to help burn off some of its exuberant energy, but rewards its owner by being easy to train and happy to act as a dutiful watchdog. The long coat needs careful grooming.

PORTUGUESE WATER DOG

Origins This dog probably arrived in Portugal with Moorish traders from North Africa. For centuries, the breed's great love of water has been put to good use by Portuguese fishermen who use the dog for salvaging tackle and nets from the water and for guarding the boats. Webbed feet help the dog to swim. The dog comes in two different coat types – a long, wavy coat and a shorter, curly coat. The coat is usually clipped short over the hindquarters and most of the tail.

Appearance A rectangular, muscular dog reminiscent of a Poodle. The head has a long skull and a strong, slightly-tapering muzzle. The eyes are round and are dark brown or black in colour. The drop ears are heart-shaped. The neck is short and straight and is carried on a short, deep-chested body. The long legs are well boned and muscular and end in webbed feet. The tail is long and tapering and is carried in a ring-shaped arch over the back; a plume of hair is left on the end.

Coat *Long-coated:* Thick and loosely waved; fairly glossy. *Short-coated:* Harsh and dense with tight curls; not glossy. Coat clipped into characteristic style. Colours are black, white, brown, black-and-white, or brown-and-white.

Size *Height:* dog 19.5–22.5in (49.5–57cm); bitch 17–20.5in (43–52cm). *Weight:* dog 42–55lb (19–25kg); bitch 35–48lb (16–22kg).

Characteristics and Temperament The Portuguese Water Dog is cheerful, intelligent and energetic, with excellent swimming ability. The breed can be obstinate, so needs firm training.

As its name suggests, the Portuguese Water Dog loves water and has webbed feet to make swimming easier. It is an intelligent and lively dog, but quite difficult to train and not for the inexperienced handler.

The beautiful Pyrenean Mountain Dog was originally used to protect flocks of sheep against wolves, but found a new role during the Second World War as a messenger dog. It is now mainly used as a companion animal and family pet.

PYRENEAN MOUNTAIN DOG

Origins For centuries, this large and impressive dog was used to guard flocks against wolves, bears and other predators in the Pyrenees of France. A descendant of the herding and guard breeds of southern Europe, the breed was a favourite with French noblemen, and it was named the Royal Dog of France by Louis XIV. In the Second World War, the Pyrenean Mountain Dog was used as a pack dog and messenger by French troops. Today it is a popular companion dog. It is also known as the Great Pyrenees.

Appearance Strong, well balanced and elegant. The head has a broad, fairly-arched skull and a medium-length, slightly-tapering muzzle. The nose is black. The almond-shaped eyes have a thoughtful expression and are dark amber in colour. The ears are triangular and lie at the side of the head when the dog is resting. The neck is thick and muscular. The chest is broad and deep and the back is broad and muscular. The legs are heavily boned and well muscled, as befits such a powerful dog; the double dew-claws help the dog to tackle the mountainous terrain. The tail tapers towards the tip and is carried with the tip slightly curled.

Coat Outercoat is fairly long, coarse and thick; it may be straight or wavy; undercoat profuse; coat forms a mane around neck and shoulders. Colours are white, or white with patches of badger, wolf-grey or pale-yellow.

Size *Height:* dog 28in (71cm) minimum; bitch 26in (66cm) minimum. *Weight:* dog 110lb (50kg) minimum; bitch 90lb (41kg) minimum.

Characteristics and Temperament The Pyrenean Mountain Dog has a confident, kindly and dignified air about it, although like any big dog it needs proper handling. The breed only requires average amounts of exercise and is likely to amble about rather than take off at speed. The dog makes a good pet, but its coat needs a lot of care.

The kindly Pyrenean Mountain Dog requires moderate exercise and regular grooming to keep its beautiful coat in good condition. It is a large dog and therefore requires positive handling.

PYRENEAN SHEEPDOG

Origins This much smaller dog from the Pyrenees region of France probably originated from crosses between indigenous Pyrenean breeds and others, such as Briards. It was used for herding flocks of sheep. The breed is a fairly new arrival in Britain, and it only received Kennel Club recognition in 1988. The coat may be long or semi-long.

Appearance A small, active, rough-coated sheepdog. The head has a fairly

flat skull and a short, slightly-tapering muzzle. The almond-shaped eyes look keen and active; they are usually dark brown, although one or both may be blue or blue-flecked in merle or slate-coloured dogs. The ears are fairly short. The neck is fairly long, and is carried on a lean, strong body with slightly arched loins. The legs are lean but well muscled; the hind legs may have single or double dew-claws. The tail is medium-length with a slight hook at the tip; the tail may be docked, and some individuals may be born with a stump tail.

Coat Rather hard and dense, flat or wavy. Colours are fawn, light to dark grey, blue merle, slate blue or brindle, black, or black-and-white.

Size *Height:* dog 16–19in (40.5–48cm); bitch 15–18in (38–46cm). *Weight:* 18–33lb (8–15kg).

Characteristics and Temperament Full of energy and stamina, the Pyrenean Sheepdog makes a good watchdog. It enjoys exercise and is undemanding in terms of food.

The Pyrenean Sheepdog comes from the French side of the mountain range and was probably the result of cross-breeding between indigenous breeds and the Briard. It is agile and spirited and requires plenty of exercise.

ROTTWEILER

Origins The name of this dog comes from the Roman settlement of Rottweil in Germany. When the Roman Empire was invading Germany, mastiff-type dogs were brought along too, for guarding and herding livestock. In time, Rottweil became an important trading centre for cattle and other livestock, and butchers in the town used the dog for various duties including pulling carts. The breed's natural guarding instincts and boldness has made it a popular dog for use by police forces and other similar organizations. The Rottweiler first appeared in Britain in the 1930s and is one of the most popular dogs in America. Overbreeding produced some poor examples, but this problem has now lessened.

Appearance A compact, powerful and well proportioned dog. The head has a wide, medium-length skull and a deep, broad muzzle. The nose is black. The brown eyes are almond-shaped. The ears are small and pendent. The neck is strong, round and very muscular. The body has a broad, deep chest with a straight, strong back. The legs are well boned and muscular. The tail is normally docked at the first joint.

Coat Outercoat medium-length, coarse and flat; undercoat should not be visible through the outercoat. Colour is black with well defined tan markings on cheeks, muzzle, chest, legs, over the eyes and under the tail.

Size *Height:* dog 25–27in (63.5–68.5cm); bitch 23–25in (58.5–63.5cm). *Weight:* dog 110lb (50kg); bitch 85lb (38.5kg).

Characteristics and Temperament Bold, loyal and courageous, the Rottweiler is also an active dog that likes plenty of exercise. The short coat responds well to grooming, and a splendid sheen is easily produced. This is a willing worker and an excellent guard dog, but proper handling and training are essential requirements for ownership of such a strong dog.

The Rottweiler has a long history dating back to Roman times. It is a formidable animal and requires careful handling from puppyhood to make it manageable. Not for the faint-hearted.

The St Bernard has a placid, affectionate nature, but because of its massive size and strength requires careful training. Don't even consider owning one unless you have plenty of space to accommodate it. Remember, also, that it has a very large appetite.

SAINT BERNARD

Origins It would be difficult to mistake the St Bernard for any other dog, for this gentle giant is depicted everywhere as a symbol of rescue and care. A descendant of mastiff-type dogs brought to the Swiss Alps by the Romans over 2,000 years ago, the dog achieved fame when it was used by the monks at the Hospice of St Bernard for rescuing travellers lost in the St Gothard Pass. The dog comes in two coat varieties, a rough-coated form and a smooth-coated form.

Appearance A well proportioned, massive dog of substance. The huge head has a broad, slightly-rounded skull and a short, deep muzzle. The nose is black.

The dark eyes are medium-sized and should have a benevolent expression. The triangular ears are medium-sized and lie close to the cheeks. The neck is thick and muscular with a well developed dewlap. The deep-chested body has a straight back and muscular loins and is carried on straight, heavy-boned legs. The feet are large, which no doubt help the dog to progress through snow. The tail is long.

Coat *Rough-coated:* Flat and dense and full around the neck. *Smooth-coated:* Close-fitting and hound-like with feathering on the thighs and tail. Colours are orange, mahogany-brindle, red-brindle, or white with patches on the body of any of these colours.

Size *Height:* dog 28in (71cm) minimum; bitch 26in (66cm) minimum. *Weight:* dog 165.5lb (75kg); bitch 150lb (68kg).

Characteristics and Temperament Fortunately, this massive dog has an extremely benevolent temperament and a steady, calm nature. Walks are usually taken at a leisurely pace, but a St Bernard can pull extremely hard, so needs to be under control. Around the house, they are inclined to drool and are not one of those large breeds that can curl up into surprisingly small spaces – an owner tends to fit around whatever space is left. Feeding is also an expensive undertaking.

The Samoyed makes an excellent family pet. It is a lively, jolly animal and fairly obedient, having a mind of its own. However, the thick coat can be rather troublesome for it in hot weather and requires very regular grooming.

SAMOYED

Origins The Samoyed was originally used to guard the reindeer herds and pull the sleds of the wandering tribesmen of the Siberian tundra. Fur traders brought the breed back to Britain. Samoyeds were also used on a number of polar expeditions.

Appearance A well proportioned, graceful, spitz-type dog with a sparkling, stand-off coat. The head is wedge-shaped with a wide skull and a medium-length muzzle. The nose may be black, brown or flesh-coloured. The brown eyes are almond-shaped and enhance the 'laughing' expression so characteristic of this dog. The ears are thick with slightly rounded tips, and are held erect. The strong neck is carried on a broad, muscular body with a deep chest. The legs are very muscular and well boned. The tail is held curled over the back and to one side.

Coat A thick, close, short undercoat and a harsh, straight outercoat which grows away from the body giving protection from the cold. Colours are pure white, white-and-biscuit, and cream.

Size *Height:* dog 20–22in (51–56cm); bitch 18–20in (46–51cm). *Weight:* dog 50.5lb (23kg); bitch 39.5lb (18kg).

Characteristics and Temperament The Samoyed is a charming dog that loves human company. Fairly obedient in a rather laid-back way, the breed nevertheless enjoys life and lets everyone know it. The coat needs plenty of grooming, but the Samoyed is quite happy to submit to any amount of attention.

SHETLAND SHEEPDOG

Origins The bleak Shetland Islands off the north-east coast of Scotland are the original home of this small dog, which bears a strong resemblance to the Rough Collie. Although small, the breed was quite capable of working with the smaller Shetland ponies and other livestock of the area.

Appearance An elegant and symmetrical sheepdog. The head is in the shape of a blunt wedge. It has a flat, fairly broad skull and a long, rounded muzzle. The nose is black. The almond-shaped eyes are obliquely set and are usually dark brown, although they may be blue or blue-flecked in merles. The small ears are usually carried semi-erect with the tips falling forward. The well arched neck is carried on a deep-chested body with a level back. The muscular legs are moderately long. The tail is well furred.

Coat The outercoat of long hair is hard and straight; the undercoat is soft and short; hair forms an abundant mane and frill. Colours are sable, tricolour, blue merle, black-and-white, and black-and-tan.

Size *Height:* dog 14.5in (37cm); bitch 14in (35.5cm). *Weight:* 20lb (9kg).

Characteristics and Temperament This attractive little dog makes a good companion for people of all ages, being watchful, intelligent and active. The breed has undemanding feeding requirements, but the coat will need plenty of regular grooming.

The Sheltie has brains as well as beauty and, like the Shetland pony, has been miniaturized, in this case, from the Collie. They require regular grooming.

The Siberian Husky is not the ideal pet; it will jump over fences and dig its way out of anything. It can also be agressive with other dogs and because of its dense coat is not very happy indoors, having been bred to pull heavy loads in harsher climates.

SIBERIAN HUSKY

Origins The Siberian Husky was developed by the Chukchi peoples of Arctic north-east Asia as a fast, long-distance sled dog. Indeed, this is the fastest of all the sled-pulling breeds, and the dog seems happiest when performing this task. Although more lightly built than other sled dogs, the Siberian Husky is tough, strong and full of endurance.

Appearance A purposeful, medium-sized sled dog. The head is rather fox-like in shape, with a slightly rounded skull and a medium-length muzzle. The nose is black in grey, black or tan dogs, liver in copper-coloured dogs and flesh-coloured in white individuals. The eyes are almond-shaped and may be brown or blue, or parti-coloured. The triangular ears are held firmly erect. The neck is arched and is carried on a medium-length, muscular and deep-chested body. Well muscled, powerful legs end in oval, slightly-webbed feet with fur between the toes. The tail has a fox-like brush.

Coat Outercoat is straight and smooth-lying; undercoat soft and dense. The coat may be of any colour, including white.

Size *Height:* dog 21–23in (53.5–58.5cm); bitch 20–22in (51–56cm). *Weight:* dog 45–60lb (20.5–27kg); bitch 35–50lb (16–22.5kg).

Characteristics and Temperament

Friendly and extremely tolerant towards humans, the same cannot always be said about the Siberian Husky's attitude to other dogs, which it will usually try to dominate. Indifferent to the coldest of weather, the breed is not a typical pet by any means. It will jump over almost anything, or dig under it, and will usually pull on the leash and then take off when released. The breed is mostly kept for sled racing.

Similar in appearance to the Welsh Corgi, the Swedish Vallhund makes an undemanding pet with its moderate appetite and low-maintenance coat.

SWEDISH VALLHUND

Origins Looking very much like a Welsh Corgi, the Swedish Vallhund – also called the Swedish Cattle Dog – was rescued from near-extinction in the 1930s. The Swedish Kennel Club recognized the breed in 1948. The dog was bred to help herd cattle by nipping at their heels, thereby encouraging them to move along.

Appearance A low-slung, sturdy little dog. The head is shaped like a blunt wedge, with a flat skull and a squarish muzzle. The nose is black. The oval eyes are dark brown in colour. The ears are pricked and mobile. The neck is long and strong, and carried on a deep-chested body with a strong, level back. The legs are fairly short, well boned and muscular. The natural tail is 4-in (10-cm) long, but puppies may have their tails docked.

Coat Of medium-length; hard and close-fitting outercoat and thick, woolly undercoat. Colours are steel-grey, grey-brown, yellow-grey, reddish-yellow or reddish-brown.

Size *Height:* dog 13–14in (33–35.5cm); bitch 12–13in (30.5–33cm). *Weight:* 25–35lb (11.5–16kg).

Characteristics and Temperament A cheerful, obedient and active dog, the Swedish Vallhund makes a good family pet. Both feeding and grooming are undemanding.

The Tibetan Mastiff makes a formidable guard dog and though wary of strangers is much attached to its owners. It requires firm handling and plenty of exercise.

TIBETAN MASTIFF

Origins For centuries, this breed of dog has been used in the foothills of the Himalayas for guarding flocks of livestock from marauding predators and for guarding homes.

Appearance A massive, powerfully-built yet dignified dog. The head is large, with a wide skull and a short, square muzzle. The oval eyes are very expressive and may be any shade of brown. The ears are triangular and pendent and hang close to the head. The neck is strong and muscular. The deep-chested body is strong, with a straight back. The sturdy, muscular legs terminate in large cat-feet. The longish tail is held curled back over one side of the body.

Coat Quite long, thick and fine, with a heavy undercoat; hair forms a thick mane on the head and shoulders. Colours are black, black-and-tan, brown, and shades of gold, grey and blue.

Size *Height:* dog 26in (66cm) minimum; bitch 24in (61cm). *Weight:* 141–181lb (64–82kg).

Characteristics and Temperament Slow to mature (it takes about four years for a male to reach full maturity), the breed is fairly aloof with strangers but friendly and attached to its owner. Essentially a large breed of guard dog, and one that enjoys exercise, the Tibetan Mastiff needs proper handling.

WELSH CORGI (CARDIGAN)

Origins Originally bred as a cattle dog, the Cardigan Welsh Corgi is the older of the two varieties of Welsh Corgi, with a history going back 800 years. Nevertheless, it is the least well known of the two breeds. It is also the only one with a tail, and the Cardigan differs from the Pembroke in other respects, too, such as in coat-colour, ear-length and foot-shape.

Appearance A sturdy, short-legged and active dog. The head has a fox-like shape with a wide, flat skull and a tapering muzzle. The nose is black. The eyes have an alert but kindly expression and should be dark, although one or both may be blue or blue-flecked in merles. The ears are proportionately large with rounded tips, wide-spaced and held erect. A muscular neck is carried on a long, fairly broad-chested body. The legs are short but strong, and the feet are round. The brush-like tail is long enough to touch the ground but is usually lifted when on the move.

Coat Weatherproof; short or slightly longer, and with a hard texture. Any colours are permitted.

Size *Height:* 12in (30.5cm). *Weight:* 22–24lb (10–11kg).

Characteristics and Temperament
Active and fast-moving on occasions, the Cardigan Welsh Corgi can also take life at a steadier pace when it feels like it. Intelligent and obedient, the breed makes a good companion and watchdog.

Not to be confused with the Pembroke Corgi, the Cardigan Corgi is a much older breed and differs in several respects, having larger ears and a tail. They make rewarding pets.

WELSH CORGI (PEMBROKE)

Origins The better-known of the two breeds of Welsh Corgi, this version usually has its tail docked. Another cattle-driving dog, the Pembroke also earned its keep by nipping at the heels of cattle to encourage them to move on – a trick that has been tried on humans on occasions as well! This breed also has a long working history, as well as being the favourite pet of Queen Elizabeth II of England, who has owned many examples of this dog over the years.

Appearance A sturdy, short-legged and active dog. The head has a fox-like shape with a wide, flat skull and a tapering muzzle. The nose is black. The round eyes are brown in colour. The ears are of medium size with rounded tips, wide-spaced and held erect. A fairly long, muscular neck is carried on a long, fairly broad-chested body. The legs are short but strong, and the feet are oval. The tail is usually docked.

Coat Weatherproof; short or slightly longer and with a hard texture. Colours are red, sable, fawn, or black-and-tan, usually with white markings on the legs, neck, chest and face.

Size *Height:* 10–12in (25.5–30.5cm). *Weight:* 22–24lb (10–11kg).

Characteristics and Temperament A popular and outgoing dog, the Pembroke makes a good companion for an active family. It likes nothing more than a good romp out in the open air, followed by a square meal. Its fondness for food should be moderated, however, to avoid obesity.

The Pembroke Corgi's chief claim to fame is its popularity with the British Royal Family, since both the Queen and the Queen Mother have kept Corgis for many years. It is a low-maintenance pet, but beware of overfeeding as it puts on weight easily.

TOY DOGS

Some groups – the hounds, the gundogs and the terrier group, for instance – are made up of dogs sharing common characteristics. Within each of these groups, therefore, we find dogs with either an inbuilt tendency to hunt, or to retrieve, or to go to earth in pursuit of quarry. The toy group also includes dogs that have one overriding characteristic in common. In this case, the common feature is that they are all small – even if they come in a variety of different shapes. In this respect, therefore, the toy group shares a common link with the aforementioned groups, yet it also has similarities with the working dog group and the utility dog group, both of which also have a heterogeneous collection of breeds within them.

The dogs in the toy group are bred with a different purpose in mind, too. Although many breeds within the other groups are kept solely as pets, their original purpose is to perform some kind of work or other. Toy dogs are bred primarily to be companions (although many of them also make excellent watchdogs and some can catch vermin very adequately).

Despite their small size, toy dogs are still dogs, and they should be treated as such. They may not need to expend as much energy as some other

Despite its diminutive size, the Chihuahua is a spirited and intelligent dog that moves in a swift and purposeful way. It is friendly but will raise the alarm at the approach of unknown visitors. However, its fragility makes it unsuitable for small children. (Page 364.)

breeds, but they still need adequate amounts of exercise and a proper canine diet. Being carried around all day and fed sweets and other inappropriate food is a demeaning way to treat a dog. Given the chance, most toy breeds will enjoy a romp in the open air and can normally give a good account of themselves when confronted by larger varieties of their

species. A properly treated dog, whatever its size, will pay back the kindness shown to it with affection and by being an amusing and stimulating companion. Most toy breeds are highly intelligent and can quickly be trained. Another feature shared by most toy dogs is that they are attractive and neat-looking animals.

and for grace and elegance it would be hard to find a better example than the Italian Greyhound – truly a Greyhound in miniature. And for sheer character and a look of pure mischief nothing can beat the Griffon Bruxellois.

FAR LEFT
The Havanese is a tough little character that can stand up for itself in most situations but fits well into family life.

BELOW LEFT
When prepared for a show, groomed impeccably and with bows in its hair, it is easy to forget that the Yorkie is a typical terrier, bred originally for work and still full of energy and ready for action. (Page 394.)

The toy group has representatives drawn from many other breed types, as well as some which are unique to the group. The terriers are represented in the shape of the Affenpinscher, the Australian Silky Terrier, the English Toy Terrier, the Yorkshire Terrier and the Miniature Pinscher. These dogs, although small, have typical terrier characteristics of bravery and dash.

For admirers of spaniels the choice in the toy dog group includes the Pekingese, the King Charles Spaniel and the Cavalier King Charles Spaniel. Lovers of spitz-type dogs will find the Pomeranian has all the spark and energy – and the voice – of its larger cousins.

Exotic, long-coated dogs come no better than in the form of the Papillon, the Pekingese and the Yorkshire Terrier,

Also known as the Black Devil, on account of its mischievous expression, the plucky Affenpinscher makes an excellent companion and watchdog and is quick to see off strangers.

AFFENPINSCHER

Origins There is some disagreement about the exact origins of the Affenpinscher, with some authorities believing it to be a descendant of wire-coated terriers from Scandinavia, while others think the dog has a link with breeds from Asia. The dog in its present form comes from Germany, and has been known there for centuries, where it is also known as the Black Devil because of its mischievous expression.

Appearance A rough-coated, robust-looking dog with a monkey-like face. The head has a rather broad skull and a short, blunt muzzle. The nose is black. The dark, round eyes have a glint to them. The ears are small and may be drop or erect. The short neck is carried on a body with a short, straight back. The legs are straight, and the tail is carried high.

Coat Short, dense, hard and wiry; the head has prominent whiskers. The colour is usually black, but there may also be grey in the coat.

Size *Height:* 9.5–11in (24–28cm). *Weight:* 6.5–9lb (3–4kg).

Characteristics and Temperament Full of character and energy, the Affenpinscher is a delightful small companion dog that will also fearlessly confront any uninvited visitor to its home.

The Australian Silky Terrier has all the 'terrier' instincts still intact, despite its elegant appearance. It is a lively little dog with plenty of stamina.

AUSTRALIAN SILKY TERRIER

Origins This breed came about in the 1800s as the result of crossings between the Yorkshire Terrier and the Australian Terrier. It was formerly known as the Sydney Silky Terrier, after a well known breeder of these dogs moved to the city of that name with his kennels.

Appearance A low-slung, long-coated dog with a refined look about it. The head is wedge-shaped, with a moderately-broad, flat skull. The nose is black. The eyes are round, small and have an alert expression. The ears are V-shaped and pricked. The neck is slightly arched and is carried on a longish body. The legs are short and finely-boned. The tail is usually docked and carried erect.

Coat Fine, straight, long and glossy with a silky texture. Colours are blue-and-tan, and grey-blue-and-tan.

Size *Height:* 9in (23cm). *Weight:* 9lb (4kg).

Characteristics and Temperament The long, fine coat and generally elegant appearance of this breed should not disguise the fact that the Silky is a real terrier! Keen, active and ever-ready, this dog makes a friendly companion with plenty of stamina.

The enchanting little Bichon Frise is an undemanding pet and enjoys partaking in family activities. However, the coat requires regular grooming to retain its beautiful appearance.

BICHON FRISE

Origins This sprightly little dog originated in the Mediterranean region, possibly as long ago as the 14th century. Later, it found favour in the royal courts of Europe. After the French Revolution, the dog became a familiar part of circus acts, but by the 19th century its popularity had declined. However, the breed's fortunes were restored when it was recognized by the French Kennel Club in 1934.

Appearance A sturdy, lively little dog with a thick woolly coat. The head has a broad skull with a shortish muzzle. The nose is black. The eyes are large, dark and round and face forward prominently; their expression is one of alertness. The ears are pendulous. An arched, moderately-long neck is carried on a body with a well developed chest and broad loins. The legs are straight and well boned. The tail is usually carried in a curve over the back.

Coat Thick, silky and loosely curled; coat is often clipped into a distinctive shape. The colour should be solid white.

Size *Height:* 9–11in (23–28cm). *Weight:* 6.5–13lb (3–6kg).

Characteristics and Temperament
Lively and confident, the Bichon Frise is happiest when receiving plenty of attention from its owners. It likes to join in family games and is undemanding both in terms of diet and exercise.

The Bolognese is a compact, squarely-built dog. The coat is usually left untrimmed but not ungroomed, which is unusual for toy breeds.

BOLOGNESE

Origins The city of Bologna in northern Italy gives its name to this dog. Similar in style to many of the bichon breeds, the Bolognese has existed in Italy for hundreds of years but is not very common elsewhere. The dog is also known as the Bichon Bolognese.

Appearance A compact, squarely-built dog with a distinctive coat. The head has a broad skull and a short, strong muzzle. The nose is black. The eyes are large, round and dark in colour. The ears are long and pendulous and are carried in such a way that they help to make the head appear wider than it actually is. The neck is of medium length. The body has a level back and slightly arched loins and is carried on short, well muscled legs. The tail is carried curled over the back.

Coat Long, dense and curly, but shorter and softer on the muzzle. The colour should be pure white.

Size *Height:* 10–12in (25.5–30.5cm). *Weight:* 6.5–9lb (3–4kg).

Characteristics and Temperament The Bolognese is another small breed that delights in taking part in as many activities as possible. Intelligent and affectionate, the breed is unusual among toy breeds in that the coat is left untrimmed – although not ungroomed – and hence appears slightly 'unkempt'.

The Cavalier King Charles is the ideal companion. Playful and with a cheerful disposition, it loves to run around, but is equally happy sitting by its owner's side.

CAVALIER KING CHARLES SPANIEL

Origins This breed has been known for several centuries, and was a popular dog in European courts in the 17th century. Larger than its relative the King Charles Spaniel, and with less of a snub nose, the Cavalier King Charles Spaniel achieved Kennel Club recognition in the 1940s.

Appearance An attractive, well balanced small spaniel. The head has a flattish skull and a short, square muzzle. The nose is black. The large, round eyes are dark in colour and have a trusting, endearing expression. The ears are long and pendulous, with good feathering. The neck is of medium length and slightly arched. The body is short with a level back and is carried on moderately-boned legs. The tail is fairly long, although sometimes it is docked by one-third.

Coat Long and silky with, sometimes, a slight wave; ample feathering. Colours are black-and-tan, ruby (rich red), Blenheim (chestnut-and-white) or tricolour (black, white and tan).

Size *Height:* 13in (33cm). *Weight:* 12–18lb (5.5–8kg).

Characteristics and Temperament One of the most popular of all the toy breeds, the Cavalier King Charles Spaniel seems to offer everything – it is friendly, happy to run in the fields or sit by its owner's side, it is built like a proper sporting dog and is easy to feed and groom.

The Chihuahua, despite its small stature, has a large spirit and brave heart. It requires little food or exercise and makes an ideal pet for an elderly person.

CHIHUAHUA

Origins This dog gets its name from the Mexican state of Chihuahua where, around the mid 1890s, it first became well known to the Western world – although there is evidence that it may have actually originated from the Orient. Soon after, the dog was introduced into the United States, where the breed standard was improved. The Chihuahua comes in two varieties – a smooth-coated and a long-coated form. This is generally considered to be the world's smallest breed of dog.

Appearance A tiny, neat-looking dog with a prominent head. The head has a broad, rounded skull and a short, pointed muzzle and a distinct stop. The large, round eyes are set well apart; several colours are possible, according to coat colour. The distinctive ears are large and flared and set at the side of the head. The slightly-arched neck is carried on an elongated body with a level back. The legs are moderately well boned and of medium length. The tail is carried over the back.

Coat *Smooth-coated:* Smooth, soft and glossy. *Long-coated:* Soft, and flat or wavy; feathering on feet, legs and ruff. Any colours are permissible.

Size *Height:* 6–9in (15–23cm). *Weight:* 2–6lb (1–3kg).

Characteristics and Temperament
Despite its diminutive size, the Chihuahua is a spirited and intelligent dog that moves with a swift and purposeful action. It is friendly but will raise the alarm at the approach of unknown visitors. Although undemanding to feed, groom and exercise, the dog is not suitable for small children.

The Chinese Crested Dog is an ancient breed from the Han Dynasty, and if you are looking for an unusual pet, then this is the one for you. Be careful, however; the hairless one is liable to get sunburn.

CHINESE CRESTED DOG

Origins A favourite dog of the Han Dynasty in ancient China, the Chinese Crested was used to guard treasures and even in some forms of hunting. The dog was first shown in America in 1885. The breed comes in two coat forms: the hairless (with a crest of hair on the head, hair covering parts of the legs and feet and a plume of hair on the tail) and the powder puff (with a body covered in fine hair).

Appearance An active and graceful dog. The head has a moderately-broad, elongated skull and a medium-long, tapering muzzle. The nose may be any colour. The almond-shaped eyes are almost black and are set wide apart. The large ears are held erect in the hairless variety, but in the powder puff variety drop ears are permitted. The neck is long and lean. The body is of medium length with a deep chest. The legs are long and lightly-boned and end in hare-feet. The tail is long and tapering.

Coat *Hairless:* Hair confined to head crest, lower legs and feet and tail plume; the skin may be plain or spotted and may lighten in summer. *Powder puff:* Coat consists of a soft veil of long hair. Any colours are allowed.

Size *Height:* dog 11–13in (28–33cm); bitch 9–12in (23–30.5cm). *Weight:* 12lb (5.5kg).

Characteristics and Temperament
Happy, lively and affectionate, the Chinese Crested Dog is a tough breed that keeps itself very clean. The dog enjoys reasonable amounts of exercise. The hairless variety in particular can suffer from sunburn.

The English Toy Terrier has a wonderful flowing action when it moves. It is alert and intelligent, makes a delightful pet, and is a good deterrent to rats and mice.

ENGLISH TOY TERRIER

Origins The English Toy Terrier, once known as the Toy Black-and-Tan Terrier, has an ancestry which includes Black-and-Tan Terriers and Italian Greyhounds. During Regency and Georgian periods, the English Toy Terrier was a familiar sight in rat pits, where this active little dog would be set against the clock, with wagers being placed on the number of rats it would kill in an allotted time.

Appearance A well balanced, elegant and compact toy dog, reminiscent of a small, prick-eared Manchester Terrier. The head has a long, flat and narrow skull and a narrowing muzzle. The nose is black. The almond-shaped eyes are small and dark with a bright and lively expression. The ears are held erect by the time the dog is mature, and are described as 'candle-flamed' in shape. The long, arched neck is carried on a short body with a slightly curving back and a deep, narrow chest. The legs are long and fine-boned. The tail is long and tapering.

Coat Thick, close, smooth and glossy. Colour is black-and-tan; the standard is very precise about the distribution of tan markings.

Size *Height:* 10–12in (25.5–30.5cm). *Weight:* 6–8lb (3–3.5kg).

Characteristics and Temperament A sound example of this breed moves with a smooth, flowing action and is a delight to watch. The English Toy Terrier has all the characteristics of a true terrier – alertness, speed of movement and excellent vermin-catching qualities. It is also friendly and watchful.

GRIFFON BRUXELLOIS

Origins This dog originates from Belgium, where it was used in stables for keeping down vermin and for raising the alarm if anyone approached. Dogs very similar to the Griffon Bruxellois were depicted in paintings in the 1400s, and the breed was well established in the 1600s. There is a mixture of breeds in its ancestry, including the Affenpinscher, Pug and various terriers. Two varieties exist – a rough-coated form and a smooth-coated form called the Petit Brabançon.

Appearance A square, well built little dog with a monkey-like face. The head has a broad, round skull, a short, wide muzzle and a prominent chin. The nose is black. The eyes are large and round. The ears are semi-erect. The medium-length neck is slightly arched, and the deep-chested body is carried on straight, medium-length legs. The tail is usually docked.

Coat *Rough-coated:* Hard and wiry, but not curly; prominent walrus moustache. *Smooth-coated:* Short and tight.

Size *Height:* 7–8in (18–20.5cm). *Weight:* 5–11lb (2.5–5kg).

Characteristics and Temperament No other dog has such a mischievous face, and this is especially apparent in the rough-coated variety. Lively, fearless and alert, the Griffon Bruxellois makes a happy and amusing pet dog for owners living in town or country.

The Griffon Bruxellois was bred to catch rats and guard property. As its name suggests, it originated in Belgium, taking its name from the city of Brussels. It has a lively, alert and mischievous nature and makes a delightful pet.

HAVANESE

Origins Known as the national dog of Cuba, the Havanese was probably brought to the country by traders or Spanish colonists. Many of these dogs were subsequently taken to the United States when their owners fled the Cuban communist revolution. The dog is also known as the Bichon Havanais.

Appearance A long-coated, well built, bichon-type dog. The head has a broad skull, a pointed muzzle and a moderate stop. The nose is usually black, but may be brown in some coat shades. The large, almond-shaped eyes are dark and have a kindly expression. The drop ears are moderately-pointed. The neck is of medium length, and the body has a level topline with a slight rise over the loins. The legs are fairly short and medium-boned and end in hare-feet. The tail, usually carried high over the back, is covered in long, silky hair.

Coat Soft and silky, with a dense crest on the head. Any colour is allowed, such as white, cream, black, blue, chocolate or silver.

Size *Height:* 8–11in (20.5–28cm). *Weight:* 7–12lb (3–5.5kg).

Characteristics and Temperament Friendly, lively and intelligent, the Havanese is a tough little character that can stand up for itself in most situations but fits well into family life.

Also known as the Bichon Havanais, the Havanese is the national dog of Cuba. Even though it looks cute and pretty, it is a tough little character and knowns how to look after itself.

The Italian Greyhound is a perfect miniature of its larger cousin. However, it is quiet and gentle and would perhaps feel happier in a home that has no young children.

ITALIAN GREYHOUND

Origins Dogs very similar in appearance to this breed can be seen depicted in the tombs of ancient pharaohs, although the modern Italian Greyhound was probably bred more recently in Roman times. This is the smallest of the sighthounds, and its diminutive size precludes serious chasing as part of a hunt. Instead, it is admired for its small-scale elegance, ease of keeping and gentle nature.

Appearance A Greyhound in miniature. The head has a long, flat, narrow skull and a fine, long muzzle. The nose may be any dark colour. The eyes are expressive, large and bright. The delicate, rose-shaped ears are set well back on the head. The long neck is gracefully arched and is carried on a narrow, deep-chested body; the back is slightly arched over the loins. The legs are long and well muscled and end in hare-feet. The tail is long and fine, and carried low.

Coat Satin-like, fine and short. Colours are black, blue, cream, fawn, red, white – or any of these colours with white.

Size *Height:* 13–15in (33–38cm). *Weight:* 6–10lb (3–4.5kg).

Characteristics and Temperament
Despite its fragile appearance, the Italian Greyhound is brave and energetic. It has a good turn of speed over the countryside, moving with the same long-striding gait as its larger cousins. The dog is also affectionate, and happy to sit at home next to its owner.

The Japanese Chin is the perfect pet for those who cannot walk too far. The coat needs regular grooming to keep it in good condition.

JAPANESE CHIN

Origins This attractive little dog is also known as the Japanese Spaniel, although it has a strong resemblance to the Pekingese. The breed probably arrived in Japan as a gift from the Chinese royal court.

Appearance A lively and dainty little dog with a distinctive face. The head is large, with a broad skull, rounded in front, and with a short, wide muzzle and deep stop. The nose is usually black, but in reds and whites it may be of a colour to harmonize with the coat. The eyes are large and dark and set wide apart. The small, V-shaped ears are well feathered. The body is compact with a broad chest and is carried on straight, fine-boned legs which end in hare-feet. The tail is well feathered and carried curved over the back.

Coat Long, silky, soft, straight and profuse. Colours are black-and-white or red-and-white.

Size *Height:* 7in (18cm). *Weight:* 4–7lb (2–3kg).

Characteristics and Temperament The Japanese Chin is a tiny dog with a cheerful and friendly nature. The breed's characteristic facial expression is one suggesting surprise. Although happy to go for leisurely walks, it is unfair to expect it to undertake anything too demanding. The coat needs regular grooming to keep it in good condition.

KING CHARLES SPANIEL

Origins Also known as the English Toy Spaniel, the King Charles Spaniel is so named because it was a favourite at the court of the English king Charles II. Many paintings from the period also depict one or more of these spaniels somewhere in the scene, such was their popularity. This spaniel is closely related to the Cavalier King Charles Spaniel. The King Charles Spaniel, however, has a shorter nose and a slightly more domed skull than the Cavalier.

Appearance A cobby and aristocratic-looking small dog. The head has a broad, arched skull and a short, square, upturned muzzle. The nose is black. The eyes are large, set wide apart, and have a friendly expression. The well feathered ears are long and pendulous. The arched neck is carried on a broad, deep-chested body. The legs are short and straight. The tail, also well feathered, may be docked.

Coat Long, silky and straight. Colours are black-and-tan, ruby (rich red), Blenheim (chestnut-and-white) or tricolour (black, white and tan).

Size *Height:* dog 10in (25.5cm); bitch 8in (20.5cm). *Weight:* 8–14lb (3.5–6.5kg).

Characteristics and Temperament An appealing small dog with a gentle and affectionate nature, the King Charles Spaniel is undemanding both in terms of feeding and exercise.

The King Charles Spaniel was the preferred pet of the English King Charles II, so it has been around for quite a long time. It is much in evidence in the paintings of the period.

The charming Löwchen is gaining in popularity, though it has been known in Europe for centuries. Eager to please, lively and intelligent, it is a fun dog for all the family to enjoy.

LÖWCHEN (LITTLE LION DOG)

Origins The Löwchen has been known in European countries such as France, Spain and Germany since the 1500s. By 1960, however, the popularity of the Löwchen had declined to such an extent that it was listed as the rarest dog in the world – although numbers have improved since then, and the breed has gained new fans. This bichon-type breed gets its other name, Little Lion, because of the characteristic lion-like shape into which its coat is sometimes trimmed.

Appearance A well built, active dog with a coat clipped into a shape resembling that of a male lion. The head is short and broad, with a flat skull, a short, strong muzzle and a well defined stop. The eyes are large and round, with an intelligent expression. The ears are pendent. The body is short and strong and is carried on strong, straight legs. The tail is of medium length and is clipped into a tuft of hair at the end, resembling a plume.

Coat Long and wavy. Any colours are permissible.

Size *Height:* 10–13in (25.5–33cm). *Weight:* 6.5lb (3kg).

Characteristics and Temperament A friendly, lively and intelligent little dog, the Löwchen makes a good family pet and is robust enough to enjoy plenty of games with children.

MALTESE

Origins The Maltese, or Maltese Terrier, is one of the oldest breeds in Europe. It was probably introduced to Malta by Phoenician traders sailing around the Mediterranean, and there is evidence of the dog being admired by early civilizations such as the Ancient Greeks. The Romans also kept these small dogs as pets, and they were popular again in the Middle Ages.

Appearance A neat little dog with a profuse white coat. The head has a flat skull and a short, broad muzzle. The nose is black. The eyes are dark brown and have an intelligent expression. The ears are long, well feathered and pendulous. The body is short and cobby and carried on short, straight legs. The tail, also well feathered, is carried arched over the back.

Coat Long, straight and silky. The colour should be pure white, although occasional lemon markings appear.

Size *Height:* 10in (25.5cm). *Weight:* 4–6lb (2–3kg).

Characteristics and Temperament The Maltese moves with a free-flowing action, seeming to glide along with the coat wafting around it. Although small, this is a tough, friendly and alert dog that likes to play and enjoys exercise. The coat needs plenty of grooming to keep it in peak condition.

The ancient Maltese has been celebrated since Roman times. It was especially favoured by women, no doubt because of its feminine appearance, but it is tough for all that.

Despite its small stature, the Minature Pinscher has lost none of the bravery and alertness of its larger cousins.

MINIATURE PINSCHER

Origins A German breed, the Miniature Pinscher is – as its name suggests – the smallest of the pinschers. The Miniature Pinscher was bred from German terriers about 100 years ago and is now widely popular.

Appearance A compact, elegant, smooth-coated small dog. The head is long with a flat skull and a strong muzzle. The nose is usually black, but in blue- or chocolate-coated dogs it may harmonize with the coat colour. The eyes are usually black. The ears may be carried erect or in the half-dropped position. The neck is graceful and arched and carried on a short, moderately deep-chested body. The legs are straight and medium-boned. The tail may be docked short or left natural – if the latter, it is often carried arched over the body.

Coat Smooth, straight, hard and glossy. Colours are black, blue, chocolate with tan markings, or various shades of red.

Size *Height:* 10–12in (25.5–30.5cm). *Weight:* 7.5lb (3.5kg).

Characteristics and Temperament Small it may be, but the Miniature Pinscher is a fearless, active and alert dog. It moves with a characteristic, high-stepping gait, and it also has a good sense of hearing and will bark to alert the household if strangers approach.

384

PAPILLON

Origins The Papillon, also known as the Butterfly Dog because of the shape of its ears, is recognized as a Franco-Belgian breed. In fact, there are two versions of this dog – one with erect ears (the origin of the name 'Papillon') and the other with drop ears. Once popular in the royal courts of Europe, the dog is still much admired today.

Appearance An alert, silky-coated dog. The head has a slightly rounded skull and a pointed muzzle with a well defined stop. The nose is black. The medium-sized eyes are dark and alert. The ears are of two types: either erect and held like the open wings of a butterfly, or carried dropped; in either style the ears are well fringed with hair. The body is long, with a level back, and is carried on finely-boned legs that end in hare-feet. The long tail is arched over the back and falls to one side.

Coat Full, flowing, long and silky; the chest has a profuse frill. The coat is white with patches of any colour except liver; the preferred markings on the head include a white stripe down the centre of the skull that helps to accentuate the butterfly effect.

Size *Height:* 8–11in (20.5–28cm). *Weight:* 7.5lb (3.5kg).

Characteristics and Temperament
Intelligent, affectionate and easy to train, the attractive little Papillon proves a star performer in obedience tests. The dog is a delightful companion, but is not recommended as a pet for small children.

The charming Papillon remains the heart-stealer it was when it was a member of the French Court. Today, it is still loved for its playfulness and strong sense of fun.

The Pekingese is not the most active of dogs and is content to amble along at its own pace. It does, however, require regular grooming to prevent the long coat from becoming hopelessly tangled.

PEKINGESE

Origins Once the sacred dog of China and named after the capital city of that country, this little dog is another of those breeds that is recognized by people the world over. Its ancestry can be traced back to at least the 8th century Tang Dynasty, and for centuries the Pekingese was highly prized at the Imperial Court. Perhaps this royal patronage explains something of the sense of self-importance which the Pekingese seems to convey. In the 1860s, some examples of the breed were brought to England after Peking was overrun, and in the early 1900s it was introduced to America.

Appearance A small, well balanced and long-coated dog with a characteristic monkey face. The head is large, with a broad skull and a short, broad, wrinkled muzzle with a strong under jaw. The flat nose is black. The eyes are large and round. The ears are heart-shaped and pendulous. The short neck is carried on a short body with a broad chest. The short legs are well boned, the hind legs being lighter. The well feathered tail is carried curled tightly over one side of the back.

Coat Long and thick with a full mane and good feathering on the ears, legs,

tail and feet; the outercoat is coarse and there is a thick undercoat. All colours are allowed except liver or albino.

Size *Height:* 7in (18cm). *Weight:* dog 11lb (5kg); bitch 12lb (5.5kg).

Characteristics and Temperament
Playful and fearless, the Pekingese is

also an affectionate dog that makes a highly individual pet. However, this is not a breed that takes kindly to long walks in the country, preferring to amble along at its own speed with a characteristic rolling gait. The coat needs lots of regular grooming to keep it in peak condition.

Like all spitz-type dogs, the Pomeranian – the smallest of the breed – has a good deal of energy. It makes a lively little companion and had a high-pitched bark to warn of the presence of strangers.

POMERANIAN

Origins This is the smallest of the spitz-type dogs and is a descendant of the big sled-pulling dogs of the Arctic region. This German dog came to Britain in the late 1870s, and its popularity later received a boost when Queen Victoria decide to keep the breed.

Appearance A small, compact, fox-faced dog with a profuse coat. The head has a slightly flat skull and a short, pointed muzzle. The nose is black in white, sable or orange dogs, brown in chocolate-tipped sable dogs, and self-coloured in dogs with other coat colours. The eyes are bright and dark with an intelligent expression. The ears are small and held erect. The body is short, with a deep chest, and is carried on fine-boned, medium-length legs. The tail is carried over the back in spitz fashion.

Coat The outercoat is long, straight and harsh, and very thick around the neck and shoulders; undercoat is soft and thick. All colours are permitted, such as white, black, cream, brown, orange, beaver or sable.

Size *Height:* 8.5–11in (21.5–28cm). *Weight:* dog 4–4.5lb (1.8–2kg); bitch 4.5–5.5lb (2–2.5kg).

Characteristics and Temperament
Pomeranians have plenty of energy, just like their larger cousins. Extroverted and vivacious, the dog makes a lively companion. It also has a shrill bark to alert its owner when anyone approaches the house.

The Pug is a sturdy, muscular little dog, rather like a miniature mastiff. It may look tough but it is actually quite a softie – gentle, even-tempered and good with children.

PUG

Origins The Pug is thought to have originated in China, where the dog was the companion of monks. It arrived in Europe with traders in the 1500s and subsequently became very popular in the Netherlands and in Britain.

Appearance A square, muscular dog reminiscent of a miniature mastiff. The head is large and round with a short, blunt muzzle; the skin has clearly-defined wrinkles. The huge, dark eyes are set in the sockets in a way that makes them seem globular; they are also highly expressive. The ears are small and thin, and there are two types – drop rose ears or folded button ears; the latter are preferred. The neck is strong and thick and is carried on a short, wide-chested body. The fairly long legs are strong and straight. The tail is curled tightly over the hip.

Coat Short, smooth, soft and glossy. Colours are silver, fawn, apricot or black; light colours should have clearly contrasting markings including a dark mask and ears.

Size *Height:* 10–11in (25.5–28cm).
Weight: 14–18lb (6.5–8kg).

Characteristics and Temperament The
sturdy Pug is a real character among
dogs. The body language and the almost
talking eyes can express all manner of
moods from alert watchfulness to an
appealing request for attention. A
playful and hardy dog, the Pug enjoys
exercise and is easy to feed and groom.

YORKSHIRE TERRIER

Origins The result of crossings involving the Black-and-Tan Terrier, the Skye Terrier, the Dandie Dinmont and the Maltese, the 'Yorkie' first came to prominence in the 1850s. Originally the Yorkshire Terrier was bred as a rat-fighting dog; then, the breed was larger than the show and pet dogs seen today.

Appearance A compact, long-coated small terrier. The head is quite small with a flattish skull and a short muzzle. The nose is black. The dark eyes are medium-sized and have an intelligent, alert expression. The small V-shaped ears are carried erect. The compact body has a level back and is carried on shortish, straight legs. The tail is usually docked to about half its natural length.

Coat Long and straight and glossy with a silky texture; hair longer on the head. The main body colour is dark steel-blue, with the hair on the head a rich golden-tan, and the hair on the chest a bright tan colour.

Size *Height:* dog 8in (20.5cm); bitch 7in (18cm). *Weight:* 7lb (3kg).

Characteristics and Temperament Groomed to the peak of perfection for the show ring, it is hard to believe that this dog with its lustrous, flowing coat and colourful bows in its hair is also, given half the chance, a typical terrier. This means that it is tough, active and ready for a romp whenever the opportunity presents itself.

Despite its dainty and feminine appearance, the Yorkshire Terrier is a true terrier at heart, having been bred to fight rats. It is alert and spirited and ready for action at any time.

DOG CARE

BRINGING YOUR DOG HOME

At last the time has come to introduce your new dog to your family home; but remember that this will be a strange experience for you both. An older dog needs to be treated with tact, diplomacy and kindness. If he has come from a dog's home he is likely to have had limited space at his disposal, and while the staff try to give as much love as they can, their attention is inevitably overstretched. Consequently, the new arrival may either be overwhelmed or thoroughly overexcited. Allow time for him to settle, then let him have a good sniff around the house and garden so that he can become accustomed to the new sights and scents that will be bombarding his senses. This is also the best time to firmly establish any areas that are forbidden to him; once he has been allowed upstairs or on the sofa you will find it very difficult to stop him in future.

Once all the excitement has subsided, show him his bed. Ideally, you will have managed to keep something from his former home which he recognizes. This will make him feel that this is now his place and offer him a little comfort in his new environment. The bed itself should be large enough to accommodate him comfortably, made of

396

a sturdy material and filled with comfortable washable bedding. Give him a small portion of food to begin with, as he may be disoriented by the journey, and show him where his water bowl is.

Good preparation is most important. A puppy can be messier than a baby – you can hardly protect a dog with a diaper! For most of the time it is advisable to restrict him to a place that is not carpeted or covered with difficult to clean flooring material. The kitchen, though not the ideal location, will possibly be chosen as the room most frequented by the family and will ensure that the puppy does not feel lonely or excluded. Allocate a place for his food and water bowls and make him a comfortable bed; puppies feel happier in a warm enclosed space – a box turned onto its side and filled with washable bedding is ideal and can easily be replaced when chewed, or you can buy ready-made enclosed beds. Site the bed where it is warm and away from draughts in a place where he will feel part of the family. While he is sleeping, leave him in peace and remember that puppies can sleep for up to 20 hours a day, requiring ample rest as part of the growing process. Don't let your children disturb him, however eager they are to play with him.

Puppies love to chew things up and will easily ruin an expensive bed. It may be cheaper to use a cardboard box until he has grown out of this destructive phase. This Labrador puppy seems quite happy with his favourite blanket.

An enclosed pen is often a good idea. This will limit the area which a dog can soil and keep him out of trouble when you are unable to keep an eye on him. However, don't use it as a constant excuse to keep him out of the way; puppies need to play and socialize with the family and they also need to be trained to defecate outside. He will never learn if he is kept constantly cooped up. Keep plenty of newspaper and disinfectant to hand and clean up any accidents immediately.

Settling In

The first few days of your dog's arrival are going to seem strange to you both. If you have a puppy, by now you will be getting more familiar with house-training (pages 406–407). A puppy must not be allowed to run around in public places until he has had all his vaccinations when he is about 12–14 weeks old, so he will have to be confined to house and garden. Use this time to get acquainted, introducing him to other members of the family and praising him regularly so that he learns to recognize your voice.

Night-times may prove troublesome when the puppy may fret because he has been left alone. While he is very young, a clock wrapped in a cloth and placed beside him can fool him into thinking it is his mother's heartbeat, and give him a little comfort. Gradually, he will come to

realize that night is a time for settling down to a good long sleep.

Introduce the new arrival to other pets very gradually, as they may be rather indignant at losing their prime positions of importance in the household. A good way is to put the puppy in a pen so that the others can sniff him through the bars. Once they have met properly, make a huge fuss of all the animals to minimize the risk of jealousy. Feed separately to avoid quarrels until all are comfortable in each other's company. Once firm friendships have been established, the other animals may well be a source of comfort and companionship to the new arrival and even cats may enjoy cuddling up to a dog for warmth.

Things You Need to Buy

Before bringing your dog home, you will need to buy a certain amount of equipment, and it is a good idea to obtain this beforehand so that everything is to hand when you need it. In any case, it will be more difficult to go shopping once he has arrived. This is not dissimilar to preparing for a new baby when you want everything to be perfect and just so right from the start.

Bowls

Your dog will require his own selection of feed and water bowls. Buy ones that

Hard plastic beds are very durable, more than suitable to withstand the considerable weight of this Bullmastiff.

This Lurcher is very much at home and more than happy to contentedly pass the time, basking in the sun in his own back yard.

of an appropriate length and width and which is long enough so that you do not have to stoop when walking. Make sure the leash is fitted with a secure clip fastener. There is no good or bad type of leash: choose the one that is the most comfortable for you. Your dog will inevitably try to chew it; discourage this rather than buying one of the chain types which is unpleasant to hold, particularly in winter.

LEFT
Dog bowls come in a variety of materials and sizes.

BELOW
A harness can be an effective form of restraint and can also be more comfortable for a smaller dog.

are suitable for his size, and which are made of heavy stainless steel or ceramics so that they stay in one place as he feeds and do not move along the floor or get knocked over, which is a common failing with plastic ones. Always make sure that he has fresh water and clean bowls with each feed. Show him where his bowls are and keep them always in that place.

Collars and Leashes

It is vital that your dog is fitted with a collar straight away. For adult dogs, there is a huge variety of collars available, from the most ornately worked leather to plain nylon. A dog's first collar should be of the buckled variety and should be fitted with an identity tag enabling him to be

instantly returned to you in the event of him straying. Even dogs fitted with an identity chip should have a tag as an extra precaution. The collar should fit so that it is comfortable, not so loose that it can slip over his head, and you should be able to comfortably fit two fingers between the collar and the dog's neck.

Puppies have delicate skin, so find a collar that is soft and comfortable and not too expensive, as they grow rapidly and may go through several before they are fully grown. In this case, nylon ones are probably best as they are relatively chew-proof. In both cases you will also require a leash, as even a puppy which cannot yet go outside will need to be trained to walk while being restrained. Choose one

Make sure your dog can be easily and speedily identified should he decide to wander. This little terrier is wearing a leather collar with a metal identity disk. There are other types, such as barrels, but these have a tendency to fall apart, when the information can be easily lost. Even if your dog has an identity chip, it is still wise to fit a collar and tag as an immediate source of identification.

There are other types of collars and leashes which are used as methods of control. If your dog has a tendency to pull, it is preferable to teach him some manners and how to walk to heel. However, and as a last resort, these items have their uses. (See page 417 for a more advanced method of control.)

Extended Leashes

These are useful if you wish to give your dog a little more freedom when it is too dangerous for him to be allowed to run free or he is difficult to catch. They have comfortable plastic handles and easy controls which allow you to quickly let him out or reel him in as necessary.

Safety in the Home

It is of utmost importance to go over your home beforehand and remove anything that may be dangerous or harmful; also move precious items to prevent them from being destroyed. There is nothing a lively dog enjoys more than charging around, so remove valuable items of furniture, secure electric cables, and unplug electrical appliances, such as lamps, which may be pulled to the floor. Keep all harmful chemicals such as cleaning fluids, rat poison and insect sprays well out of reach and preferably locked away.

Remember that puppies love to chew things up; don't leave shoes or bags lying around. Also place all houseplants well out of reach; many are actually poisonous, so don't take any chances and remove them all.

Puppies have a natural urge to chew. From the age of 3–6 months, the adult teeth will begin to emerge, forcing the milk teeth out. This can cause pain and irritation, as in human babies, so be sure to provide toys which are the equivalent of teething rings. Unfortunately, dogs never seem to grow out of their desire to chew, even when the adult teeth appear. However, there are a variety of objects which they can legitimately chew up, which include hard nylon toys and objects made from rawhide and sterilized bone. Provide plenty of these as it will help preserve your furniture. Also get toys you can both play with, especially toys that can be pulled against; dogs love playing tug-of-war.

Safety Outside

There are some people who prefer their dogs to live outside, in which case they must be sure that there is a warm, water- and wind-proof kennel, and that it is big enough. Place it in a sheltered area, add plenty of warm, washable bedding and a safe form of heating, if

possible. Many thick-coated dogs thrive outside and some even prefer it, for example dogs with very dense coats designed to withstand harsh weather, e.g. the Husky. This arrangement should not be an excuse to leave a dog on his own for hours on end; he requires just as much love and attention as the dog which lives indoors.

Your yard or garden must be adequately fenced to prevent your dog from roaming. Even in country areas where there is less traffic, a fatal accident could still occur. A boundary fence of 4-ft (1.2-m) high for small dogs and 6ft (1.8m) for large dogs should be adequate, making sure that the fence is securely fixed at ground level. Dogs are keen diggers and talented burrowers, so make it a rule to regularly check that fences and gates are secure.

Identity Chips

Recent technology has made it possible to have all pets electronically tagged. A tiny microchip is painlessly injected into the loose skin around the neck, where it should stay forever.

The chip contains a number which is logged into a central computer on which is recorded the owner's name, address and telephone number. Have your dog chipped as a back-up to an identity disk.

SAFETY IN THE HOME CHECK LIST

Keep all poisonous plants out of reach

•

Keep poisonous household products locked away

•

Unplug appliances not in use and remove dangling cables

•

Remove small objects that could be swallowed or cause choking

OUTDOOR SAFETY CHECK LIST

Remove any poisonous plants

•

Ensure that boundaries are adequately fenced and that gates are secure

•

Fence ponds and cover swimming pools when not in use

•

Lock away garden tools and mowers

•

Lock away garden fertilizers and weedkillers

TRAINING YOUR DOG

To make them easier to live with, it is vital that dogs are adequately house-trained and have learned to be obedient. Dogs cannot be allowed to run riot making nuisances of themselves, and need to be taught what is acceptable and what is not. Dogs need training from an early age, but it is not too late to teach older ones, although they will be rather slower to mend their ways.

Handling

During a dog's lifetime there will be many times when it will be necessary to handle him, whether it be grooming him, cleaning his ears or paws, or giving him medicine. Consequently, it is a good idea to teach your puppy to accept being handled before it actually becomes necessary. Choose a time when he is relaxed and sleepy and practise lifting his ears, examining his paws, touching his body and opening his mouth. At the same time, talk kindly to him, then offer him a treat. By doing this regularly from an early age, you will find that when he needs to be examined, especially by a vet, he will not be unduly alarmed.

As he gets older, and to prevent him from becoming aggressive and possessive with his food, kneel beside him while he is feeding and gently cover the bowl, perhaps dropping in a

morsel of something he particularly likes. He will begin to see the act of feeding as a shared experience and stop snapping at people and other animals at mealtimes.

Playing

All puppies love to play and it is an important part of their development. However, playing with a human being is rather different from playing with another dog and the puppy must be made aware of that important difference. He may try to bite you, and when this happens, tell him sharply NO; if he persists, put him in a room on his own until he calms down. When dogs play with one another, mock fighting instincts come to the fore, inherited from their wolf ancestry. This is fine between dogs, but they must be made to understand what is acceptable when playing with you. If you watch two puppies at play, you will notice that they see how hard they can bite without hurting one another; if one yelps with pain, the other will moderate his biting. If your puppy bites you, 'yelp' too, and support this with an 'ouch' or NO. Don't strike him or push him away, this will only excite him further. If he persists, shut him away on his own; puppies are unhappy when isolated and will soon learn to behave.

House-Training

Begin house-training straight away. Even before you introduce a puppy to his new home, show him a place outside in the yard or garden where he can urinate and defecate as it is more than likely that, after a car journey, he may make use of it. If he doesn't, never mind, if he does, praise him warmly. From now on you will have to watch him closely to see what is on his mind. Puppies usually feel the urge to evacuate on waking and about 10–20 minutes after feeding. This is the optimum time to take him outside to the appointed place, especially if you see him circling or sniffing at the floor. Don't carry him out unless evacuation appears imminent; let him follow you outside. Once the deed is done, praise him, make a fuss of him, and tell him what a good boy he is. If he does soil indoors, which is inevitable as you cannot watch him constantly, unless you actually saw it happen, merely ignore it and quietly clean up. If you catch him in the act, tell him firmly NO and OUTSIDE, and take him to the proper place to show him what you mean. Never strike or rebuke him after the event as this could easily develop into behavioural problems, such as submissive urination.

At night, or if you have to go out, use the paper-training method below. If he performs in the night, when morning comes take him outside anyway, and go through the usual process of encouragement, then clean up the mess inside without fussing.

Paper-Training

For those who live in an apartment or cannot be with their pet all day, paper-training is another option. Teach him to evacuate by himself onto newspaper. First start by placing newspapers all over the floor, when he will gradually develop a preference for a particular spot. This is the time to remove the newspapers, putting only a few in that particular place. Hopefully, he will come to regard this as a spot where he can evacuate. Once this is established, and you wish him to go outside, gradually move the paper to the door and then eventually outside, leaving the paper there so that he can use it for a few times before you remove it completely. With a little luck, he will now associate going out with evacuation. When this happens, praise him every time he does the right thing.

In the case of an adult dog, you will usually be able to tell if he is house-trained. However, if he does have a few accidents, and he may because of the change in his routine, follow the same procedure as with a small puppy.

OPPOSITE and LEFT
Play is a vital part of training and dogs like nothing better than to chase a ball or toy. Teaching them to 'fetch' is a fun form of obedience training, as well as an excellent source of exercise.

Obedience

There are many different ways of training your dog to be obedient, but the most up-to-date and popular method is that of positive reinforcement. This relies heavily on the dog's natural wolf-like characteristics and the way wolves establish a natural pecking order within a social group.

Begin training puppies from day one. Because they are essentially pack animals, they will naturally look to a leader, and it is vital at this stage that you are recognized as such. Establish simple rules and boundaries for the puppy to follow. For example, try banning him from a particular room. If he attempts to enter, tell him NO in a firm voice. He will soon learn to comply with your demands as it is in his nature to obey; there are many exercises in obedience which can be practised in the home using patience and kindness. Above all, remember that all good behaviour should be rewarded with praise and perhaps a treat. Don't overdo this aspect of training so that your dog becomes bored; once he loses interest he will be far more difficult to train in future. Avoid trying anything too difficult to start with – you will only manage to confuse him.

If your dog is older, he may already understand some commands. Establish how much he already knows, reinforcing his successes with praise and rewards. On the other hand, he may have no idea what is required, or may have developed some bad habits. If this is the case, start from scratch as you would with a new puppy. With older dogs and puppies you will soon establish a way of training which is enjoyable to you both, and which will further strengthen the bond of friendship between you.

Once you are both proficient in the basics of training and your puppy has had his vaccinations, it is time to take him out into the big wide world. Suddenly, he will be bombarded by different sounds, smells and situations. His attention will at once be distracted and you may think that everything you have taught him has gone in one ear and out the other. Allow time for him to become accustomed to his strange new surroundings.

It is best to teach your dog new commands off the leash. However, don't take a new dog or puppy into an open space for the first time without one; spend the first few days walking him on it, making a start on his basic training by using commands such as HEEL, SIT and STAND. One useful command which can be performed anywhere is WATCH ME, maintaining eye contact with your dog for about 10 seconds while using the command. This is a useful basis for all training and brings to the dog's attention the fact that it is time for work. Use hand movements to reinforce your voice commands and reward with a treat as well as praise when he performs correctly. However, refrain from giving a treat every time; he needs to know that he must behave solely to please you, but always offer praise. Always end the training session with something he can do well, and finish with praise and a game he really enjoys.

Once your dog is comfortable in his surroundings and you are confident that he will stay and not run off, you can let him off the leash. Find a quiet place with no distractions, and begin training using the commands you have already taught him at home or when on the leash. Keep the sessions short – no more than 15 minutes for a puppy, slightly more for an older dog. Any one person in your family can try his hand at training, but only one person at a time should issue commands to avoid confusing the dog and upsetting him. Don't make the sessions too regular; be spontaneous. If he begins to equate going out with a training session he may become difficult. Intersperse his training with lots of walks and games.

COME

Teaching your dog to come is difficult, but is one of the most important commands to establish and could be vital to his safety. It is not easy to teach because asking your dog to come to you is often for negative reasons, for example to leave something which he thinks is interesting or great fun. So you may often be tempted to shout at him in frustration and admonish him when he eventually does decide to come.

HEEL

Prompt obedience is vital when you are walking a dog on a leash. There are many times when a dog cannot go unrestrained, so he will be required to walk quietly at heel, without pulling on the leash. Dogs which pull are extremely tiring on their owners' arms and can damage themselves, producing distressing wheezing noises in the process. If you cannot make your dog come to heel on the leash you may both benefit from dog-training classes or, as a last resort, you may wish to try out some of the various control collars (pages 412–413).

When obedience training, it is usual to bring your dog to heel on your left. Ask him to sit next to you and say WATCH ME, assuming that you have

One of the most important commands you can teach your dog is to sit to command. This is particularly important when crossing a busy street.

already taught him this command. Take a couple of steps forward, and if he has true eye contact with you he should move with you. If the dog stops when you stop, give him praise and perhaps a treat. Repeat the exercise, gradually increasing the number of paces.

Another method is to begin by making the dog sit. Hold a treat in each hand, placing your left hand near to him so that he can see and smell it, saying HEEL as you move forward. Then raise this hand and, using the other hand, go through the SIT exercise offering treats and praise. At times, repeat without the treat until the dog reacts to the command HEEL automatically.

SIT

Getting your dog to sit to command is important and can be used when it is vital for him to stay still, for example, in a hazardous situation such as preparing to cross a busy street. It is obvious that dogs already know how to sit, but they need to be able to immediately react to the command to do so; this is easy to achieve making use of the dog's natural conformation. Dogs have relatively inflexible spines, so the action of moving his head up will force him to sit down.

The process is best taught using a treat. Take the morsel between your

finger and thumb, holding it slightly above his nose so that he can see and smell it. As you perform this action, say SIT. As the dog visually follows the treat, his head will come up and he will sit. Reward and praise him. Try this several times with and without a treat, but always with plenty of praise.

STAND

To ask you dog to stand on command, begin by placing him in the lying position. Place a treat in front of his nose and move it up and away from him, using the command STAND. Finish by offering the treat and praising him.

Now try combinations of all three commands, HEEL, SIT and STAND, with or without the treat, until he is proficient in all of them. An obedient dog which promptly adopts these positions on command is easy to control in a multitude of situations, such as putting on or taking off a leash, making him stay put or asking him to lie down quietly.

DOWN

This action is much more difficult, so take your time and be patient. Once again using a treat, ask the dog to SIT, then say DOWN, then hold the treat in front of the dog's nose and move it downwards with the dog's nose following until it is between his front

legs. This movement should make his back end slide down as he follows the treat. Once performed correctly, offer the treat and praise. If this method doesn't work, try pulling the treat from between his front feet forwards.

STAY

Another useful command and one which could avert an accident in a hazardous situation. Once again, it is a difficult exercise and the aim is to make the dog "stay" when the distance between you both is at a minimum until he understands what you require. Only then, gradually increase the distance, rewarding with treats at first, then with praise only.

First ask your dog to sit, then raise your open palm above his face and say STAY in a firm voice. Then gradually back away. If he manages to stay for more than 5 seconds, reward him. Repeat until you can move quite some distance away.

FETCH

This has no other purpose than to provide your dog with much-needed exercise while saving your own legs. Being able to 'fetch' depends largely on the breed type; retrievers have the ability inbred, while terriers find it more difficult. Fetching is fun and all part of

This Labrador has become distracted and his first instinct is to investigate. His owner is trying to restrain him, but the situation could become dangerous near a busy street. This dog needs training so that he knows the difference between having fun and knowing when to behave.

Aggression is the worst form of bad behaviour, as the bite from even a small dog can be serious. Unfortunately, aggression may have been learned in a previous situation – maybe the dog has been ill-treated in the past – in which case you will need to seek professional advice to remedy the situation.

the throwing game. An easy way to teach your dog this trick is to throw a ball a short distance and say FETCH. When the dog picks it up, say COME, and praise him when he does. To teach him to drop the ball on command, hold up a favourite toy and say DROP; the dog should relinquish the ball in favour of the toy, when you should praise him and throw the toy. Repeat until he gets the idea, gradually eliminating the toy.

Training Aids

It has been mentioned that when teaching your dog to 'come to heel', you may encounter difficulties. Listed here are some artificial methods of control. However, they should only be used when all other avenues have been explored and found unsuccessful.

Slip- & Half-Check Chains

These are useful for dogs which pull on

the collar to a lesser extent. They are ideal for small or delicate dogs and are much kinder than the check chain. They are also much safer, especially when utilized by the heavy-handed. They are not as effective as the check chain but rather more preferable.

Head-Restraining Collars

These look much the same as a horse's bridle, but of course without the bit. The idea is that when the dog pulls, its head will turn inwards, which significantly reduces his power to pull. It is preferable to seek advice from your vet before fitting your dog with one of these as they are not suitable for some breeds of dog and can damage the eyes; also dogs which are susceptible to neck injuries should not be fitted with one. They are effective for stopping a dog from pulling, but are of little use as a training aid to correct the problem, as the restraining collar merely blocks the desire to pull rather than training the dog not to do it.

Harnesses

Harnesses may be useful when a conventional collar is causing the dog breathing problems and soreness from constant pulling. However, it will not cure the problem – if anything, it is more likely to compound it.

Spiked Collars

An unfortunately-named piece of equipment. When used to control a pulling dog, the 'spikes', which are in fact blunt prongs, tighten as the dog pulls, pinching the skin of the neck. It is not a pleasant form of control and its use is banned in some countries.

Unwanted Behaviour

To understand why a dog is behaving in an unacceptable manner you will need to find the root cause of the problem. Understanding why he is misbehaving is the first step towards a cure. Striking the dog or shouting at him is likely to make matters worse. Be calm and patient and eventually the problem will be solved. There follows some of the more common forms of unwanted behaviour. For more complex problems you may require the help of your vet or an animal behaviourist.

Aggression

The most serious problem, even in the smallest of breeds, is the dog which bites and its bite can cause serious damage. Other aggressive traits are some types of barking, growling, baring of the teeth, and lunging or snapping. A prelude to aggression is that the dog may stand very still and square with an alert expression on his face with his hackles raised. (The

This little Basset puppy is having a game of tug-of-war with his owner's sleeve. It is important to teach your puppy from an early age the difference between harmless fun and more aggressive behaviour.

hackles are a ridge of hair which rises from the nape of the neck and trails off down the spine.) Aggressive behaviour towards other dogs is common in unneutered males, so the obvious solution if you wish him to interact happily with other dogs is to have him neutered, preferably before puberty. Other causes of aggression are fear and nervousness (often the result of previous ill-treatment), and these forms are often the most dangerous as they are directed at people. If your dog has attacked or bitten anyone, be it a member of your family or a stranger, you must tackle the problem immediately. Ask your vet, he may be able to recommend a suitable animal behaviourist who specializes in this type of aberration. Happily, by correctly training your puppy from an early age you are less likely to encounter aggressive behaviour later or. We have already discussed how you have gradually established yourself as your dog's pack leader by handling him; also practise taking food away from him, then returning it with praise. This will stop him being aggressive at mealtimes. You can do the same with a favourite bone or toy. You should also approach your pet when he is sleeping, waking him up gently so as not to upset him when he is at his most vulnerable.

Accustomize your puppy to strangers and other dogs as soon as possible. Early socializing will make him feel more confident with strangers in the future and less likely to be aggressive through fear or uncertainty.

Never physically reprimand a dog; this is more likely to make the situation worse. Instead, tell him firmly NO, and couple this with a stern and disapproving look.

When new people come to the house, utilize your dog's new-found obedience skills. Ask him to sit, and get the stranger to give him a pat and a treat. This way a visitor will be someone to be welcomed rather than feared.

Don't leave your dog tied up in a confined space for too long; because he is a territorial animal he may well try to defend his space in an aggressive manner. If he does begin to show signs of aggression or if you have just acquired an older dog and are unsure how he will react, never let him off the leash until you are happy that his problems have been sorted out, and never think that your dog will grow out of aggressive behaviour; in fact, the problem is likely to become worse, so tackle it straight away and seek any professional advice you may require.

Muzzles

Much controversy surrounds the use of these, though many countries have made it illegal for some dangerous breeds, such as the Pit Bull Terrier, to frequent public places without one. However, many experts are convinced that they actually make the problem of aggression worse, causing the dog frustration and discomfort. Great care should always be taken when de-muzzling a dog as the muzzle will tend to make him momentarily more aggressive. Always consult your vet before muzzling a dog as there may be other kinder and more effective ways of curbing him, such as re-training, as mentioned above.

Excessive Barking

All dogs bark from time to time – it is the canine form of communication. It would be unkind to totally deter a dog from barking as it is often a sign that he loves life and wants someone to play with him.

Radio-Controlled Collars

These should only be used as a last resort and only on the advice of your vet or a qualified animal behaviourist. They are designed for dogs which are out of control and constantly escaping. The dog's unruly behaviour is in fact curbed by a mild electric shock. There is a great deal of controversy surrounding their use, but they are becoming ever more popular and many people swear by them. It is claimed that once the dog has had one or two shocks he will establish the parameters of his territory and stay

within them, while others maintain that such an unnatural form of control could well cause a dog severe psychological damage.

There are similar versions designed to stop constant barking which, once again, should only be used as a remedy of last resort. There is a much kinder method called the olfactory collar; when the dog barks, the collar emits a squirt of citronella oil which is activated by a microphone. The dog soon links barking with what is to him an unpleasant odour and stops the irritating habit.

Jumping Up

Some dogs have the annoying habit of jumping up at their owners as well as strangers as they are greeting them or when something has particularly excited them. While small dogs do little harm, apart from their dirty paws and scratchy claws damaging clothing, it can nonetheless be extremely tiresome. However, a large dog is an entirely different matter, as a frail person or child could quite easily be pushed over and badly frightened. If you want your dog to jump up as a trick, teach him by command, using the various methods outlined in this chapter; but if you want him to stop the habit, rush towards him; this will throw him off balance and distract him from his purpose. Alternatively, you could try the SIT and STAY commands. Another ploy, when you arrive home, is to ignore the dog until he has calmed down, then make a

Excessive barking is a nuisance which may drive you and your neighbours to distraction. It is possible to train your dog not to bark, or if this fails, there are products available to help alleviate the problem. If your dog won't stop barking, don't leave him out on his own; this will only exacerbate the problem.

OPPOSITE

The instinct to dig is strong in most dogs and is very difficult to cure. The best thing to do is to give him his own place in the garden where he is allowed to dig. Bury his favourite things in it to get him started.

fuss of him with praise and a treat and hopefully he will begin to relinquish his antisocial behaviour. Once control is established, keep to the routine, letting him know that he will receive no attention until he is sitting calmly. If you cannot stop him from jumping up, keep him on a leash and pull him down, or try a head-restraining collar. This gives you fuller control of the neck, allowing you to pull him away more effectively without causing damage.

Digging up the Garden

Digging is a deeply-rooted part of a dog's instinctual behaviour and many have actually been bred for the purpose; for instance, terriers are sometimes required to dig for small animals which burrow underground, while many dogs feel the need to dig a hole to bury a bone. This goes back to their lupine ancestry when wolves would bury their kill to save it for another day.

Once again, try to get to the root of the problem. If he persists in digging in one spot, you may be able to train him to LEAVE by command, using treats to distract him. However, there may be a smell which is stimulating him. Try to find the source and if it is in one particular spot you could try replacing the old soil with new, or planting some large shrubs to deflect him from the area.

He may be digging to make a cool place to lie down in; if this is so, create a shady spot for him elsewhere, or keep him indoors on hot days. However, he may just like digging as a hobby, when you are better off giving in and making him his own special place in which to dig, perhaps in the form of a sandpit, or an area of bark chippings. Encourage him to bury his favourite toys there; he will soon latch on to the fact that this is his very own play area. If he persists in digging in a no-go area, reprimand him with a firm NO, and return him to the place where he is allowed to dig; start off by flicking at the sand which may stimulate him to begin digging there again, and when he does, praise him for it.

Stealing

Puppies and older dogs love to hold objects in their mouths and may run off with your precious possessions. Don't leave portable objects of value lying around in the first place, but if your dog has grabbed something he shouldn't have, don't shout at him, as he will probably run off with it; equally, don't chase him as he will immediately think that you are playing a game and you will have great difficulty in getting him to come back. The most effective way is to crouch down beside him and offer a treat, followed by the command DROP,

---

FOLLOW THESE SIMPLE RULES FOR HAPPY AND SUCCESSFUL TRAINING

Never use physical punishment

•

Never reprimand for not performing correctly

•

Keep the training session short, and make it interesting with plenty of variety

•

Space training sessions irregularly so that the dog doesn't begin to anticipate

•

Initially, use tasty treats to help reinforce the command, reducing them to occasional use once proficiency has been achieved

•

Give praise after every correctly performed task, while ignoring those which have been unsuccessful

•

End the training session on a good note. Finish with a task which your dog does well and praise him warmly, perhaps rewarding him with a treat. He is then more likely to remember that training sessions are fun

when he will most likely relinquish your property in favour of the treat. You can practise this with him using worthless objects so that, from an early age, he learns to drop them on command.

The Check Chain

Only to be used on a dog which persists in pulling at its leash, the check chain should never be used by an inexperienced handler. The effect of a sharp jerk, coupled with the word HEEL, for example, will hopefully correct the problem. It is a valuable aid for handlers who require their dogs to be on the leash for long periods, and prevents the dog from making the distressing 'wheezing' sound which results from constantly pulling on a collar. Make sure the chain is correctly fitted, as one that is incorrect could potentially result in strangulation. Always have an expert demonstrate the chain's use before buying one. There exists much controversy regarding the use of the check chain, and many insist that it should never be used in any circumstances. However, it is thought preferable to include it to warn people of the hazards rather than to ignore the matter altogether, when the inexperienced may be tempted to use one. REMEMBER: always remove the chain when letting the dog run free.

FEEDING AND EXERCISE

Correct feeding is the most important aspect of dog care and is vital if your dog is to stay healthy and happy. As previously mentioned, there are similarities between people and dogs. They, like us, eat most things, which means that they require both meat and vegetables in their diet, which must also contain the correct levels of carbohydrates, vitamins and minerals to keep them well. Dogs also require as much water as they can drink, which is an important aid to digestion. Like us, they require feeding according to their size, shape, age and lifestyle. The diets of a sheepdog working on a farm and a pampered pet living in an apartment will differ considerably. The diet of a pregnant female will also be different, as will that of puppies which need higher levels of nutrients for healthy growth. It is most important to avoid overfeeding: you may think that you are being kind by offering large meals and tasty treats; however, the opposite is true and will inevitably end in obesity and even illness.

There are many different varieties of proprietory foods on the market, all of which contain the correct levels of minerals, vitamins and other additives which go towards creating a well balanced diet for a dog.

OPPOSITE
The working Bernese Mountain Dog requires very much higher levels of energy foods when compared to less active dogs.

LEFT
Your dog's eating habits and the amount of exercise he has are directly linked. He requires a well balanced diet containing proteins, carbohydrates, fats, vitamins and minerals.

Canned Foods

These come in a variety of brands and differ considerably in price and quality. They contain approximately 75 per cent water mixed with various meat and fish products and cereals. Needless to say, they are very convenient. However, because they produce quite low energy levels, you would have to feed a large dog quite a lot, which would make them very expensive. For larger dogs it is advisable to mix them with dried food to bulk them up and add more calories.

All-Meat Canned Foods

As the name suggests, these contain only meat and to provide your dog with the levels of energy he requires you would have to feed him a large amount which would produce an unhealthy, unbalanced diet. Consequently, they should always be combined with mixers.

Semi-Moist Foods

These have a much higher concentration with only 15–30 per cent water content which allows lesser quantities to be given. They contain meat, vegetables, cereals, fats and sugars, and are easy to digest and very palatable. They come in a huge range and are a popular method of feeding. They can be stored without refrigeration but are rather expensive. However, they are particularly suitable

Dried foods contain nearly all cereal and should be offered as a mixer or supplement to canned or fresh meat for a well balanced diet.

for small, fussy dogs. Not to be fed to dogs which are diabetic as they contain high levels of sugar.

Dry Foods

These contain only about 10 per cent water and have a high-energy content. However, they mostly contain cereal so should only be used as mixers or as a supplement to canned foods to provide a well balanced diet. These foods contain all the important proteins; for example, meat, bone meal and soy flour, but have little in the way of an appetizing smell

and are therefore not very palatable. Some are used as mixers to boost the energy content of canned foods. The advantages are that they can be stored in large quantities and are cheaper than other foods; however, don't keep them past their sell-by date as they will have lost most of their vitamin content. Be careful when feeding these as it is easy to give too much, which could lead to obesity.

Home Cooking

It is quite possible to feed your dog food which you have prepared and cooked yourself at home. However, it is most important that it contains the correct dietary requirements and there are various recipe books on the subject. Don't attempt this without advice as you could deprive your dog of all-important nutrients.

It is vital that the correct levels of proteins, fats, carbohydrates, vitamins, minerals and fibre are fed, together with water.

Proteins

Vital for development, a dog's ability to digest protein varies. In the form of meat, 90 per cent is digestible while a dog can digest only around 70 per cent vegetable protein, such as soya. However, feeding high levels of vegetable protein can cause bowel upsets.

Fats

Fats in the form of fatty acids are a vital part of the diet and are essential to a dog's well-being; deficiencies can cause skin and ear problems and nervousness. They offer high levels of energy which means that the dog has to digest less protein, which reduces the work the liver and kidneys have to do. A dog can digest virtually 100 per cent of fats.

Carbohydrates

These are the highest energy producers in a dog's diet and consist of starches, sugars and cellulose. To provide him with the required levels of carbohydrates, feed boiled potatoes or rice, with dried foods and mixers to a lesser extent. Some canned foods have between 12 and 15 per cent carbohydrate, while fresh meat and fish have none at all, so it is important when feeding these that you include a mixer which contains some carbohydrate.

Fibre

High-fibre diets have become popular with the human population and have proved to be beneficial, and this also applies to dogs. Add about 5 per cent fibre to the total diet, which is what you will find added to meat and cereal-based dog foods and biscuit-based mixers. Fibre is an important aid to digestion and

It is not a good idea to feed your dog at table when you yourself are eating; give him his own meal away from the table at family mealtimes, which will discourage him from begging from you.

speeds up the movement of food through the gut, reducing the risk of bowel disorders such as diarrhoea and flatulence. It also helps absorb toxins, by-products of digestion, which as a consequence ease stress on the liver. It is also an excellent idea to increase the amount of fibre fed to obese dogs, filling them up without adding to their weight problem. It is also useful for diabetic dogs as fibre absorbs glucose.

Vitamins and Minerals

As in all animals, the correct balance of vitamins and minerals is vital for the proper functioning of the body; they are also an important factor in the prevention of disease. Ready-prepared dog foods already contain a careful balance of these elements to provide all that a dog needs. Particularly important are calcium and phosphate, which play a vital part in a dog's development, including the formation of bones and healthy teeth. If you are feeding fresh food you will have to make sure that you are providing your dog with enough minerals and vitamins. Many are contained in dried foods which can be added as a supplement.

Energy

Feed your dog according to the amount of energy used. Some dogs are extremely athletic and have a fast metabolic rate.

These will require foods with a higher energy content. However, others may be far less active, in which case they will require much less food. Never be tempted to overfeed a growing dog, even a large one. Overeating can cause growth abnormalities and even shorten a dog's life. The chart below provides a rough guide to the energy levels in the form of calories required for dogs of different sizes. However, this should be increased or decreased according to activity, age, pregnancy and lactation. All ready-prepared dog foods will have a feeding chart on the packaging. Use it as an important guide, but watch out for signs of obesity and reduce the feed accordingly. A sign that you are overfeeding is that your dog may vomit or develop diarrhoea. In extreme cases, consult your vet who will plan a special diet for him.

Feeding Times

Most adult dogs only require one meal a day and most people prefer to feed this in the evening. A good idea is to let it coincide with your own evening meal which will deter your dog from begging at table. Some dogs with an evening meal inside them cannot last the night without having to go outside; in which case, feed earlier in the day. Smaller dogs may not be able to eat a meal in one sitting, so

OPPOSITE
Seeing your dog so alert and full of vitality is a joy that can only be achieved by a correct balance of food and exercise.

LEFT
A dog likes nothing better than to gnaw on a juicy bone, which benefits the teeth and exercises the jaws. Only give him a raw knucklebone, as cooked bones tend to splinter.

APPROXIMATE ENERGY REQUIREMENTS

Average weight of dog		Energy required (kcals per day)
Sml breeds	2kg (2.2Ibs)	230
	5	450
	10	750
Med breeds	15	1010
	20	1250
	25	1470
Lge breeds	30	1675
	35	1875
	40	2070

APPROX. CONTENTS OF BRANDED DOG FOODS

Food	Pr	Car	Fa	Wa	Kc
Dry (complete)	22%	51%	7%	15%	3.4
Semi-moist	19%	38%	10%	26%	3.0
Canned (complete)	8%	12%	5%	73%	1.0
Canned (all meat)	9.5%	1.5%	5%	82%	1.3
Biscuit		10%	69.9%	6.1%	8.4%	3.5

Pr=Protein **Car**=Carbohydrate **Fa**=Fat
Wa=Water **Kc**= Kcals per gram

Hide chews are a good safe alternative to bones; they exercise the jaws and clean the teeth without making too much mess on the rug!

GOLDEN RULES OF FEEDING

Never overfeed your dog

•

Feed according to size, age and lifestyle

•

Feed a well balanced diet which contains correct levels of proteins, carbohydrates, fats, fibre, vitamins and minerals

•

Always provide a constant supply of fresh water

•

Don't constantly feed fresh food without taking advice, otherwise your dog may go short of vital nutrients

divide the amount into two and feed half morning and evening. Puppies and lactating mothers require a different regime of feeding. Your vet will give advice here.

Always feed your dog in the same place, offering clean bowls with every meal, and also fresh water. Place the bowls on an easy-to-clean surface such as the kitchen floor. Remove any uneaten food immediately and discard.

Don't be tempted to feed your dog titbits from the table or snacks between meals. This will encourage begging and

Include you dog in as many family activities as possible. He would much rather be out and about with you than stuck at home on his own. While sailing isn't particularly good exercise for a dog, he will enjoy the trip and perhaps get an opportunity for a swim!

scrounging and is most annoying as well as likely to make him fat. You may feed small treats when training, but only in moderation, and you can break them up into smaller pieces to make them go further. There are dog treats available on the market for this purpose, but remember that they are fattening. The best option is a dog biscuit, which is high in carbohydrate but low in fat.

Bones

A meat bone not only provides hours of pleasure, but also exercises the jaws and cleans the teeth. Offer a raw knuckle bone as this is unlikely to splinter. Avoid cooked bones, especially chicken; these will splinter and could cause severe internal damage.

Exercise

Exercise and feeding go hand-in-hand. Your dog's level of exercise will depend on his size, age and breeding. It is not necessarily the case that large dogs require more exercise, in fact a Jack Russell Terrier requires more exercise than a Great Dane.

Walking your dog and playing games with him is not only beneficial to you both but is part of the joy of dog ownership. Exercise plays a vital part in your dog's well-being, and will keep him fit, healthy and happy. A dog which is

confined to the house all day will become lethargic, dull and fat; he may also develop behavioural problems such as excessive barking and destructive habits.

We have already discussed the wisdom of acquiring a breed of dog which suits your needs, so if you are unable to walk far yourself, you should choose a dog which requires a small amount of exercise.

All dogs require daily exercise, be it a walk round the block twice a day for the more sedate breeds, to a ramble in the

countryside or a strenuous game in the park for more energetic types. Working breeds, such as sheepdogs, will obviously get all the exercise they need in the course of their working lives. Before beginning any form of exercise, especially in the case of an older dog, it is a good idea to have your vet check him over first, as he may be suffering from a heart problem or stiff joints which energetic exercise could aggravate.

Walking

This is an excellent form of exercise for both you and your dog, as the gentle movement tones muscles, and is beneficial to heart and lungs. If your dog is unfit, start with a short walk of no longer than 15 minutes and build it up slowly as he becomes fitter. Old or ill dogs will still benefit from some exercise – ask your vet's advice.

Playing and Running Free

Should you live in an area where there are lots of people around, keep you dog on the leash; if there is nowhere to let him run free, you will have to walk further with him to give him the exercise he requires. Young and active dogs really do need to run free, but only attempt this if your dog is obedient to your commands, you are sure that he is not aggressive, and that dogs are

OPPOSITE
Playing ball on the beach is the perfect way to exercise your dog and you will both enjoy the fun. Check first that dogs are allowed on the beach as some have seasonal restrictions.

LEFT
Dog owners should have respect for others and arm themselves with scoops or bags to remove their dogs' excreta from public places. Many towns provide special receptacles for the purpose, so use them, as dog mess is not only unpleasant but harmful to young children and expectant mothers.

Whatever the situation, work or play, correct feeding will ensure that your dog never runs out of energy.

actually permitted to be off the leash. Bring a ball or frisbee for him to chase, or arrange to meet up with other dog-owners so that the dogs can run around and play together; this is good, strenuous exercise, great fun to watch, and is a way of getting dogs to interact socially with one another.

If you are a keen walker yourself, nothing could be better than a long walk with your dog in the countryside. He will love sniffing about and will probably cover three times your distance as be runs backwards and forwards, searching out interesting smells. Follow the country code: don't let your dog anywhere near livestock. If there are notices demanding that dogs be kept leashed, obey them. If you are likely to be out for a long time, make sure you bring some water with you and that he does not become overheated. Watch out for hazards such as deep holes or barbed wire and do not let your dog eat anything that could be poisonous.

Another form of exercise is to take your dog jogging with you, but exercise common sense; make sure that he is fit enough, keep to soft ground to save his paw pads, and avoid doing it in hot weather. Don't take a puppy with you which is under 6 months old as serious damage could be done to soft bones.

Be Responsible

Before taking your dog to a public place you should familiarize yourself with any local laws and regulations regarding the right to keep a dog. Some countries insist on a dog being licenced, others have restrictions regarding dogs in public places. Be aware of laws concerning certain breeds which may require muzzling; in the UK, some breeds are totally banned.

Finally, remember always to clean up after your dog, as its excrement can be extremely harmful, particularly to children and pregnant women; it is also extremely unpleasant and antisocial when it sticks to shoes. There are various products available, from elaborate scoops to simple bags, and most public areas are provided with a special disposal bin for the purpose. So use it.

Although not relevant to the presence of dogs in public places, you should also be aware of rules regarding tail-docking and ear-cropping, which is banned in the UK but still practised in the United States. While tail-docking is not actually banned, it is increasingly finding disfavour.

GROOMING

Grooming a dog is not solely for cosmetic reasons, it is an important aspect of his overall care. Regular grooming helps to keep the coat clean and the skin in good condition. It also provides an excellent opportunity to check for ticks, fleas, and skin abnormalities.

All dogs require grooming to a greater or lesser extent. It is obvious that longhaired types will need more attention, but breeds with shorter coats will benefit from a brisk grooming, if only to bring out the natural shine of the coat.

Longhaired varieties such as Yorkies, Afghans and Shih Tzus require at least one hour's grooming a day, so unless you are prepared to put in this amount of work, don't buy a longhaired breed. For those who wish to show their dogs, professional clipping and grooming may be required, and is an extra expense.

A dog should eventually grow to enjoy grooming sessions, having been shown from an early age that it is pleasant by having a soft brush run gently over his body, or by using the handling techniques on page 404.

Start off the grooming session with an examination to satisfy yourself that your dog is healthy; check that the skin

Longhaired dogs, such as this Bearded Collie, require daily grooming to prevent matting and keep his luxurious coat in first-class condition.

is clean and free from dandruff; if there is evidence of fleas, see page 440. Check that the body is free from lumps and abrasions, that the ears have no discharge, and that the eyes are clear and bright. Should he begin to object, offer a treat and praise him warmly.

Then, using a wide-toothed comb, gently remove the excess dirt and knots from the coat, finishing off with a suitable brush. Then, using separate pieces of cotton wool moistened with

water, gently remove any discharge from the eyes, and clean and remove dirt from ears and nose. You will also need to clean the teeth. Do this using either a flannel face-cloth or a toothbrush and some canine toothpaste. Don't use your own toothpaste as it is strictly unsuitable. Finally, check to see if the claws need clipping; the need for this will vary according to the amount of exercise the dog takes, but may be necessary every few weeks or so.

The Coat
Dogs have varying types of coat, and each one requires a different type of grooming.

Long with an Undercoat – Seen in breeds such as the Pomeranian and Samoyed. The coat should be brushed thoroughly forward and then back; once the knots have been removed, tackle the fluffy undercoat with a comb.

Silky – As in Yorkshire and West Highland Terriers. Brush daily, trimming or stripping out the loose older hair every three months.

Smooth – As in Dobermans and Labradors. Most dirt will brush off easily. Use a comb and bristle brush and a hound glove to give shine and improve the circulation.

Curly – As in Poodles. This type of dog never sheds its coat, so mats and knots will develop very quickly and remain there unless extra attention is paid to them. Groom daily using a brush and comb. A regular professional clip will go a long way to making your task easier.

Wiry – Groom twice a week. Coat can be stripped or clipped to make it more manageable.

Equipment
There are many types of brushes and combs available; choose those which are suitable for your dog's coat. Other tools you may require are stripping combs, shears and scissors which are used to thin and trim the coat. Don't use electric clippers unless you have received training in their use. To prolong the life of your equipment, clean it thoroughly after use.

Combs
You will require two of these, one wide-toothed with rounded edges and ends to protect the skin, and a fine-toothed version. These come in either plastic, or metal, which will obviously last longer but are likely to be more expensive. The wide-toothed comb is first used to break up mats and tangles and remove large patches of mud. The finer comb is used

Grooming not only keeps your dog's coat in good condition, it will also give you the opportunity to check him over for parasites or other problems.

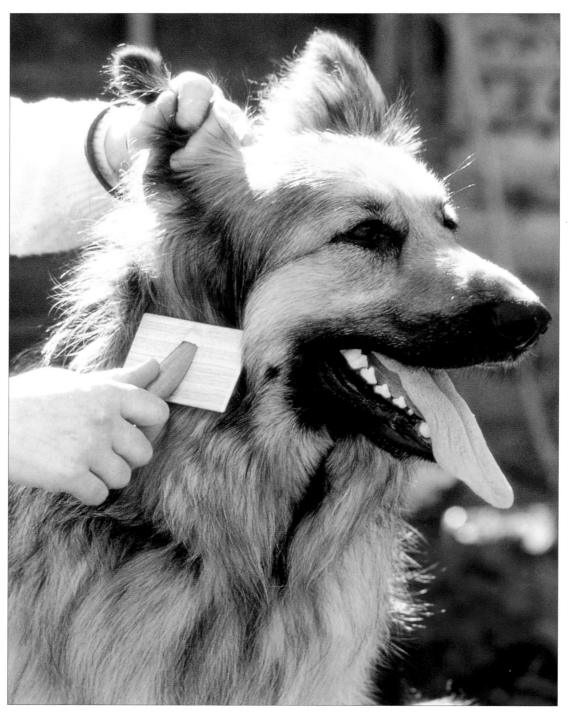

on the undercoat to remove loose hair. Don't tug the comb through the hair; if you meet with resistance, remove the comb and gently work on the knots little-by-little, using your fingers and the comb. The fine comb will also help you to detect the presence of fleas.

Bristle Brush

The brush does most of the work and should be used after all the knots have been removed. It can also be used to give a dog which is well groomed a once-over to tidy the coat. For longhaired dogs, the brush should have bristles which are long enough to penetrate the coat as far as the skin, thus preventing matting of the undercoat. For shorter-haired breeds, use a shorter-bristled brush. You are advised to use a brush composed of natural bristles as the synthetic varieties can cause static as well as damage the hair and skin.

When brushing a longhaired dog, brush against the 'lie' of the coat using short strokes. Work on small patches at a time and don't tackle the whole coat by brushing in the wrong direction as you may damage the hair.

When brushing a medium-coated dog, pay particular attention to the quarters as it is here that much of the loose hair accumulates.

A selection of grooming tools. Shorthaired dogs won't require many of these.

unwelcome in the house. Time for a bath. If your dog is a persistent roller he will obviously require bathing more often; however, the rule is not to bath more than once a month unless it is really necessary. Only use a shampoo which has the pH balance suitable for dogs, and not for people, which will dry out the skin causing irritation and flaky patches. Avoid bathing working dogs too much as shampoo strips the fur of its natural oils which are important for waterproofing the coat.

Summer is the ideal time to wash your dog outside, using a garden hose, and he will probably enjoy being cooled off on a hot day. In cooler conditions, either wash him in the bath, or the sink if he is small. Before bathing, and especially if he is longhaired, give him a thorough grooming, removing all knots; then place wads of cotton wool in each ear if he will let you. Before placing a dog in the bath, prepare the water. It is best to use a shower hose, making sure that the water is lukewarm. Remove his collar and lift him gently into the bath (you may need a helper at first to hold him steady). Using the hose, wet him thoroughly, avoiding the ears, eyes and nose. Apply the shampoo, rubbing it in well, and include the legs, tail and paw pads. Wash the head carefully. Rinse off thoroughly, removing every trace of

Carder

This is a rectangular board on which short bent-wire teeth are mounted. Its purpose is to remove the loose undercoat on shorter-haired varieties, but it can also be used on longhaired dogs by working the carder into the skin, then twisting away through the hair to the surface.

Hound Glove

Used solely on shorthaired dogs such as

Labradors, it is composed of short bristles, rubber bumps, or wire teeth. You can wear it like a glove, working over the dog to remove loose hair and add shine.

Bathing

By our standards, dogs are dirty creatures: they like nothing better than to snuffle through mud, and enjoy rolling in unspeakable things with terrible odours, making them offensive and

433

RIGHT
This Irish Terrier is an active dog always on the go; he will rarely need his claws clipping as regular exercise will wear them down naturally. Check them regularly, however.

OPPOSITE
Choose a dog according to the amount of time you have available. The Weimaraner (left) is a low-maintenance dog, requiring little grooming, but the Rough Collie (right) will require considerably more attention.

shampoo. Before he can shake himself everywhere, cover him with a towel, dry him vigorously, and leave him somewhere warm to dry, or in summer, put him in the garden in the sunshine. You may use a hair drier if your dog will tolerate it, but don't hold it too close as you may burn him.

Claw-Clipping
You will need to attend to your dog's claws regularly, so invest in a good quality pair of clippers. The most suitable types are the ones which cut sharply like a guillotine as opposed to those which merely crush the nail. These can cause a great deal of pain, making claw-clipping a

dreaded experience. When clipping, be extremely cautious. If your dog has a pale nail you will easily be able to see the quick and a pink area coming down the centre. If you cut through this, it will bleed and be very painful. So cut well away from this. If your dog has black nails, take off only the thin tip at the end.

434

Remember that dogs as well as humans can suffer from heatstroke. Make sure that you always provide adequate shelter for him, particularly when it is hot and sunny.

TRAVEL

The dog as part of a family (pack) thrives on human companionship, so it is hardly surprising that he loves going on holiday with his owner. This is perfectly possible as long as you make the proper preparations. If you are planning to provide your own accommodation, i.e. in tents or a trailer, then there is no problem. However, if you are staying at a hotel you will need to check in advance that dogs are allowed. Many hotels will welcome them in all rooms, while others will allow dogs only in the bedrooms; if you are planning long evenings out you will need to make sure that you have a dog-sitter.

There are times, however, when you will need to weigh up the pros and cons of taking your dog on holiday at all; does he get travel sick? Will he end up in a crate in the hold of a plane? Is the climate at your destination very hot, or are you planning outings to restaurants and theatres in the evenings? If so, he may be happier staying with a relative or boarded out in kennels, especially where quarantine regulations exist.

If you decide to take him with you abroad, you will need to take a supply of drinking water from home. Dogs suffer from stomach upsets as well as human beings, so unless you want to give him expensive bottled water, bring your own.

Some dogs love being in cars, others don't. Get your puppy used to travel from an early age, even if it is just a trip around the block. Don't feed dogs that get sick while travelling beforehand, and give him a good walk before you set off, when hopefully he will go to sleep.

If all the conditions are right, your dog will like nothing better than having some time away from home with the family.

(For the same reason, bring a supply of his usual brand of food with you.) Make sure that all vaccinations are up to date, check with your vet to see if further ones are required, and take proof of vaccination with you. Make sure that the dog's identification tag is legible and have an identichip fitted as an extra precaution. Bring his licence or passport, if necessary, and his own bed for comfort as well as his favourite toys and grooming tools.

Travel by Motor Car

Make sure that your dog is adequately restrained, either in a crate or in a seat belt designed for dogs. Don't let him run loose around the car; he could distract the driver and in the event of a crash be badly injured or killed.

If he gets travel sickness, don't feed him until the journey is over. Stop for regular breaks, taking him for short walks to stretch his legs and allowing him to urinate and have a drink.

Don't under any circumstances leave your dog alone in a car if you value his health and safety. Many have been stolen, and others have become overheated and died, causing heartbreak to their thoughtless owners. Even on a cool day, a dog left for any length of time confined to a car may be overcome by heatstroke. (If you see a dog left in a car

and it appears to be in distress, call the police straight away.)

Travel by Air

This is quite a traumatic experience for a dog and should only be undertaken if really necessary. Some airlines will allow a small dog to travel in an approved carrier under the seat, while larger animals will have to be put in a crate in the hold. You will need to book early as space allotted to animals is limited. Try to reserve places on a non-stop flight and travel in the coolest part of the day if possible.

Tranquillizers

If your dog is a bad traveller your vet may prescribe tranquillizers; these are not the perfect solution as breathing difficulties may occur. A better idea is to take your dog for a good walk or run which will tire him out so that he will sleep throughout the journey.

Boarding Kennels

If you are going away and don't want to take your dog with you, you will have to find alternative accommodation for him. The best option is for him to stay with a relative or friend with whom he is on good terms; alternatively, have someone move into your house. Don't leave him at home on his own, even with someone

coming in to feed and exercise him regularly; he will be very lonely on his own and may become destructive, causing damage or even behaving in a manner likely to endanger himself.

The other option is to lodge him in a boarding kennel, and many of these are excellent. However, the best way to find one is on the recommendation of a friend or your vet. Take a look at the establishment before you book the dog in; there should be someone living on the premises at all times as well as quick access to a vet in emergencies and an adequate place in which to exercise the animals. The kennels themselves should be warm and dry and not too cramped and the food should be of good quality. Once you are satisfied that all is well, book your dog in. You will need to do this well in advance of your holiday, particularly if you are planning to travel at holiday peak periods. A reputable kennel will not take your dog unless he is fully vaccinated, so make sure that these are up to date. When you drop him off, provide him with his own bedding and some toys to make him feel at home.

HEALTH

Vaccinations

It is of the utmost importance that your puppy is started on a programme of vaccination. Puppies are very vulnerable to disease and should not be allowed to go outside or have any contact with unvaccinated dogs before they have had the full course as recommended by your vet. Vaccination is done three to four times between the ages of 12 and 14 weeks and guards against many life-threatening diseases.

Rabies – This is a deadly virus which attacks the nervous system and can affect all mammals. In many places, such as the U.K. and parts of Europe, the disease has been virtually eradicated, so vaccination will only be given where the disease is endemic. The puppy should be vaccinated at 3 months with a booster around 10 months, followed by a further booster at approximately 1–3 years.

Canine Distemper – Often fatal, this is a viral disease which affects the respiration, intestines and the nervous system. It is vital that a puppy is vaccinated every 3 weeks until he is 12–14 weeks old, followed by an annual booster. This is a multi-vaccine which also protects from Canine Hepatitis, a virus which attacks the liver, and

Parainfluenza, which is the broad term for a group of viral and bacterial diseases which cause kennel cough, and which is similar to our common cold. Canine Parvovirus is a dangerous disease which attacks the intestines and can be fatal to puppies. Some vets vaccinate for Parvo separately at up to 5 months. Leptospirosis is a bacterial disease which can cause kidney and liver failure. Some vets don't vaccinate for this until 9 weeks.

There are other vaccines which your vet may advise, but this largely depends on where you live. Examples are Lyme Disease, which is carried by ticks and transmitted through a bite and can affect much of the body, and Coronavirus, another intestinal disease which can prove fatal to puppies.

Skin Problems

Fleas – When giving your dog his regular check-up when you are grooming him, it is important that you look at the skin. A sure sign that something is amiss is excessive itching and scratching. Then the obvious thing to look for is flea infestation and you can confirm this by running a fine-toothed comb over the dog's coat, when you may catch some of the offenders. Concentrate on the rump and the area between the back legs and around the neck where you may also

find evidence in the form of a reddish-black substance which consists of blood and flea faeces. The flea is a very common parasite and plagues many animals besides cats and dogs. They survive by sucking the animal's blood and the bite causes an itchy irritation. Sometimes, the dog may develop an allergy to the flea's saliva which will make him scratch frantically, resulting in sore and weeping skin. The flea, if eaten by the dog, is also responsible for the spread of tapeworms, so if your dog has fleas you should worm him as well.

The flea is quite a difficult pest to eradicate as it spends a part of its life cycle living apart from the dog, laying its eggs deep in the weave of your carpet. Merely to treat the dog is not enough. Start by thoroughly vacuuming the carpet, paying particular attention to the edges where fleas tend to congregate. Wash the dog's bedding and treat the carpet with a household flea-killer (your vet will recommend one which is safe for pets), applying it over the carpet and especially around the edges. Dispose of the vacuum cleaner bag when you have finished, preferably by burning it.

Next treat the dog. There are many different preparations on the market, but it is advisable to consult your vet. There is one type which can be sprayed onto the dog which is very effective and lasts for months and there is an anti-flea drug which can be administered by either tablet or injection. These are becoming very popular, are effective for up to a year, and dispense with the need for sprays and powders.

Shampooing your dog regularly, though no more than once a month, will also help keep the flea population down. You may wish to buy a special flea shampoo, but others are just as effective. When he is dry, comb him through thoroughly to catch any fleas which may have survived. Combing is also a good way of keeping fleas at bay, as the combing action breaks the fleas' delicate legs, when they drop off and die.

Ticks – Most common in the countryside where they inhabit woods and long grasses, fields and hedgerows, attaching themselves to dogs as they run by. The tick causes a great deal of irritation and can be particularly harmful as it is a carrier of Lyme Disease in some areas. If the disease is prevalent where you live, ask your vet to vaccinate your dog against it.

Ticks are easy to spot; they attach themselves to the hair and sink their mouths into the dog's skin to suck the blood, with the result that its stomach becomes engorged with blood until it resembles a large apple pip. It will

eventually drop off and attach itself to another animal, but it is desirable to kill it before this stage is reached.

If your dog frequents areas where ticks are prevalent, check him over, paying particular attention to the underside and legs. Once detected, dab the tick with alcohol, vodka or methylated spirits, or apply a flea spray which kills ticks as well, leaving for a few minutes or as recommended if you are using a spray. Then, with a pair of tweezers, grasp the tick just above the mouth parts, pulling it out sharply and making sure that you have removed the mouth parts as well.

Mites – These are tiny parasites which can only be detected under a microscope. There are two varieties, *demodex* and *sarcoptes*, and both types cause mange. They occur naturally in all dogs, living in the hair follicles and under the skin and only become a problem then the dog's immunity is at a low ebb due to illness or an incorrect diet. The mites multiply rapidly, causing itching and hair loss, which can lead to serious skin infections. They may also transfer to human beings. During grooming, you may notice that your dog has some bald patches which are sore and crusty, and he may be scratching frantically. Take him to the vet who will

take a skin scrape to examine under a microscope, when all should be revealed. Mites can be treated with pesticide shampoos and other treatments can be injected or given orally.

Lice – These are particular types of lice which only affect the dogs in your home; they cannot live on cats or humans. There are two kinds, one which bites the skin, feeding on the skin flakes, and the sucking louse which will cause even more irritation. Lice are relatively large, approximately 0.08in (2mm) long, and they lay eggs or nits which stick to the base of the dog's hair until they hatch. Treatment is by insecticide sprays or baths as recommended by your vet.

Gastric and Intestinal Disorders
Worms – These are parasites which live in the dog's intestines. They are extremely common; puppies are even born with them or pick them up early from their mother's milk. Unless the adult worms are present in the dog's faeces, there is little other evidence that there is a problem; the only way is for your vet to examine the faeces under a microscope. To eliminate these pests, a regular worming programme is vital. Your vet will recommend the correct wormers to use as well as the correct dosage. From the age of 4 weeks, treat

your puppy for roundworms and repeat the treatment until he is 6 months old. Pregnant bitches will require a special worming programme and all adult dogs should be wormed every 6 months. Most wormers supplied by the vet will get rid of the common varieties your dog is likely to pick up, the most usual being roundworms and tapeworms.

Roundworms – Several of these parasites inhabit the dog's small intestine, the most important belonging to the *ascarid* family; but some varieties, such as *toxacara*, also infest the large intestine, while others live in the blood vessels and respiratory tract. They feed on digested food passing through the dog's intestine and are most harmful to puppies, the worms being capable of passing through the gut wall, through the blood supply to the liver and lungs, where they are coughed up and swallowed, repeating the process. Puppies may develop liver infections such as hepatitis, pneumonia and fits and obstruction of the intestines may also occur. In adults, the worms migrate to the muscles where they lie dormant as cysts; in pregnant bitches the worms attack the embryo and settle in the puppy's lungs, which is the reason why virtually all puppies are born with them.

This type of worm is harmful to children as they may become encysted in the child's eye, in severe cases causing eye loss. However, this is thankfully rare, and can be avoided by immediately disposing of the dog's faeces, washing your hands thoroughly before handling food, and ensuring that your children wash their hands regularly. They should be trained not to put their hands in their mouths after touching the dog.

Hookworms and Whipworms – Both live in the intestines and are invisible to the naked eye, so they can only be detected by faecal examination. Both can cause diarrhoea and the hookworm can cause anaemia, both the result of poor hygiene. They should be treated by a vet.

Heartworms – *Angiostrongylus* is a potentially fatal parasite. It lives in the blood vessels and is transmitted by slugs which have been eaten. The larvae leave the dog via the lungs when they are coughed up and swallowed, eventually ending up in the faeces. These are difficult to treat as the worms live in the dog's circulatory system and a drug administered to kill the worms in the bloodstream could well cause a thrombosis. It is therefore necessary for the dog to be treated by the vet in his surgery where he can be monitored carefully.

Tapeworms – *Dipylidium caninum* is picked up when a dog inadvertently eats fleas in which the tapeworm larvae have developed. The worm is composed of segments which resemble grains of rice. They can cause itching and discomfort around the anus and the segments are clearly visible in the faeces. It is advisable to treat a dog for tapeworms regularly; eradicating fleas will greatly help the process.

Bloat – This is a serious condition and should be treated as an emergency. At the first sign, take your dog to the vet immediately. Gastric dilatation and volvulus (GDV) occurs when the stomach becomes bloated with air, causing it to rotate and in effect blocking the escape of air from the stomach. Signs to look out for are a heavily distended stomach; the dog will also be retching without producing vomit. He will be in severe discomfort and the condition can lead to shock and even death. Surgery is required to decompress the stomach and to ensure that it is returned to its correct position. Bloat is most common in the larger, deep-chested breeds.

Vomiting – All dogs vomit from time to time and as they habitually eat such extraordinary things, it is just as well that they do. They also tend to vomit when they have overeaten. Eating grass to induce vomiting is often an indication that your dog is unwell, so keep a close eye on him. However, and to add to the confusion, they also eat grass because they like it.

If a dog has been vomiting, leave him to rest in a quiet place and withhold food for 24 hours, apart from a little water. Then reintroduce food slowly, choosing bland foods such as chicken and rice. Once fully recovered he can be returned to his normal diet.

If he cannot stop vomiting and continues to do so after fasting, or if there is blood present, take him to the vet immediately as the cause may be serious, indicating poisoning, an intestinal obstruction, kidney or liver failure, inflammation of the pancreas, or an infectious disease such as *parvovirus*. If the dog has been sick for a prolonged period he will be very dehydrated and your vet may decide to put him on a drip.

Diarrhoea – All dogs suffer from diarrhoea at some time or another, the usual cause being overeating or a change of diet. In these cases, follow the same procedure as if he had been vomiting. If diarrhoea persists over the next two days, he may be suffering from something more serious, such as worms, kidney disease, cancer or a viral disease, so consult your vet.

Flatulence – This is usually caused by overeating or a reaction to diet. A little wind is perfectly natural, but if flatulence becomes a problem, feed small meals at shorter intervals and avoid soy-based products which are a prime cause of the trouble.

Anal sacs – These are glands situated on either side of the anus and contain an noxious discharge, which is normally expelled when the dog defecates. In some cases, however, the sacs become blocked, causing discomfort. The dog will begin to drag his bottom along the floor or continually lick his anus. When this occurs, take him to the vet who will empty the sacs which is a simple procedure; ask him to show you how to do this as the problem is likely to recur. Never ignore this as the sacs may become infected; if they do, antibiotics will be required.

Urinary Disorders

Keep a watchful eye on your dog's urinary habits; any changes such as straining to go, more frequent than normal urination, or signs of blood in the urine, should be regarded as serious and may require immediate veterinary attention or even surgery. An infection of the urinary tract could be the cause of any of these symptoms as well as disease of the prostate gland in male dogs; a blockage caused by kidney stones can be fatal it not treated at once. Other diseases which cause increased urination are kidney failure and diabetes, both common in older dogs. An indication of this is increased thirst. While diabetes can be kept in check with insulin injections, kidney failure will eventually cause death, but with a low protein diet, plenty of fluids and regular exercise, the progress of the disease can be decelerated.

Incontinence can easily be distinguished from a behavioural problem because the dog will leak in his sleep, leaving wet patches. However, there are many causes of incontinence, such as prostate trouble in males and cystitis predominately in females, the latter being treatable with medication. Older dogs may become incontinent due to a variety of causes, many listed above; all can more or less be controlled and you can help the problem by taking your dog for plenty of walks, or by letting him out as often as possible to relieve himself.

The Eye

The dog's eye is very similar in structure to our own, so it follows that similar problems will occur. Keep a close check on your dog's eyes, checking for discharge, redness, swelling or cloudiness. A healthy eye should be clear and bright, the white parts should be white not pink, and the under parts of the eyelids should be a healthy pink with no redness or inflammation. If your dog does lose his sight for whatever reason, it is not the end of the world; all of the dog's senses are sharp, particularly those of smell and hearing, and blind dogs learn to manage quite well. They will soon memorize the layout of your house and will happily go for walks while staying close to your side.

Conjunctivitis – This is one of the most common diseases of the eye in both humans and dogs. It is an inflammation of the conjunctiva, the membranes lining the eyelids. The infection can be caused by a foreign body in the eye, or a scratch or tumour on the eyelid: it can also occur because of a congenital disorder which is a deformity of the eyelid, *entropion*, in which the eyelid grows inwards, causing the eyelashes to scrape the surface of the eye, or *ectropion* where the eyelid turns outward. Tears then flood into the pouch formed by the lid, leaving the cornea unlubricated so that it dries out. Both can be corrected by surgery. In other cases, the eyelashes

may grow in the wrong direction, called *trichiasis*, causing pain and redness. The hairs are removed using electrolysis, which makes the dog instantly more comfortable. Conjunctivitis can be treated with eyedrops or ointment prescribed by your vet.

Dry Eye – *Keratoconjunctivitis* is a condition where the eyes produce insufficient tears to adequately lubricate the eye. Symptoms are redness, severe discomfort, and a greenish discharge. This should be treated at once to save the eye from permanent damage. Medication can also be provided to keep the eyes moist.

Glaucoma – This is caused by a disorder of the drainage system inside the eye. Some of the drainage outlets can become blocked, causing the fluid to build up to dangerous levels inside the eye, when it becomes painfully stretched. The dog will require immediate treatment in the form of either surgery or drugs to reduce the fluid to save his sight. Symptoms to look out for are swelling, excessive tear production, pain and sensitivity to light.

Cataracts – This is usually a condition of old age. However, it can be hereditary or caused by a mother's poor condition

during pregnancy. Symptoms are a cloudy cast which appears over the lens which can be surgically treated in severe cases.

Corneal Injury – These are caused by external forces such as a scratch to the eye from an overhanging branch. Damage to the cornea should be treated immediately as the eye may become infected and ulcerated leading to blindness. Prompt action will save a dog's sight.

Dental Care

Clean your dog's teeth every time you groom him. Use a small toothbrush or a flannel cloth and a toothpaste for dogs, and check that the teeth are clean with no tartar build-up. This irritates the gums resulting in a disease called *gingivitis*, which can also be caused by the milk teeth not falling out when they should. Get your vet to check your dog's teeth every year.

To keep the teeth clean and the gums healthy, let your dog chew on a knuckle bone or hide chew, which will also exercise the jaw. He is likely to have bad breath if there are problems with his teeth; other signs are drooling, pain when eating, nasal discharge, or a swollen jaw. If he has any of these, take him to the vet.

Disorders of the Ears

Deafness – The main cause of deafness in dogs is hereditary, through selective breeding, and is particularly common in dogs which are predominately white such as Dalmations. It is so common that you should always have a dog's hearing tested before buying it. Infections of the inner ear can also cause deafness, nerve damage and loss of balance.

The ear consists of four different parts: the flap, the external ear canal, the middle and inner ears. The ear flap is vulnerable to injury and can easily be torn on branches when dogs run through undergrowth; in the event of injury, hold a towel tightly over the wound and take to the vet immediately for stitching. *Haematomas* are another problem connected with the ear flaps; these are lumps caused by a small injury or by excessive head-shaking which fill with blood, and are common in older dogs. *Haematomas* do not disappear of their own accord, but must be treated by a vet as delay may cause the ear to become deformed.

Otitis Externa – This is an inflammation of the external ear canal caused by ear mites, yeast and bacterial infections, and is also common in dogs which like to swim. In this instance, it can be avoided by drying inside the ears thoroughly, the best method being a mixture of half vinegar, half rubbing alcohol, which, when inserted, helps to dry out the ear. Signs of *otitis externa* start with head-shaking and scratching the offending ear, which may be inflamed and painful to touch, emitting a foul-smelling discharge. The ear mite produces a thick discharge which has a gritty consistency. At the first sign of this disease, take you dog to the vet.

Cleaning the Ears

Only clean your dog's ears if they are dirty or if there is a waxy discharge. Don't insert anything into the ear canal, use a piece of damp cotton wool to clean around the outer area of the external ear canal.

Disorders of the Bones

Osteoarthritis – The most common bone disease, this manifests itself in inflammation of the joints. It is a degenerative disease most common in older dogs, the underlying causes being an old injury, an inherited malformation, such as hip dysplasia, or simple wear and tear. Symptoms are an initial stiffness after rest which eventually wears off after exercise. In more extreme cases, the dog will walk with a stilted gait or have a pronounced limp. A visit to the vet will determine the severity of your dog's condition, when he will usually be given anti-inflammatory drugs, a diet sheet, and a specially designed exercise regime.

Hip Dysplasia – This is an inherited abnormality which mostly affects the larger breeds, the most common example being the German Shepherd, which has been bred with a sloping rump. This abnormal positioning of the hip joint can be painful, particularly when arthritis inevitably sets in. In extreme cases surgery is required to re-build the joint: in less severe cases, the same treatment as for arthritis is usually given.

Back Pain – Like us, dogs also suffer from back pain. In some cases it may only be sore muscles resulting from strenuous activity, in others the dog may have a partially slipped disk when he may be reluctant to climb stairs or jump; he may also cry out when picked up. Complete rest and treatment with muscle relaxants and anti-inflammatory drugs will possibly be all that is required. However, if the disk has slipped severely, the dog may suffer a partial or total paralysis, in which case urgent surgery is required.

Back pain is a common complaint in long-backed, short-legged breeds such as Corgis and Dachshunds.